TORTURE

TORTURE

EXPANDED EDITION

Edward Peters

PENN

University of Pennsylvania Press

Philadelphia

Library of Congress Cataloging-in-Publication Data

Peters, Edward. 1936–
    Torture / Edward Peters. — Expanded ed.
        p.   cm.
    Includes bibliographical references and index.
    ISBN 0-8122-1599-0 (alk. paper)
    1. Torture — History.   2. Torture (International law)   3. Torture — Europe —
History.   I. Title.
    K5410.T6P48   1996
    341.8'1 — dc20   96-32654
                                                                            CIP

Contents

Preface to the Expanded Edition

Torture was first published in Oxford and New York in 1985. It was translated into Spanish in 1987 and into Portuguese in 1989 (São Paolo) and again in 1994 (Lisbon). The book had the honor of being removed from the UK exhibit stand at the 1985 Moscow Book Fair. The German translation of 1991 added a very brief bibliographical supplement. The text of the original edition has been left intact with the exception of the correction of a few minor errors.

Because the text has not been changed, several points made by earlier reviewers may be conveniently addressed here. The reviews were encouraging; that paragraphs contain no sour grapes. Two reviewers regretted that the book focused narrowly and specifically on torture without directly linking it to (and discussing) what one called, "all those other crimes against humanity perpetrated by modern regimes, from genocide to the political manipulation of mass starvation." These are fair points, but the book could not have retained its focus if it had included them in any detail. Perhaps this book may help some other book do so at adequate length and breadth. Another reviewer expressed concern that the book did not describe the experience of the victims in adequate detail. It did, however, indicate where such descriptions could be found, and the anamnestic literature has increased and circulated substantially since 1985. This literature is discussed in the New Addendum to the Bibliographical Essay, pp. 200–210 this edition.

A fourth reviewer raised a more serious problem: the novelist David Bradley, in one of the reviews for which I am most grateful, expressed concern that my insistence on so narrow a definition of torture restricts the application of the term to an excessively narrow field of action, denying it not only to the rhetorical action of writers, but also to instances in which abuse permitted by law might very well fit into a slightly expanded definition. I do not profess to be any more of a policeman of rhetoric than I thought was necessary to clear the air of some of the most misleading uses of the term in modern sentimental journalism. Bradley is right. The definition should be expanded.

Finally, one reviewer resorted to what can only be called the pointlessly instrumental application of heuristic concepts to a book that was originally written to help restrict them. Complaining that I had failed to distinguish in modern history between torture under an "authoritarian" regime and that under a "totalitarian" regime (the heuristic difference apparently being that the former can change policy and the latter cannot), the reviewer neglected to note that it does not matter to victims whether they are tortured by authoritarian or totalitarian regimes. The experience of torture is the same. In any case, the events of 1989 and since suggest that the original distinction needs rethinking.

The main feature of this edition is the two appendices. The first offers a much more extensive bibliographical survey of the literature on both the history and the contemporary practice of torture between 1985 and 1995; the second provides a number of English translations of original documentary sources on the subject from the Roman Empire to the twentieth century. Many of these originally appeared in my edition of Henry Charles Lea, *Torture* (Philadelphia, 1973), now out of print. I have revised the commentaries to these texts and added relevant bibliographical information.

I am grateful to all those colleagues and friends (and sometimes perfect strangers) who have expressed an interest in seeing the book return to print. I am also particularly grateful to a number of institutions and individuals who have communicated with me about the book in correspondence and conversation and have advised me on bibliographical and other matters. Prominent among these are the RCT in Copenhagen and its director, Dr. Inge Kemp Genefke; Darius Rejali, particularly for his generous and extensive bibliographical suggestions; Rita Maran, Sarah Terry, Mika Haritos-Fatouros, Ronald Crelinsten, James M. Powell, Kate Nelligan, and John Murphy.

Editor's Preface

Ignorance has many forms, and all of them are dangerous. In the nineteenth and twentieth centuries our chief effort has been to free ourselves from tradition and superstition in large questions, and from the error in small ones upon which they rest, by redefining the fields of knowledge and evolving in each the distinctive method appropriate for its cultivation. The achievement has been incalculable, but not without cost. As each new subject has developed a specialist vocabulary to permit rapid and precise reference to its own common and rapidly growing stock of ideas and discoveries, and come to require a greater depth of expertise from its specialists, scholars have been cut off by their own erudition not only from mankind at large, but from the findings of workers in other fields, and even in other parts of their own. Isolation diminishes not only the usefulness but the soundness of their labours when energies are exclusively devoted to eliminating the small blemishes so embarrassingly obvious to the fellow-professional on the next patch, instead of avoiding others that may loom much larger from, as it were, a more distant vantage point. Marc Bloch observed a contradicton in the attitudes of many historians: 'when it is a question of ascertaining whether or not some human act has really taken place, they cannot be too painstaking. If they proceed to the reasons for that act, they are content with the merest appearance, ordinarily founded upon one of those maxims of common-place psychology which are neither more nor less true than their opposites.' When the historian peeps across the fence he sees his neighbours, in literature, perhaps, or sociology, just as complacent in relying on historical platitudes which are naive, simplistic or obsolete.

New Perspectives on the Past represents not a reaction against specialization, which would be a romantic absurdity, but an attempt to come to terms with it. The authors, of course, are specialists, and their thought and conclusions rest on the foundation of distinguished professional research in different periods and fields. Here they will free themselves, as far as it is possible, from the restraints of subject, region and period within which they ordinarily and necessarily work, to discuss problems simply as problems, and not as 'history' or 'politics' or 'economics'. They will write for specialists, because we are all specialists now, and for laymen, because we are all laymen.

Torture provides a telling index of the nature of states and societies, and of the relation of power to the individual. Our great-grandfathers regarded its abolition as one of the definitive achievements of their age, a prepotent symbol of emancipation from the long reign of superstition and force which had been the Middle Ages and the *ancien régime*. Its revival – torture is currently practised by one government in three – is one of the most brutal evidences of the fragility of their confidence in human progress. But though torture poses the clearest of moral challenges neither its decline nor its resurrection can be understood in simple moral terms. They were part of more complex changes, not always beneficent in the first case, or unambiguously malevolent in the second. In this remarkable book Edward Peters deploys the resources of legal and intellectual history, of political analysis and contemporary experience to bring this most repugnant of subjects into the realm of systematic understanding. As always, understanding must be the first condition of cure.

R.I. Moore

Acknowledgements

My colleagues at the University of Pennsylvania in several academic departments and on the staff of the Van Pelt Library have been immensely helpful to me in the research and writing of this book, as have Professor James Muldoon of Rutgers University, Camden, and John T. Conroy, MD, of West Hartford, Connecticut. I express particular gratitude to Alan Kors, Martin Wolfe, Jack Reece, Thomas Childers and David Ludden. Elliott Mossman helped me considerably with Soviet legal theory, and Elaine Scarry forced me to distinguish between moral and sentimental definitions of torture in a long discussion over her own forthcoming book *The Making and Unmaking of the World: The Body and Pain.* The Interlibrary Loan Section of the Van Pelt Library quickly and expertly provided books that would otherwise have proved very difficult for me to obtain. Ms Joan Plonski rapidly turned disordered typescript and handwritten corrections into a clear and accurate text. Without her services the book would have taken much longer to write. If I have ventured far from my usual fields of research in the later parts of this book, I have done so with the help of these colleagues and with the encouragement of R.I. Moore and Patrick Wormald, and I am grateful to the former for having invited me to write it at a moment when neither of us had the vaguest idea of what it would be when it was finished.

This book is dedicated to those human beings who work in – or pass through – the RCT, Copenhagen, Denmark, and to the memory of F.S. Cocks.

Full citations of sources cited in parentheses in the text will be found in the bibliographical essay.

E.P.

Introduction: Torture – Past and Present – and the Historian

What is torture? From the Roman jurists of the second and third centuries to the historians and lawyers of the present, those who have taken the most trouble to consider the question have come up with remarkably similar answers. Thus the third-century jurist Ulpian declared:

> By *quaestio* [torture] we are to understand the torment and suffering of the body in order to elicit the truth. Neither interrogation by itself, nor lightly inspired fear correctly pertains to this edict. Since, therefore, *quaestio* is to be understood as force and torment, these are the things that determine its meaning.

In the thirteenth century, the Roman lawyer Azo gave this definition:

> Torture is the inquiry after truth by means of torment.

And in the seventeenth century, the civil lawyer Bocer said that:

> Torture is interrogation by torment of the body, concerning a crime known to have occurred, legitimately ordered by a judge for the purpose of eliciting the truth about the said crime.

In our own century, the legal historian John Langbein has written:

> When we speak of judicial torture we are referring to the use of physical coercion by officers of the state in order to gather evidence for judicial proceedings . . . In matters of state, torture was also used to extract information in circumstances not directly related to judicial proceedings.

Article 1 of the Declaration against Torture adopted by the General Assembly of the United Nations on 9 December 1975 reads thus:

> For the Purpose of this Declaration, torture means any act by which severe pain or suffering, whether physical or mental, is intentionally inflicted by or at the instigation of a public official on a person for such purposes as obtaining from him or a third person information or confession, punishing him for an act he has committed, or intimidating him or other persons. It does not include pain or suffering arising only from, inherent in or incidental to, lawful sanctions to the extent consistent with the Standard Minimum Rules for the Treatment of Prisoners.

Finally, there is a somewhat more elaborate definition by another twentieth-century legal historian, John Heath:

> By *torture* I mean the infliction of physically founded suffering or the threat immediately to inflict it, where such infliction or threat is intended to elicit, or such infliction is incidental to means adopted to elicit, matter of intelligence or forensic proof and the motive is one of military, civil, or ecclesiastical interest.

The first three of these definitions applied to torture as a legal incident, first in Roman, then in European civil law systems until the nineteenth century. The fourth is a modern legal historian's definition of torture during that long period. The fifth is the most recent diplomatic definition. The last is intended to apply to the historical circumstances, but with an eye toward the recent reappearance of torture and the concern it has generated since the end of the Second World War, creating a definition that is applicable to the present as well as to the past.

Yet it is likely that people using the term in the second half of the twentieth century may find these definitions too narrow. Is not the key to torture simply the physical or mental suffering deliberately inflicted upon a human being by any other human being? In many respects the meaning of the term in the common usage of most western languages might well support such a question. From the seventeenth century on, the purely legal definition of torture was slowly displaced by a moral definition; from the nineteenth century, the moral definition of torture has been supplanted largely by a sentimental definition, until 'torture' may finally mean whatever one wishes it to mean, a moral-sentimental term designating the infliction of suffering, however defined, upon anyone for any purpose – or for no purpose.

The capacity on the part of human beings to inflict pain on other human beings, in the name of the law, the state, or simply for personal gratification, is so widespread and enduring that to single out one aspect of it for discussion, and historical discussion at that, may seem invidious or pedantic. Yet, in spite of the moral and sentimental outrage that the word generates in the late twentieth century, its longest and surest definition is a legal – or at least a public – one. The lawyers and historians cited above all find one common element in torture: it is torment inflicted by a public authority for ostensibly public purposes. The semantic history of the term *torture* invariably possesses a public dimension, in much the same manner as do the terms *execution* and *assassination*. By analogy, it might be said that torture stands in the same relation to such private offences as trespass, battery or aggravated assault as a state execution stands in relation to murder. Torture is thus something that a public authority does or condones. From Ulpian to Heath its public dimension distinguishes torture from other kinds of coercion or brutality. Part of the argument of this book will consist of an account of the various kinds of meanings the term 'torture' has possessed, and it will attempt to relate these meanings to the reality of torture in the late twentieth century. One of the lesser-known functions of apparent invidiousness and pedantry may be their insistence upon clear definitions. As means of objectifying and therefore better understanding some of our most pressing but least considered ideas and terms, otherwise pedantic and invidious analyses may prove to be worth a little cognitive investment.

This approach to torture runs somewhat against the grain of a number of current considerations. A recent collection of essays published in the ongoing series Concilium: Religion in the Seventies was entitled *The Death Penalty and Torture*. Both institutions were discussed by the contributors in the light of the policies of recent state practices, and it has been in the light of concerns over modern state power that torture has generally been discussed. Although this approach is a valid one, it is not the approach of this book. I have attempted to single out the problem of torture alone for analytical treatment, perfectly aware that some very closely related ideas and practices will be neglected. Just as this book does not deal with the death penalty and other forms of state coercion, so it will not deal with other manifestations of public horror; there is not a word here about the Wars of Religion or the holocaust, and very little on the various inquisitions. By isolating the phenomenon of torture I have attempted to describe the history of a single practice; my failure to mention others is deliberate, but it reflects no indifference toward them. I have written the history of a subject that requires a detailed history. Narrowing down the focus may well intensify it; and torture needs all the intensity of attention it can get.

Just as this book will not consider torture in relation to the death penalty, neither will it, except incidentally, consider it in relation to aggravated forms of punishment, capital or other. The opening section · of the last chapter will consider modern international concern with both torture and 'cruel, inhuman, or degrading treatment or punishment', including punitive mutilation, but the practice of modern legislators concerned with human rights distinguishes between the two, and this book will respect that distinction. It is true that a moral position may be taken concerning torture, the death penalty, and various other forms of statutory punishment considered together, and that a sentimental position may be taken as well. But our concern is with torture alone. Although this book will consider the historical connections between legal procedure and moral thought, it will do so in terms of torture and not of those aspects of public coercion that are often associated with it.

These restrictions have not been adopted merely to suit the convenience of the author. Torture began as a legal practice and has always had as its essence its public character, whether as an incident in judicial procedure or as a practice of state officials outside the judiciary proper. In the Judaeo-Christian and Islamic worlds the term intermittently possessed a moral dimension, and since the eighteenth century it has also possessed a sentimental dimension. Thus, its meanings in the twentieth century may range from the technical and legal (as they do in various instruments of international law) to the sentimental (as they do in much popular, including journalistic) usage. The history of these different meanings will be touched upon in this book, but torture will always mean a public incident, however broadly 'public' may be interpreted.

Other kinds of people using the term might raise another objection. Is the modern revival of torture in the twentieth century to be regarded as the revival of an ancient though interrupted tradition, or as the child of a particular kind of modern state? After all, statutory abolition of torture in criminal law swept virtually all of

Europe during the eighteenth and early nineteenth centuries, to the extent that Victor Hugo could announce in 1874 that 'torture has ceased to exist.' Is not twentieth-century torture, then, something new, unrelated to the ancient legal history of torture? All historians and readers of history must constantly make distinctions between that which is particular and discontinuous and that which is general and continuous; each technique is suitable for different purposes. Let us consider history in the long range first.

Although many ancient societies experienced the transition from primitive and domestic to sophisticated and public systems of law, not all of them came to use torture as distinctively as did the Egyptians, the Persians, the Greeks and the Romans. Some societies, notably those of the Babylonians, the Hindus and the Hebrews, seem to have developed a system of ordeals that never permitted torture to be introduced. These consisted of physical tests undergone by one contending party, assuming that success or failure depended upon divine intervention. In northern Europe before the twelfth century, early Germanic law also permitted a wide variety of ordeals but did not autonomously develop a doctrine of torture; nor, apparently, had Celtic laws done so earlier. Later, despite the introduction of torture into the legal practices of western Europe after the twelfth century, eastern Europe continued to cling to the ordeal until the beginning of modern times.

Thus, the history of torture in western Europe may be traced from the Greeks, through the Romans, through the Middle Ages, down to the legal reforms of the eighteenth century and the abolition of torture in criminal legal procedure virtually throughout western Europe by the first quarter of the nineteenth century. Removed from ordinary criminal law, however, torture was re-instituted in many parts of Europe and in its colonial empires from the late nineteenth century on, and its course was greatly accelerated by changing concepts of political crime during the twentieth century. The best recent evidence indicates that torture is used, formally or informally, in one country out of every three.

Such a history may seem at first perplexing, but it *is* a history. From the nineteenth century on, political crime has been conceived in much the same way as simple criminal law had been earlier, and a similar need for confessions troubles the officials and jurists of twentieth-century states who employ or permit torture as troubled the jurists of the Middle Ages or the *ancien régime* when faced by the procedural or tactical requirement of a confession from the accused.

A number of superficial surveys of the history of torture simply accept the idea that torture occurs in cycles of legalization and abolition; indeed, such a view easily presupposes the existence of torture as something with a natural history and makes the history of torture then an account of these cycles. But the notion of abstract entities that occur in cycles does not take our understanding very far. Moreover, it suggests a certain inevitability about the whole process, one that implicitly urges resignation in the face of something resembling a force of nature.

In fact the history of torture can be quite specific. It is not, for example, clear to what extent the Greeks owed their procedures of torture to Egyptians and Persians, so it is possible and plausible to begin with what we know of the Greeks – because some of their law does seem to have influenced that of Rome, and the law of Rome that of medieval and early modern Europe. The flurry of successful abolition movements during the eighteenth and early nineteenth centuries abolished torture chiefly as a part of criminal procedure only, and here those movements comprised not only rulers and legislatures, but the judicial profession itself, which remained procedurally liberal while often socially very conservative. But Bench and Bar alone had ceased to comprise the entire legal power of the state by the late nineteenth century. Then, particularly where the power of state agents escaped routine judicial control and review, and in areas that were relatively new, such as military information, espionage, police work and political supervision, new state powers were developed, particularly in those areas in which European states had always been especially sensitive – those that touched upon the safety and security of the state itself.

From the thirteenth century at the latest, European lawyers had developed a category of the exceptional crime – the *crimen exceptum* – one so dangerous to society and outrageous to God that its prosecution procedure was permitted enormous latitude. Once torture had been abolished from ordinary criminal law, the possibility of a new kind of *crimen exceptum* permitted the reintroduction of torture in order to deal with 'extraordinary situations'. Much of modern political history consists of the variety of extraordinary situations that twentieth-century governments have imagined themselves to face and the extraordinary measures they have taken to protect themselves. Paradoxically, in an age of vast state strength, ability to mobilize resources, and possession of virtually infinite means of coercion, much of state policy has been based upon the concept of extreme state vulnerability to enemies, external or internal. This unsettling combination of vast power and infinite vulnerability has made many twentieth-century states, if not neurotic, then at least extremely ambiguous in their approach to such things as human rights and their own willingness (the states would call it 'necessity') to employ procedures that they would otherwise ostensibly never dream of. It is in this sense that torture may be considered as having a history, and its history is part of legal procedure as well as later governmental exercises of power, whether officially or unofficially. The purpose of a long-ranging history of torture is to emphasize its public dimension and permit the reader to see both the twentieth century in a wider context and earlier European history from an unaccustomed point of view. By focusing upon the public character of torture – whether in strict legal procedure or in the hands of sub-legal or paralegal agencies – we may be able to regard torture in the twentieth century no longer in the simplistic terms of personality disorder, ethnic or racial brutality, residual primitivism, or the secularization of ecclesiastical theories of coercion, but as an incident of some forms of twentieth-century public life, no longer, as in the past, restricted to formal criminal legal procedure, but occurring in other areas under state authority less regulated than legal procedure, less observed, but no less essential to the state's notion of order.

This book will deal with the historical dimension of what Ulpian, Bocer, Langbein and Heath, implicitly or explicitly, call *judicial* torture, but it will not use that adjective. It will argue instead that judicial torture is the *only* kind of torture, whether administered by an official judiciary or by other instruments of the state. It will also argue that other things sentimentally called 'torture' had better be called something else. The juxtaposition of familiar terms from one area of meaning to another for dramatic effect is a device of rhetoric, not historical or social analysis. And semantic entropy does not clarify understanding. Although I am under no illusions about the capacity of one book to effect a semantic revolution, I do hope that the argument in the following chapters will make as strong a case as possible for verbal precision, particularly in matters as pressing as the one under consideration. Moral outrage and sympathy require no historical understanding, but historical understai ưng may sharpen both. And both need to be sharpened.

And so we begin with history. The first chapter gives an account of the emergence of torture in western culture in Greece and Rome; the second deals with the long age of torture in early European legal procedure to the end of the eighteenth century. Chapter 3 considers the statutory abolition of torture and the emergence of a moral dimension to the term in the polemics of Enlightenment reformers; chapter 4 traces those circumstances in the nineteenth and twentieth centuries when torture reappeared, to use the phrase of the eighteenth-century English jurist William Blackstone, as an 'engine of the state, not of law' (*Commentaries on the Laws of England*, 4 vols, Oxford, 1765–9, IV:321). The final chapter looks at the recent past and present, from the United Nations Declaration of Human Rights in 1948 to the publication of Amnesty International's report, *Torture in the Eighties*, in March 1984.

For purposes of accuracy and reference, I have kept a number of words and phrases in their original language, but I have consistently provided English equivalents. Since one purpose of this book is to point out the differences between a professional technical vocabulary such as that of the law and wider moral and sentimental vocabularies, verbal precision remains important throughout, and this includes precision in describing the often deliberately misleading euphemisms frequently employed to designate torture in the twentieth century.

A few modern studies of torture in the twentieth century offer passing glances at its history in early Europe, but because these are remote and seem to occur in different circumstances from torture in the twentieth century, such historical accounts are often too brief, too superficial, or even wrong. The most reliable accounts, those of John Langbein, *Torture and the Law of Proof* (Chicago, 1977), and Piero Fiorelli, *La tortura giudiziaria nel diritto comune* (Milan, 1953–4), gain much of their effectiveness from their specific and technical detail. In his excellent study, Langbein remarks upon this aspect of his work, and he then notes that he has 'left it for others to draw the implications for European political, administrative, and intellectual history'. The present book is an attempt to take up the history of torture at that point. If it succeeds at all that will be because it owes much to the work of scholars like Langbein and Fiorelli as well as to those colleagues cited in the acknowledgements above.

Scholars who must write without footnotes are like workers who must make bricks without straw. The bibliographical essay at the end of this book combines notices of the most useful scholarship with an essential set of references to passages cited in the text. Although there are few individual references, every passage cited in the following chapters will be found in a work cited in the text itself or in the bibliography. I have included a considerable number of these, many in translation, because they offer important documentary and critical evidence which should not be entirely paraphrased.

Two of the main themes of this book are the public character of torture in both its earlier and later forms and the differences among its legal, moral, and sentimental conceptualizations at different periods in its history. There is a third: the place of legal history itself in such an account. It is remarkable that, with a few stunning exceptions, legal history is the kind of history least integrated with other kinds, and therefore generally the least well understood. Yet it is crucial in the history of torture to understand certain technical procedural aspects concerning the early history of torture as an incident in European criminal law, and it is equally important to understand the place of the law in modern states that deliberately and philosophically subordinate law to other public interests and institutions. The last two chapters of this book take up the implications of this theme again, but at its outset it is proper to regard the law neither as an independent, beneficial institution, nor, in a structuralist-reductionist mode, simply as one more instrument of a ruling class. E. P. Thompson, in one of these few stunning studies, *Whigs and Hunters* (New York, 1979, p.266), makes an observation to which I wholeheartedly subscribe:

There is a difference between arbitrary power and the rule of law. We ought to expose the shams and inequities which may be concealed beneath this law. But the rule of law itself, the imposing of effective inhibitions upon power and the defence of the citizen from power's all intrusive claims, seems to me an unqualified human good. To deny or belittle this good is, in this dangerous century when the resources and pretentions of power continue to enlarge, a desperate error of intellectual abstraction. More than this, it is a self-fulfilling error, which encourages us to give up the struggle against bad laws and class-bound procedures, and to disarm ourselves before power. It is to throw away a whole inheritance of struggle *about* law, and within the forms of law, whose continuity can never be fractured without bringing men and women into immediate danger.

In this most dangerous of centuries, any fresh perspective on its chief instruments, even a historical one, may not be entirely without interest – or use.

1

A Delicate and Dangerous Business

The emergence of torture in Greek law

Twentieth-century people, although they may easily recognize the existence of privilege- or status-distinctions in institutions which profess to operate democratically and impersonally, often know little about societies – or earlier periods in our own history – in which privilege and status were the only elements that determined social identity, nor about the processes in early European societies that transformed them from communities based upon status distinctions to communities based upon shared rights. Yet in terms of legal history alone, these processes were fundamental to the emergence of the idea of 'law' itself and to the role of law and its incidents in social, cultural and political history ever since.

For, once the Greeks had succeeded in inventing the idea of an abstract 'law' (*nomos*) and the Romans had followed by inventing the first legal science, an entirely new element entered the history of human social relations. Citizens and historians alike have disputed its importance and character ever since. Individual incidents of legal procedure – not only torture, but the concept of evidence, the character of witnesses, and the functions of advocates and magistrates – thus emerged from earlier unarticulated custom, closely attuned to the needs of new cultures, but also leading those cultures in distinct directions. It is in this context that we must look for the emergence of torture as a distinct phenomenon.

At the beginning of the history of torture among the early Greeks we find for the first time in western history the transition from an archaic and largely communal legal system to a complex one in which the problem of evidence and the distinction between the free man and the slave are particularly striking. The problem of evidence had emerged from archaic Greek custom, in which the 'law' had consisted of the conflict between two litigants exercising self-help in a contest, an *agon*, surrounded by family, friends and dependents, guided only by *themis*, custom, and *epikeia*, appropriate behaviour. *Themis* and *epikeia*, the 'rules' of particular legal conflicts, came to be pronounced first by voluntary arbitrators, whose decisions in favour of one or the other party were called *dikai*, 'statements'. These accumulated over time into a recognized body of opinion, until the popular perception of their abstract moral quality made the term *dike* come to mean Justice itself. These early legal conflicts probably made little use of evidence, just as they reflected little or no notion of crime as distinct from personal injury. Their outcome depended rather upon the social standing of the litigants and the opinion of the community's most substantial members. The first personal offence was tort (civil injury to person, property, or reputation) rather than crime, and the ambition of the injured party was to have that injury acknowledged and made good.

The transformation of Greek society from the eighth to the fifth centuries BC included the shift from feud, or *agon*, to trial. The poet Hesiod, himself a disgruntled litigant, argued that for the sake of fairness laws should be written, that standards of judgement be clearly stated, and that the most frequent causes of disagreement be surrounded by witnesses who will later testify to fact. The importance of membership in a *polis*, a city-republic, was that it placed each citizen within a much broader legal context in which 'the law' was abstracted from the earlier web of particular events, relationships and experiences and made autonomus. No longer was 'the law' the outcome of a series of household-feuds. The law of the city began to displace the laws of household at the same time as private ethics was conceptually separated from public behaviour. Written law emerged almost as soon as the first recognizable city-republics, and written law defined procedure and characterized those who had different kinds of access to it.

By the sixth century BC, free citizens of the Greek city-republics willingly submitted to many restrictions on their personal actions that would have outraged Homer's aristocratic warriors. But they submitted willingly because they knew the laws, respected those who administered them, and accepted that even legal procedure was generally beneficial, rather than coercive, to those who were free – and citizens. Those who possessed no ascertainable honour or citizenship status – strangers, slaves, those in shameful occupations, or those whose shame (*atimia*) was publicly acknowledged –

possessed no right, neither the right not to be coerced nor the right to litigate.

Concepts of honour and status thus stratified Greek urban society. In the fourth century Aristotle summed up the development that he perceived over the preceding two centuries in the matter of legal protection. He observed that, in the early sixth-century reforms of Solon, no citizen could be made a slave for personal debt; certain acts could properly be prosecuted by the public; citizens might appeal from the decisions of magistrates to those of popular courts. These protections greatly strengthened citizenship status. They emphasized the citizen's unique access to the law, the importance of his knowledge of it and its procedures, his obligation to plead his case in person, and his necessary experience of sitting in the assembly as a juryman himself. Such a citizen clearly possessed honour (*time*), and there were limits to the degree of coercion to which he might be subjected, as well as to the nature of evidence that might be used against him, or by him against another free citizen.

The honour of the citizen lent great importance to his sworn word. The doctrine of evidence itself may be said to have been defined by the importance of a citizen's testimony. Therefore, one possessing no such citizen-status could not provide 'evidence' as the Greeks understood that term. The legal procedural protection of the free citizen and his sharp differentiation from other, far less privileged, classes of people led the Greeks to the conclusion that those without legal privilege had to be coerced into a special status in which their testimony became acceptable. Their testimony became equal to that of citizens by means of physical coercion. The origins of this notion are obscure, although they may lie in the power of a head of household over slaves and dependents. Originally, then, the importance of the honour of a citizen created a classification of evidence that distinguished between a 'natural' kind of evidence that might be obtained readily from the word of a citizen and a coerced kind of evidence that had to be extracted by force from everyone else.

This argument for the honour of the citizen may be illustrated by an event that took place in 415 BC. In that year a number of statues of the god Hermes were desecrated, outraging Athenian popular opinion and precipitating a large number of accusations against citizens. One of the accused citizens, Andocides, accused his own accusers of wanting 'to abrogate the decree voted during the archontate of Skamandrios and to put to the torture those whom Dioclides has accused [of desecrating the Herms]'. Although nothing else is known of the 'decree of Skamandrios', it seems to have served as the charter of the citizen's exemption from general legal disabilities, particularly torture, respected sufficiently to be cited in a case where there was great pressure to discover the culprits and, evidently, an explicit suggestion that some citizens' exemption from torture be abrogated.

In the fifteenth chapter of his *Rhetoric*, Aristotle gives a list of five 'extrinsic' proofs that may be used in a legal process, besides the figures of rhetoric which may also be used: the laws, witnesses, custom, torture and oaths. Aristotle's term for torture, and the general Greek term, is *basanos*, which is philologically related to the idea of putting something metallic to a touchstone in order to verify its content. Thucydides uses a very similar word to describe the work of the historian: the historian must work with a critical spirit and he must not simply accumulate all sorts of records without a critical principle, but must test them with a touchstone to be sure of their truth; he must inquire critically about them. 'Judging from the evidence which I am able to trust after most careful inquiry . . .' (*Peloponnesian War*, I.1) is Thucydides' formulaic description of the historian's task. *Basanos*, torture, evidently connoted a kind of necessary critical inquiry, but it was not the kind of inquiry that could be made of a free man. Put in slightly different terms, Aristotle's *basanos* is a kind of inquiry whose results may serve as evidence in a sub-procedure within a larger legal procedure that is essentially adversarial but whose citizen-litigants may not be subjected to the sub-procedure of *basanos*.

Our sources for the history of evidence and procedure in Greece are unanimous on the question of who can be subjected to *basanos*: it is the slave and, under certain circumstances, the foreigner. The Greeks, however, left no works on civil or criminal procedure, and our chief sources for the torture of slaves are the legal orators and the comic playwrights. The former, in a series of written speeches to be delivered by their clients or to serve as models for forensic rhetoric, and the latter, in dramas that touch upon daily life, are not the lawyer's nor the historian's ideal sources, and there has been much scholarly dispute concerning the Athenian attitudes towards evidence derived from the torture of slaves and the frequency of their use of it. A well-known collection of speeches by the fifth-century orator

Antiphon illustrates the general idea concisely: a choregus (one who was responsible for the civic duty of paying the chorus at religious festivals, and later at dramatic festivals as well), accused of murdering one of the boys who was trying out for a place in the chorus, describes the terms of investigation:

> [My accuser] may take as many witnesses as he likes, examine them, examine witnesses who are freemen, as becomes the examination of freemen, and who, out of self-respect and justice are naturally disposed to speak the truth about the facts. In the case of slaves, he may interrogate them if their statements seem truthful to him. If their statements do not, I am prepared to deliver all my own slaves to him so that he may have them put to the torture. If he requires the testimony of slaves that do not belong to me, I promise, after having obtained the permission of their owner, to deliver them also to him so that he may put them, too, to the torture in whatever manner suits him.

There are a number of legal problems about this passage, one being that the choregus seems to be referring to an informal investigation designed to avoid a trial. In any case, the right of a citizen in a criminal (or indeed a civil) suit to demand the torture of slaves seems to have been generally accepted, whether in an informal exchange of investigations or in a trial proper. In another speech, Antiphon offers one reason for the practice of torturing slaves: a perjured slave cannot suffer the penalties of a perjured free man, that is, he cannot be declared legally infamous (*atimos*), with the attendant disabilities of that status, nor can he be fined. That slaves could be tortured is also clear from some papyrus evidence from Greek Egypt, which states that if judges cannot form an opinion after all the evidence is in, they may apply corporal torture to slaves after their testimony has been given in the presence of both parties to the case. That this was a general Greek practice is evident from the fact that the Roman emperor Hadrian cites it in a rescript (*Digest* 48.8.1.1) evidently derived independently from other Greek practice.

The modes of torture are described offhandedly in a scene from Aristophanes' *The Frogs*. Dionysius, having changed places and dress with his slave Xanthias, has forgotten the right of a master to prove his own innocence by offering his slaves for torture. Shortly after they have changed places, Xanthias is accused of theft, and he sees a way out; he tells his accuser:

> I'll make you a fair offer;
> Arrest my slave and put him to the torture,
> and if you get your proof, put me to death.
> *Aiacos.*   What kind of torture?
> *Xanthias.*   Any kind you wish.
> Tie him to a ladder, suspend or, whip him.
> Pile rocks upon him, put vinegar in his nose,
> Whip him with bristles: but not with leeks or onions.

But it is also possible that the speech reflects a considerable degree of exaggeration and that the very details of Xanthias' *panta tropon* suggest that such a variety of tortures may have been more encyclopaedic in a comic sense than a description of actual practice.

It is also necessary to point out that the power of masters to punish slaves corporally was generally accepted among the Greeks, slaves sometimes being referred to as *andrapoda* – 'human-footed stock' – in contrast to *tetrapoda* – 'four-footed stock'. Although Greek attitudes toward the proper treatment of slaves improved between the sixth and the third centuries, such a power on the part of masters suggests that it was not a long step to permit the judicial torture of slaves, since they were routinely subject to physical coercion of the most severe kind even outside the sphere of the law.

Although at least one scholar has claimed that torture of slaves was the survival of a type of ordeal that was only later worked into the Athenian rules of evidence, our earliest sources, the fifth-century Greek orators, refer to the interrogatory torture of slaves as if it were a commonplace. A well-known example of this literature is the following passage from the orator Isaeus:

> Both personally and officially you regard torture as the surest test. Whenever freemen and slaves appear as witnesses, and it is necessary that fact in the case be discovered, you do not employ the testimony of freemen, but by torture of the slaves you seek to find the truth of the circumstances. And that is natural, men of the jury, for you know that some of the witnesses have appeared to give false evidence, but none of the slaves has ever been proved to make untrue statements as a result of their torture.

Such a statement implies an Athenian view of the reliability of torture that contrasts sharply with other aspects of Athenian culture. Indeed, this and similar statements in other orators have been dismissed as fictions, chiefly because there is also no evidence as to widespread or even customary torture of slaves in Athenian law. The same orators upon whose evidence for the torture of slaves we are forced to rely also imply that threats to torture slaves were part of the rhetorical display of the court and that some orators could also give perfectly plausible arguments against the truthworthiness of slave testimony. In short, the fifth and fourth centuries provide some ambiguous evidence that the judicial torture of slaves was acceptable in theory, but very little evidence either that many slaves were tortured or that Athenians thought very highly of such testimony.

But Greek law had two facets: on the one hand, a body of civil law was slowly built up possessing its own rules and procedures; on the other, the law was often in danger of being exploited for political reasons, and there is much more evidence that in political cases torture may have been more frequent than in routine civil or criminal litigation.

After the Athenian defeat at Syracuse in 413 BC, the Syracusans put the Athenian leader Nicias to death because, as Thucydides says, 'certain Syracusans . . . were afraid . . . that on some suspicion of their guilt he might be put to torture and bring trouble on them in the hour of their prosperity.' (*Peloponnesian War*, VII.86) The possibility that Nicias might have been tortured by the Lacaede-monians appears to have been a justified expectation of the Syracusans, perhaps because interrogatory torture under the extenu-ating circumstances of battle or capture by an enemy power was not part of the routine law of the Greeks and offered freer opportunities for torture and aggravated punishment.

The exceptional character of political life, whether in the hands of the enemy or in those of one's political enemies at home, suggests that whatever the facts of slave torture, the torture of freemen proved to be exceptionally difficult, even in a period of general unrest such as had been the case in the desecration of the Herms. But the fear of the Syracusans over the possible incriminating testimony of Nicias was not unfounded in the political atmosphere of the fifth century. In 411, Phrynichus, a leading member of the oligarchy of the Four Hundred in Athens, was assassinated, and although the assassin, a soldier, escaped, an accomplice was taken and, as Thucydides says (*Peloponnesian War*, VIII.92), was tortured by order of the Four Hundred, although he revealed very little information under torture. Such irregular torture of freemen (although the victim of the Four Hundred was not an Athenian, but an Argive) seems to have been rare in Greece, perhaps the best-known case having occurred a century before in the torture of Aristogiton in 514 for his part in the assassination of the Peisistratid Hipparchus.

Torture in Roman law

Since Roman law, shaped by some Greek influences, constituted the greatest body of learned jurisprudence known to western tradition, its doctrine of torture influenced strongly the two revivals of torture that the western world has experienced – those of the thirteenth and twentieth centuries.

Briefly put, in the earliest Roman law, as in Greek law, only slaves might be tortured, and then only when they have been accused of a crime. Later, they might be tortured as witnesses, although with severe restrictions. Originally only a criminal accusation against a slave could elicit slave testimony, but by the second century, slaves could be tortured in pecuniary cases as well. Freemen, originally preserved from torture (and from the forms of capital punishment reserved for slaves), come under its shadow in cases of treason under the Empire, and then in a broader and broader spectrum of cases determined by imperial order. The division of Roman society into the classes of *honestiores* and *humiliores* after the second century AD made the *humilioris* class liable to the means of interrogation and punishment once appropriate only for slaves. And even the *honestiores* could be tortured in cases of treason and other specified crimes, as defendants and witnesses.

As in Greece, Roman slave-owners under the Republic had the absolute right to punish and torture their own slaves, when they suspected them of offences against themselves within their own property. This right was not abolished in Roman law until 240 AD, by a rescript of the emperor Gordian (*Code* 9.41.6). Cicero's speech *Pro Cluentio* recounts a case in which Sassia, the mother-in-law of Cluentius Avitus, put one of her own slaves to torture in her own house. The slave confessed, was tortured a second time, and was then killed, Cicero argues, because of Sassia's fear that he might retract his testimony elicited by torture. Such treatment of slaves seems to have been common in Rome, and led the great historian Theodor Mommsen to argue that Roman domestic discipline was the basis of later Roman penal procedure in civil and criminal law, a view that has much to recommend it.

Since Roman law constituted part of the pattern for torture in later European law until the nineteenth century, some consideration of its character and details ought to be given here. There is no better place to start than with Mommson's argument from domesticity.

The shift of law in any culture from a conflict between individuals and families to a public trial is always a complex matter. Much of the legal procedure of the Roman Republic can only be understood from the point of view of private 'justice'. From feud, even blood feud, and private revenge the next step led easily to voluntary arbitration by a third party, from voluntary or communal arbitration to arbitration imposed routinely by the state in the *legis actiones* (forms of legal action), then to a wider formulary procedure and finally to the procedure *cognitio extra ordinem*, in which the state wholly administered judicial proceedings. As Alan Watson (*The Law of the Ancient Romans* (Dallas, 1970), p.10) has argued, some of these developments took place quite early among the Romans. In the *cognitio extra ordinem* the parties to a suit lose control over its course and the private citizen acting as an arbitrator gives way to a public official delegated by the emperor or by an official high in the imperial administration. In the course of this transition the power of the state increased from its original role in the *legis actiones* of controlling vengeance and organizing arbitration. In addition, certain actions came to be considered *crimina*, acts which put the security of society in danger and threatened the loss of the *pax deorum*, the peaceful benevolence of the gods, and these were distinguished from those purely private conflicts known as *iudicia privata*.

This brief summary reflects the generally recognized divisions of Roman legal history: the period of ancient law (to the third century BC); the classical period (from the second century BC to the beginning of the third century AD); and the law of the later Empire (from the third century AD to the sixth century AD). Historians of Roman law, unlike those of Greek law, regard even the earliest Roman legal procedure as a collective process rather than exclusively one of self-help; the community voice was heard in any case early and consistently throughout a legal dispute, whether in the person of a voluntary arbitrator or that of a public magistrate.

It has been argued that one of the great forces that transformed Roman law from the primitive and sacral stage to a rationalized and secular stage was the influence of Greek thought from the fifth century BC on. During this long and slow process, the oath and the testimony of witnesses acquired greater recognition, as did the formal character of complaints and the method of arbitrating them. The formulary procedure represented a greater sophistication in categorizing and weighing evidence, particularly that of written evidence. The later development of the early *cognitio extra ordinem* made it the standard form of the Roman trial, governed totally by a single magistrate who, usually a member of a class below the highest in Roman society, was professionally informed about legal matters.

In the process of ancient classical law, the principle of the inviolability of the freeborn citizen was strictly adhered to. Theodor Mommsen pointed out that never in the history of the Republic was there any indication that that principle had been violated. Even Roman slaves outside of the household appear to have been vulnerable to torture only in criminal proceedings and not, like their counterparts in Greece, in civil cases indiscriminately. In his *De partitione oratoria* (34.117–18), written around 45 BC, Cicero discussed the advocate's approach to evidence produced by torture:

> If examination of witnesses held under torture or demand to hold such examination is likely to help the case, you must first support that institution, and speak about the efficacy of pain, and about the opinion of our ancestors, who undoubtedly would have repudiated the whole thing if they had not approved of it; and about the institutions of the Athenians and Rhodians, highly cultivated people, with whom even freemen and citizens – most shocking as this is – are put to the torture; and also about the institutions of our fellow-countrymen, persons of supreme wisdom, who although they would not allow slaves to be tortured to give evidence against their masters, nevertheless approved of the use of torture in cases of incest, and in the case of conspiracy that occurred during my consulship. Also the contention usually employed to invalidate evidence under torture must be scouted as ridiculous, and pronounced to be doctrinaire and childish. Then you must

produce confidence in the thoroughness and the impartiality of the inquiry, and weigh the statements made under torture by means of arguments and inference. These then more or less are the constituent parts of a case for the prosecution.

Cicero seems to be wrong, at least about traditional Athenian law, and his evidence for the case of the Rhodians is unknown. His reference to torture in the Catiline conspiracy is the only evidence that torture may have been used or contemplated in 64 BC, but his prohibition of the torture of slaves to produce evidence against their own master is generally recognized as a Roman legal principle, although possibly as the result of senatorial decree rather than from immemorial custom. Cicero here, obviously, is defending the prosecutorial use of torture and presents arguments only in its favour – or rather describes the sorts of arguments an advocate would have to use to accredit it if he needed to invoke its use. His arguments are not unlike those Aristotle had given as part of the speechwriter's stock in trade. Aristotle is specifically echoed in Quintilian's *Institutio oratoria* (5.4.1) of the second century AD:

A like situation arises in the case of evidence extracted to torture: one party will style torture an infallible method of discovering the truth, while the other will allege that it also often results in false confessions, since with some their capacity of endurance makes lying an easy thing, while with others weakness makes it a necessity. It is hardly worth my while to say more on the subject, as the speeches both of ancient and modern orators are full of this topic. Individual cases may however involve special considerations in this connection. For if the point at issue is whether torture should be applied, it will make all the difference who it is who demands or offers it, who it is that is to be subjected to torture, against whom evidence thus sought will tell, and what is the motive for the demand. If on the other hand torture has already been applied, it will make all the difference who was in charge of the proceedings, who was the victim and what the nature of the torture, whether the confession was credible or consistent, whether the witness stuck to his first statement or changed it under the influence of pain, and whether he made it at the beginning of the torture or only after it had continued some time. The variety of such questions is as infinite as the variety of actual cases.

The evidence of the Roman orators, like that of the Greek orators, is specialized and illuminates only part of the problem. Legal sources proper offer two more important kinds of information: the transformation of Roman society and the reflection of that transformation in criminal law. The Republican distinction between the free citizen and the slave became less important in two respects after the establishment of the Empire: the emergence of imperial constitutions and practices in the first and second centuries AD and their effect on the law, particularly the law of treason; and the growing social divisions of the Empire that produced the two general classes known as the *honestiores* and *humiliores*. The first of these exerted great influence upon the law itself, and the second created new categories of relative liability under the law.

Henry C. Lea, in his essay on torture (*Superstition and Force* (1866), separately reprinted as *Torture*, 1973) cites a passage from Suetonius (*August.* xxii) which suggests the ominousness of imperial privilege. During the second Triumvirate, a praetor named Z. Gallius happened to salute Octavius while he carried a tablet under his toga. Octavius, thinking the tablet might have been a sword and Gallius the agent of conspiracy, had Gallius arrested and tortured before putting him to death. The idea of majesty that had once resided collectively in the Roman people now came to reside in the person of the emperor. The emperor could not only make law, but he could make exceptions to the law which did not necessarily recognize the old Republican privileges of the freeman, particularly when the imperial safety was (or was imagined to be) in danger.

The sources for the legal history of the Republic – the Twelve Tables, the orators, the senatorial decrees, and the occasional comments of jurists, such as are found in the *Institutes* of Gaius – disappear under the Empire, and they are replaced by the edicts and constitutions of individual emperors, commentaries on these by later jurists like Paulus and Ulpian, and other literary materials. The culmination of this process in the *Corpus Iuris Civilis* of Justinian, compiled in the sixth century, presents a formidable body of law, rationally laid out and explained, that has influenced jurists ever since. But from the sixteenth century to the present, the problem of the relation between Justinian's compilation and the legal history of the period between the first and the early sixth centuries AD has occupied the labours of scholars and jurists alike. Justinian's *Corpus* cannot simply be unrolled and be expected to reveal the legal development that led up to it. However, so many of the fundamental texts of imperial Roman legal history are contained in the *Corpus* that reference to it is essential, and convenient.

Since the figure of the emperor – although normally with the advice of jurists – stands at the head of Roman law, we must consider both the growth of imperial policy in crimes of state, and the social changes that created two classes of citizenship in Roman society and two classes of liability in Roman law.

Octavius' torture of Gallius was the first, but not the worst, example of extra-procedural imperial actions towards suspected traitors. Suetonius (*Tib.* 61–2) details with great maliciousness the steps by which Tiberius sought out real and imagined conspiracies, so that 'every crime was treated as capital', even to the point at which a friend of the emperor's, invited from Rhodes, was absent-mindedly put to the torture because the emperor assumed that he was simply a new informant. 'While Caligula was lunching or revelling, capital examinations by torture were often made in his presence' (*Cali.* 32). Claudius 'always exacted examination by torture' (*Claud.* 34), and Domitian, 'to discover any conspirators who were in hiding, tortured many of the opposite party by a new form of inquisition, inserting fire into their private parts, and he cut off the hands of some of them' (*Dom.* 10).

Thus far, we have concentrated on the activities of the emperors in the area of interrogatory torture alone, but we must note that the pages of Suetonius and Tacitus are filled with extravagances of cruelty, suspicion and murderous, psychotic rage that colour the history of the Julio–Claudian dynasty. It is sometimes difficult to sort out a single thread among the blood that smears early Roman imperial history. At times, imperial anger resulted in a deliberate parody of the judicial procedure: Tacitus describes a scene in which Tiberius investigates the discovery of some mysterious marks beside the names of the imperial family in the papers of one Libo:

> As the defendant denied the allegation, it was resolved to question the slaves, who recognized the handwriting, under torture; and, since an old decree prohibited their examination in a charge affecting the life of their master, Tiberius, applying his talents to the discovery of a new jurisprudence, ordered them all to be sold individually to the treasury agent: all to procure servile evidence against Libo, without overriding a senatorial decree! (*Ann.* II.30)

Tacitus' remark about Tiberius' 'applying his talents to the discovery of a new jurisprudence', is more than bitter irony, since the emperors' position and power permitted them to develop extraordinary procedures regarding the old Roman crime of *maiestas*, or *perduellio*, the injury of the Roman people. Tacitus also tells the story of the freed slave Epicharis:

> In the meantime, Nero recollected that Epicharis was in custody on the information of Volusius Proculus; and, assuming that female flesh and blood must be unequal to the pain, he ordered her to be racked. But neither the lash nor the fire, nor yet the anger of the torturers, who redoubled their efforts rather than be braved by a woman, broke down her denial of the allegations. Thus the first day of torment had been defied. On the next, as she was being dragged back in a chair to a repetition of the agony – her dislocated limbs were unable to support her – she fastened the breast-band (which she had stripped from her bosom) in a sort of noose to the canopy of the chair, thrust her neck into it, and, throwing the weight of her body into the effort, squeezed out such feeble breath as remained to her. An emancipated slave and a woman, by shielding, under this dire coercion, men unconnected with her and all but unknown, she had set an example which shone the brighter at a time when persons freeborn and male, Roman knights and senators, untouched by the torture, were betraying each his nearest and his dearest. For Lucan himself, and Senecio and Quintianus, did not omit to disclose their confederates wholesale; while Nero's terror grew from more to more, though he had multiplied the strength of the guards surrounding his person. (*Ann.* XV.57)

It is in the light of procedures such as these that one should, for example, consider the persecution of the Christians. Originally Christians were protected by their Jewish status, since Judaism was recognized as a legal religion in the Empire, although it did not conform to normal Roman requirements for licit religions. By the last quarter of the first century AD, Roman magistrates were able to distinguish the separate Christian identity from Judaism, and Christians therefore fell into the category of followers of illegal religions and were subjected to the legal liabilities such status entailed. Although there is much scholarly disagreement over the technical reasons for the persecution of Christians, scholars are generally agreed that the torture and aggravated death sentences under Nero, beginning in 64 AD, constituted a precedent for regarding Christians as both impious and subversive and therefore subject to investigation by torture and subsequent shameful and degrading punishments. Lea astutely catches the combination of unique psychological circumstance and the legal power of the emperors in his remark that 'under the stimulus of such hideous appetites, capricious and irresponsible cruelty was able to give a wide extension to the law of treason' (*Torture*, p.10). For the law of treason, the *crimen laesae maiestatis*, constituted the rationale for the emperors' assumption of such extraordinary legal powers. The results of the development of the law of treason later affected criminal procedure in general.

Echoing Mommsen, Floyd Lear (*Treason in Roman and Germanic Law*, 1965) has suggested that the Roman doctrine of treason, the *crimen laesae maiestatis*, the injuring or diminishing of majesty, grew out of early Roman religious sanctions against the killer of a father, *parricidium*, and the actions of a Roman who becomes an enemy of his own community and aids its enemies, *perduellio*. Included in *perduellio* are desertion from the army, the delivery to the enemy of any Roman territory, giving aid and comfort to the enemy, the inciting of a war against Rome or a rebellion within, and the breaking of the ban of exile by returning illegally to Italy. *Perduellio* also included assaults on magistrates and violations of the obligations of client to patron. Again echoing Mommsen, Lear traces the history of the term *maiestas* so that it becomes associated with the dignity of the representatives, or tribunes, of the plebs, who were not protected by the patrician notion of *perduellio*. By the end of the Republic, the single term *maiestas*, majesty, had come to stand for the dignity of the Roman people and state, having absorbed earlier terms and extended itself to insult as well as injury. On occasion a temporary dictator might arrogate such status to himself as to make assaults on him technically a crime against the *maiestas* of the Roman people, as Octavius had in the case of Q. Gallius before he became emperor. Once the head of the state became the *Augustus*, he was able to cluster about himself the old sanctions against parricide, violating the duties of a patrician, injuring or insulting the tribune of the people, and violating religious sanctions, so that the *crimen laesae maiestatis* was a crime of impiety as well as insult and injury, and then not simply against a private individual, but against one who embodied the dignity, sacrality and majesty of the Roman state in his own person.

Such a spectrum of authority explains the freedom of the Julio–Claudian emperors to protect themselves against real or fancied threats that is so grimly calendared in Suetonius and Tacitus. This precocious development of the Roman law of treason survived the Julio–Claudian house and influenced not only the incidence of torture in the Roman Empire, but an extraordinarily heightened idea of the state.

Besides the transformation of the doctrine of *maiestas*, we must also consider some of the legal consequences of social change in the Empire between the first and the fourth centuries. The old Roman Republican distinctions between freemen and slaves and, among the freemen, between patricians and plebeians, effectively ended with the social wars and the fall of the Republic. The new distinctions, which appear in law by the third century AD, speak of two kinds of citizen: *honestiores* and *humiliores*. The former were privileged and served as the effective governing class of the Empire; the latter were the rest of the people, those in minor trades, the poor and the uprooted. The way in which these distinctions were translated into law may be seen in a passage from Justinian's *Digest*:

> The credibility of witnesses should be carefully weighed. Therefore, in investigating their persons attention should be paid *first of all* to the rank of each, whether a man is a decurion [an urban official ranking as *honestoris*] or a plebeian [*humilioris*] or whether his life is honourable and blameless, or on the contrary he is a man branded by public disgrace [*infamia*: see below] and is reprehensible . . . (22.5)

Justinian's directive was not limited to advising magistrates on how to estimate the character of witnesses. For by the sixth century the legal reflections of *honestiores/humiliores* and the new ruthlessness of criminal law under the emperors made the *humiliores* the first Roman free victims of judicial torture, outside of those who had been tortured under the provisions of the *crimen laesae maiestatis*. Nor was torture the only burden that *humilioris* status entailed. Certain kinds of punishment, such as corporal punishment by being thrown to the wild beasts or by being crucified, were the lot of the convicted *humilioris*. The lowest class of free citizens of the Empire, subject to such examination and punishment as had once been applicable only to slaves and to free citizens in cases of treason, had now slipped juridically down to that level itself. Citizenship no longer offered the protection to all citizens it once had done.

By the period of the early Empire several features of Roman legal history helped make the law of treason central to the question of torture. On the one hand, some categories of people were regarded as being so low, and on the other, some kinds of crime so vile, as to break down restraints otherwise present in the system. The establishment of the emperor's position as personification of the majesty of the Roman people, and the emergence of treason as a particularly vile and personal crime, help to define the context in which torture of freemen developed in Roman criminal law. But a classic case will remind us of the strength of the protection which the law afforded normally to Roman citizens around the middle of the first century AD.

One of the best-known trials in the history of Roman law, although not for legal reasons, is that of St Paul before the Roman courts of Jerusalem and Caesarea, told in Acts 22–26. Paul, charged with various crimes, was brought before a centurion who proposed to examine him by torture in order to get at the truth of the charges against him. When he was tied up in preparation for being whipped, Paul asked the centurion: 'Can you legally flog a man who is a Roman citizen and moreover has not been found guilty?' After verifying Paul's claim with his superior, the centurion not only released him, but worried, 'because Paul was a Roman citizen and that he had put him in irons'. Although the rest of the trial illustrates other points of Roman procedure, Paul's claim that citizenship exempted him from the routine criminal investigative procedures is a striking example of the sacrosanctity of Roman citizenship in a highly visible provincial administrative centre.

It should also be noted that Paul merely had to voice the claim to citizenship for the torture to be suspended. The claim had to be investigated meticulously. Nearly two centuries later Ulpian (*Digest* 48.18.12) cited an imperial rescript stating: 'When anyone to avoid being tortured alleges that he is free, the Divine Hadrian stated in a rescript that he should not be put to the question before the case brought to decide his freedom has been tried.' Thus, in cases like that of St Paul, the claim to freedom acted as a kind of interlocutory decree that had to be resolved before the original process could proceed. And from the evidence of Acts, it appears that Hadrian himself was merely restating an older principle of law.

The Romans used a number of terms to describe what we, somewhat indiscriminately, called 'torture'. The investigative process in Roman criminal procedure was called *quaestio*, which also referred to the court itself. *Tormentum* originally referred to a form of punishment, including the aggravated death penalty, to which, under the Republic, only slaves were subjected, although later freemen were also liable to it for certain crimes. When *tormentum* was applied in an interrogatory way, the technical term was *quaestio per tormenta*, or *quaestio tormentorum*, that is an investigation by means that had originally been strictly a form of punishment, and that of slaves only. Ulpian was also specific about the linking of these terms:

> By 'torture' we should understand, torment and corporeal suffering and pain employed to extract the truth. Therefore, a mere interrogation of a moderate degree of fear does not justify the application of this edict. In the term 'torment' are included all those things which relate to the application of torture. Hence, when force and torment are resorted to, this is understood to be torture. (*Digest* 47.10.15.41)

Ulpian elsewhere could remark (*Digest* 29.5.1.25): 'We, however, understand the term torture to mean not merely being put to the question, but every inquiry and defence that may be made in the investigation of the death of the master.' Evidently, by Ulpian's day, *quaestio* and *tormentum/tortura* had become virtually synonymous. This identification is preserved in French, in which the term *la question* in the criminal process was long synonymous with *la torture*. Thus, the terminology of Roman torture explains why it was originally confined to slaves, since it was a development of punishments applicable only to slaves.

Indeed, the vast bulk of the material in the *Digest* in the title 'Concerning Torture' (48.18) refers routinely to the torture of slaves. The single exception consists of a statement by Arcadius Charisius (*Digest* 48.18.10.1): 'But when the charge is treason, which concerns the lives of emperors, all without exception are to be tortured, if they are called to give evidence, and when the case requires it.' Charisius, writing around 300 AD, is a late witness, but he testifies to a practice that was clearly recognized informally in the first century, and officially during the second.

Customarily, as has been pointed out, slaves could be tortured only in criminal cases. The emperor Antoninus Pius, however, extended their liability to pecuniary cases in the second century:

> The Divine Pius stated in a rescript that torture could be inflicted upon slaves in cases where money was involved, if the truth could not otherwise be ascertained, which is also provided by other rescripts. This, however, is true to the extent that this expedient should not be resorted to in a pecuniary case, but only where the truth cannot be ascertained, unless by the employment of torture it is lawful to make use of it, as the Divine Severus stated in a rescript. (*Digest* 48.18.9)

Thus, the area of law in which slaves could legitimately be tortured expanded to certain civil areas by the second century. At the beginning of the Empire, Augustus had cautioned against the use of torture (*Digest* 48.18.8): 'I do not think that torture should be inflicted in every instance, and upon every person; but when capital and atrocious crimes [*capitalia et atrociora maleficia*] cannot be detected and proved except by means of the torture of slaves, I hold that it is most effective for ascertaining the truth and should be employed.' About jurists' and emperors' doubts concerning the efficacy of evidence obtained, by torture, we will speak below. Here it is sufficient to note that the range of torture expanded dramatically between Augustus' time and that of the Antonine emperors in the second century. The qualification 'when the truth cannot otherwise be ascertained', marks both Augustus' and Antoninus Pius' observations, but it seems to have come to mean less and less during the second and third centuries.

As the occasions for torturing slaves expanded, they also began to be extended into the lowest class of citizens. Callistratus, around 200 AD, noted a similar development in terms of the death penalty (*Digest* 48.19.28.11): 'Slaves who have plotted against the lives of their masters are generally put to death by fire; freemen sometimes also suffer this penalty, if they are plebeians and persons of low rank.' An early fourth-century rescript of the emperors Diocletian and Maximian (*Code* 9.41.8) states:

> We do not permit soldiers to be subjected to torture, or to the penalties imposed upon plebeians in criminal cases, even when it appears that they have been dismissed from the service without the privileges of veterans, with the exception of those

who have been dishonourably discharged. This rule shall also be observed in the cases of sons of soldiers and veterans. In the prosecution of public crimes, judges should not begin the investigation by resorting to torture, but should first avail themselves of all accessible and probably evidence. If, after having obtained information relative to the crime, they think that torture should be applied for the purpose of ascertaining the truth, they only ought to resort to it where the rank of the persons involved justifies such a course; for, by the terms of this law, all the inhabitants of the provinces have the right to the benefit of the natural benevolence which we entertain for them.'

Public dishonour and 'low condition' thus became two of the circumstances by which freemen might be subject to torture. Let us consider them in order.

The early distinction between slaves and freemen, and between patricians and plebeians, included, for the Romans, the idea of personal dignity, honour, esteem and reverence. In defining *dignitas*, Cicero (*De inventione* 2.166) stated: 'Dignity is honourable prestige. It is worthy of respect, honour and reverence.' The Romans, always acutely sensitive to any hint of the diminishing of dignity or reputation, recognized and named the facts of their loss – infamy [*infamia*] and [*ignominy*] – long before they made a formal legal doctrine of them. For a Roman, whether in or out of court, by formal or informal means, to lose social respect was a severe psychological and social blow. Romans could, and did, go to great lengths to prevent their honour from being lost or diminished. J. M. Kelly has recently suggested that Roman fear of shame acted as one factor inhibiting litigation, even in cases where one had right and the law on one's side. Since the Roman trial was one of the few places in which *reprehensio vitae, vituperatio* – unabashed, highly eloquent artistic insult – was the stock in trade of opposing advocates, and where the usual laws of defamation did not apply, attacks on personal honour and dignity accompanied the trial procedure. Romans also recognized *vilitas* – the practice of certain dishonourable trades or professions. On occasion, the Edict of the Praetor dictated that certain kinds of individuals could not bring suit before his court. Among those barred from the Praetor's court were homosexuals, procurers, gladiators, those who fought wild beasts in the

arena, comic and satirical actors, those who had suffered dishonourable discharge (*missio ignominiosus*) from the army, and certain
individuals condemned in shaming legal procedures. During the
second century AD the condition of infamy was recognized as
covering most of these cases. From this time on, the legal sources
concentrate much more precisely upon the juridical nature of
infamy, on the rules governing magistrates' application of it, and the
juridical consequences it entailed.

During the fifth and sixth centuries a substantial jurisprudence of
infamia developed. This development paralleled the extensions of
the occasions when slaves could be tortured, when freemen might be
interrogated and punished by formerly servile methods, and when
'low' condition exposed more and more freemen to torture itself.
These changes are not unrelated. Commenting in the second century
on the old law of the Twelve Tables, the jurist Gaius had
distinguished the *plebs* as comprising all those below senatorial rank.
By the first and second centuries, the upper rank of Roman society
had expanded to include more people than senators alone, especially
in the equestrian, or 'knightly' rank. This upper rank acquired the
older privileges of patricians and senators. Those not in the upper
rank (that is, those called by the second century the *honestiores*)
became the *humiliores*, and just as the distinction between *honestiores*
and *humiliores* grew sharper, particularly in terms of the idea of
personal dignity and legal privilege, so the distinction between the
humiliores and the slaves grew blurred, and the *humilioris*, lacking the
dignity of the upper rank, acquired some of the indignity of the
lowest rank. Arcadius Charisius makes this point (*Digest* 22.5.21.2):
'Where the circumstances are such that we are compelled to accept a
gladiator, or some person of that kind, as witness, his evidence is not
to be believed, unless he is subjected to torture.' The infamous
person, like the slave of old, lacks the *dignitas* to offer voluntary
testimony merely under questioning; torture must validate his
testimony.

The developing doctrine of *dignitas* and infamy constituted one
means of imposing upon hitherto free citizens disabilities that once
had pertained to slaves alone. That the *humilioris* class of free citizens
(made no less vulnerable by the extension of universal Roman
citizenship by Caracalla in 212) was acquiring new and formerly
servile liabilities in matters of legal procedure between the first and
the fourth centuries is amply illustrated by steps taken in imperial

rescripts to protect the *honestiores* from a similar fate. In a text already cited, Diocletian and Maximian protected the status of soldiers; the same emperors repeated a rescript of Marcus Aurelius from the second century regarding the preservation of the dignity of *honestiores*:

> It was decided by the Divine Marcus that the descendants of men who are designated 'Most Eminent and Most Perfect' to the degree of great-grandchildren, shall not be subject either to the penalties or the tortures inflicted upon plebeians, if no stigma of violated honour attached to those of a nearer degree, through whom this privilege was transmitted to their descendants. (*Code* 9.41.11)

Other instances of such efforts at protection of the *honestiores* are many. Ulpian claimed the same privileges for decurions, local town councillors, and their children (*Code* 9.41.11), a right that had to be renewed by the fourth-century emperor Valentinian (*Code* 9.41.16), who excluded only the case of treason from its defensive scope. Theodosius the Great, in 385, insisted upon the exemption of Christian priests from torture (*Code* 1.3.8), thus indicating the alignment of the Christian clergy with the *honestioris* class. That these protections were needed is indicated by a rescript of the Emperor Valentinian in 369, which indicated (*Code* 9.8.4) that although torture could be routinely applied in the case of treason, and exceptionally by personal command by the emperor, it was, nevertheless, widely and indiscriminately applied to freemen for far lesser offences.

Clearly, between the second and the fourth centuries, the privilege of not being subject to torture was being eroded, not only from the bottom of society upward but, beginning with treason and slowly enlarging to include other offences including those determined by the pleasure of the emperor, it was also being eroded from the top down. The occasional and irregular torture of freemen by the Julio-Claudians created a practical precedent that later emperors and jurists may have attempted to regulate in theory, but expanded in practice. And magistrates below the level of emperor were quick, or indifferent, to follow suit.

Nor was treason, even a vastly expanded definition of treason, the only reason that emperors legitimated the use of torture against freemen. Caracalla in 217 (*Code* 9.41.3) authorized it in cases when a woman was accused of administering poison. In the fourth century Constantius (*Code* 9.41.7) made soothsayers, sorcerers, magicians, diviners and augurs liable to both interrogatory torture and the aggravated forms of capital punishment. Constantine and Justinian (*Code* 9.9.31; *Novel* 117.15.1) authorized its use in cases of unnatural lusts and adultery respectively. Diocletian issued an edict stating that all Christians should be deprived of the privileges of status and be subject to the application of torture, an edict naturally not preserved in the *Corpus* of the Christian emperor Justinian.

By the fourth century, the old sharp line between privileges of freemen and slaves had long since disappeared, and a variety of offences brought freemen under the threat of torture. At the top of Roman society, first treason, then the expanded definitions of treason and the addition of other offences, also exposed *honestiores* to torture. The appearance of a class of bureaucratic magistrates, no longer the learned jurists of the second and third centuries, probably made the application of torture more routine and less considered. The series of imperial edicts cited above which tried to remind officials about the restrictions on torture probably reflected a real problem and real imperial and *honestioris* concerns.

The character of Roman torture

The chief legal sources for the Roman law of torture are found in the *Code* of Justinian (9.41) and in the *Digest* (48.18). The former consists of imperial constitutions, the latter of the opinions of jurists. Together, the sources discussed so far offer a comprehensive account of the occasions of torture, but they say little of methods of torture. They also contain a jurisprudence of torture and a survey of opinion on the reliability of evidence gained by torture. The remarks of Cicero and Quintilian cited above suggest that the orators were perfectly aware that the occasions of torture and the results of testimony elicited by torture had to be manipulated during the trial depending upon whether the speaker defended or opposed the evidence in question. Such purely practical viewpoints as they advocate does not suggest a particular oratorical approval or disapproval of torture, but they do suggest no absolute conviction of the reliability of evidence elicited in this manner. The *Digest*, while presenting the point of view of the jurists, is at once less ambivalent and more cautious. One of the most important texts in the *Digest* (48.18) consists of twenty-seven extracts from the lost *Treatise on the Duties of a Proconsul* by Ulpian. Ulpian's very first observation notes that Augustus had stated that 'confidence should not unreservedly be placed in torture', and that torture should not begin in inquiry. In fact, the opening of Ulpian's whole discussion deals with cautionary warnings about the place of torture in the judicial process, the requirement of other evidence, the presence of strong suspicion, the prohibitions on torturing slaves for evidence against their own masters, and the kinds of questions that should be put during torture. The *Digest* (48.18.1.23) contains a remarkable reservation concerning the whole question:

> It was declared by the Imperial Constitutions that while confidence should not always be reposed in torture, it ought not to be rejected as absolutely unworthy of it, as the evidence obtained is weak and dangerous, and inimical to the truth; for most persons, either through their power of endurance, or through the severity of the torment, so despise suffering that the truth can in no way be extorted from them. Others are so little able to suffer that they prefer to lie rather than to endure the question, and hence it happens that they make confessions of different kinds, and they not only implicate themselves, but others as well.

Thus, emperors, orators and jurists all recognized the problem of evidence extracted by torture, although such concerns seem to have been the limit of their concern for the practice. Like the Greeks, the Romans recognized in treason, and in servile or low social status, adequate causes for the continuation of practices that they themselves knew were highly unreliable. The jurisprudential safeguards the Romans devised were based not upon an anachronistic humanitarianism, but upon their conviction that the evidence produced by it was a *res fragilis et periculosa*, a 'difficult and dangerous business', and could easily be misleading or false. Valerius Maximus cited a number of cases in which torture produced evidence that proved unreliable. Quintus Curtius Rufus (*Historia*, VI.xi) tells the story of the torture of Philotas for evidence in a conspiracy against Alexander the Great. After extensive torture, Philotas promised to confess if it were stopped. When the torture ceased, Philotas turned to the investigator and asked 'What do you wish me to say?' Curtius Rufus observes that no one knew whether to believe Philotas, 'for pain elicits both true confessions and false statements'. Although they had some misgivings about the legitimacy of torture, the Romans also had few misgivings about its effect upon human beings. Between the second and the fifth centuries, they expanded and developed a method of investigation about whose reliability they had few illusions. Instead of questioning the method, they surrounded it with a jurisprudence that was designed to give greater assurance to its reliability, a jurisprudence that is admirable in its scepticism and unsettling in its logic.

To appreciate both scepticism and logic it is necessary to look at Roman methods of torture, about which both the *Code* and the *Digest* are conspicuously silent. These methods remind us of the multiple meanings of such terms as *tormentum*, since the means of interrogatory torture sometimes derived from aggravated physical punishments and sometimes offered new models for such punishments, including means of capital punishment.

The standard means of torture (later, apparently, adopted as a means of aggravated capital punishment) was the rack, a wooden frame set on trestles in which the victim was placed with hands and feet fastened in such a way that the joints could be distended by the operation of a complex system of weights and ropes. Such distension of the joints and muscles was the aim of related tortures such as the *lignum*, two pieces of wood that pulled the legs apart. A torture that seems to have been derived from capital punishment was that of the *ungulae*, hooks that lacerated the flesh. Torture with red-hot metal, flogging, close constriction of the body in confinement (the *mala mansio*, or 'evil house') – some of these techniques borrowed from the Greeks – constituted additional forms of torture. One juridicial source for other forms may be found in the *Digest* (48.19), 'On Punishments', for various forms of corporal punishment were also adapted for use in interrogatory torture. The jurist Callistratus (*Digest* 48.19.7) lists 'castigation with rods, scourging, and blows with chains' among these. Greek methods of capital punishment had included beheading, poison, crucifixion, beating to death with clubs, strangling, stoning, hurling from a precipice and burial alive. The Romans prohibited posioning and strangling, and they reserved crucifixion for slaves and particularly despicable criminals. Ulpian points out another Roman prohibition (*Digest* 48.19.8.3): 'No one can be condemned to the penalty of being beaten to death or to die under [beatings with] rods or during torture, although most persons, when they are tortured, lose their lives.' That is, although torture by rods often ends in death, the death of the person under examination cannot be the purpose of such torture. The Romans also seem not to have used the torture on the wheel, which the Greeks had used.

Aside from the titles in the *Digest*, the historians and the Christian apologists offer the most detailed accounts of Roman penal practices, including torture. Lactantius' *On the Deaths of the Persecutors* and Eusebius' *History of the Church* offer amazing detail of both formal and informal torments inflicted upon Christians, including all of those mentioned above, whether as interrogatory tortures or aggravated sentences of death. In the light of the survival of aggravated death sentences and the extent of popular resentment against Christians and other especially despised enemies, scepticism about the reliability of evidence gained from torture pales as a moderating element in a society which knew of no way procedurally to avoid torture and therefore was inevitably committed to its excesses.

Roman law and Germanic societies

In the history of the legal institutions and mentality of the Germanic invaders and settlers of the Roman Empire after the fourth century, we can see yet again the transformation of archaic legal practices into more complex ones, partly as a result of internal changes within Germanic societies and partly as a result of the availability of a developed, learned law, in this case that of Rome. As in archaic Greek and perhaps early Roman law, the concept of personal injury and self-help precedes that of crime, the concept of the feud precedes that of trial, and freeman status not only distinguishes the Germanic warrior from the slave and the stranger, but attributes to him many qualities similar to those that had once protected Athenian citizens and Roman citizens of the *honestioris* class. But the Germanic societies of early medieval Europe did not, for the most part, swiftly develop and adapt their practices and values to those of Roman law. In most cases Roman law did not become widely known and studied in northern Europe until the end of the eleventh century. Not until the twelfth did much of it influence the legal institutions of Europe.

But for those who were not freemen, or those who were disgraced freemen, Germanic law did permit torture and punishments of a kind that diminished personal honour. Slaves accused of crimes, the wives of a murdered man of rank, and the freeman publicly pronounced a traitor, deserter or coward might all be treated in this way. Tacitus' *Germania*, written at the end of the first century, clearly recognizes these characteristics of Germanic legal culture.

In many cases among the Germanic legal codes (which certainly do not comprise the sum total of actual Germanic legal practice), there is an echo of the earlier custom of the Roman torture of slaves. But even in this case, as Lea observed (*Torture*, p.26), 'the legal regulations for the torture of slaves are intended to protect the interests of the owner alone.' Even slaves accused of crimes (here, as in early Roman law, only the accused slave could be tortured) remained valuable property, and the inveterate Germanic respect for the property of a freeman tempered even its adaptation of those parts of Roman legal practice that did not violate its fundamental premise of freeman-capacity among litigants.

Tacitus' observations on the virtual untouchability of free Germanic warriors, however, can best be understood in terms of our own recently-acquired sense of the difference between shame-cultures and guilt-cultures. One did not live long or well without honour in the world described by Tacitus. But the Germanic world described by Tacitus did not live long itself. From the fourth to the sixth centuries, it broke through the Roman frontier, established peoples and kingdoms within the old provinces of the Empire, and finally supplanted the Empire itself in the West. The rapid social changes that followed from these adventures drastically reoriented Germanic society, a process that can be traced from the transformation of kingship to the appearance of written legal codes. At first the principle of the personality of the laws separated German from Roman; one went to law according to the laws of the people among whom one was born. Germanic legal practices and Roman legal practices existed side by side in many places, and perhaps it was in this way that the Roman torture of slaves was adopted by the Germans, although by the fifth and sixth centuries torture in Roman law had long since been extended to all but the *honestiores*. The Germans seem to have regarded themselves as the equivalents of *honestiores*, and, aside from occasional unsanctioned actions by their kings, seem to have preserved the freeman from torture consistently throughout most of their early legal history.

Besides the divisions of Germanic society into the ranks of slaves and free warriors, however, other social distinctions appeared after the fourth century. Gradually, the independent status of Romans and their advantage in clinging to their own law by right of the personality of law slowly faded as Roman legal institutions disappeared and the Roman subject-population merged with the Germanic population of the two kingdoms. By the seventh century, for example, the code of the Visigoths no longer recognized Gothic and Roman legal procedures; Visigothic law, at least, was on its way to becoming territorial rather than personal. Further, the differentiation among free Germanic warriors proceeded apace, and in the same Visigothic code we find references to the torture of 'freemen of the lower class', possibly an echo of late Roman legislation, but surely a sociological phenomenon that bore some meaning within Visigothic society itself. In several countries, 'freemen of the lower class' merged with upwardly mobile slaves to constitute a new half-free class of serfs, but by then these and their legal personality had virtually dropped out of Germanic legal practice altogether.

In the case of the Visigothic law alone do we see a substantial body of doctrine concerning the torture of both slaves and freemen. Although the propietary character of slaves, as noted above, is recognized, and slave testimony was considerably restricted, it seems to have been practised routinely among the Visigoths. Book VI, Title 1 of the *Visigothic Code* describes the circumstances in which torture is permitted and mandated. Torture even of freemen of the lowest class can only take place either in the case of a capital crime or in one involving a sum of money greater than 50 (later, 250) *solidi*. Only freemen can accuse freemen, and no freeman can accuse someone of a higher rank than himself. Torture must take place in the presence of the judge or his appointed representatives, and neither death nor the loss of use of a limb is permitted. Homicide, adultery, offences against the king, the people as a whole, counterfeiting and sorcery are the crimes for which, assuming the qualifications of the accuser's and the accused's rank are met, torture can be used, even upon a noble. But even when the peculiarly Visigothic characteristics are noted, it is clear that the law of the *Visigothic Code* is modelled upon late Roman imperial law, even as it mitigates its severer sanctions.

The Visigoths alone wrote this much torture into their laws, and it remained in those laws through the early medieval history of the

Iberian peninsula and was revived in the period of the *reconquista* after the eleventh century. Although a few other Germanic codes preserve echoes of the Roman law of torture, the fact of the accusatory process and the undeveloped rules of evidence worked against the practical survival of torture until the process of working Roman law into the legal culture of northern Europe began in earnest during the twelfth century.

2

The Queen of Proofs and the Queen of Torments

The legal revolution of the twelfth century

A revolution in law and legal culture took place in the twelfth century and shaped the criminal – and much other – jurisprudence in Europe until the end of the eighteenth century. It derived both from a transformation of the law as it had existed between the sixth and twelfth centuries and from an increasing awareness of the need to create universally binding and applicable laws for all of Christian Europe, and the possibility of doing so. Thus both the 'revival' of learned Roman law and the immediately subsequent formation of a universal canon law opposed themselves to what rulers and earlier scholars perceived as the provincial, 'irrational', unprofessional and archaic nature of law before the twelfth century. Generally, legal historians have agreed with twelfth-century jurists' view of the legal culture that preceded them. That culture has been termed irrational, ritualistic and primitive – and, in less charitable and understanding circles, superstitious and savage. Current research is in the process of revising such opinion. Early European law, however, operated according to certain cultural premises, and it could hardly be reformed until those premises no longer compelled assent. In the legal universe of early Europe, law was not a separately reformable part of a segmented culture; ideas of nature, reason, God and society had to change as well – indeed, before the law itself could change.

The reasons for that legal and intellectual revolution are many. They touch upon both fundamental cultural assumptions and the most important of social bonds; of, in the words of Julius Goebel, 'the deadly pressure of social change upon the outmoded structure of rights and remedies'. In spite of the intensity of that pressure, the archaic European structure of rights and remedies first had to be *perceived* to be outmoded before substantial change could be initiated.

Among the consequences of the legal revolution was the recovery and adaptation of the body of learned, written Roman law, the creation of specifically legal education, the emergence of a legal profession, and new bodies of applied law through western Europe. These changes were adaptations to the changed social conditions of twelfth-century Europe. They were preserved until the late eighteenth century, not only by the continued study and practice of Roman or Roman-influenced law, but by the printing process, law schools, courts and philosophical jurisprudence; and they circulated throughout Europe until the end of the *ancien régime*. The tradition that they created has survived until the present. In one of the most important consequences of the revolution, the inquisitorial procedure displaced the older accusatorial procedure. Instead of the confirmed and verified freeman's oath, confession was elevated to the top of the hierarchy of proofs, so elevated, in fact, that jurists called confession 'the queen of proofs'. Differently from Greek and Roman law, the place of confession in legal procedure, rather than the status of the accused or the nature of the crime, explains the reappearance of torture in medieval and early modern law.

The 'criminal law' of Europe before the twelfth century was predominantly private. Public officers did not search out and investigate crimes. Injuries were brought to the attention of the officials of justice by those who had suffered them, and it was the accuser's responsibility to see that legal officers acted. The accusation of one private party by another was, as the jurists said, the 'ordinary remedy' for what, since the twelfth century, we have called a 'crime'. Since both parties possessed freeman-capacity, litigation between them was strictly limited according to the inviolability of the person of a freeman. The accuser found the proper court (one that professed jurisdiction over both parties), made his accusation, swore an oath to its truth, and called the other party into court to answer. The accused, faced with the charge, needed in general only to take an oath that the charge was false. It might be that the court then decided that the accused's oath by itself was not sufficient for a decision and required oath-helpers, compurgators, in addition to the oath of the accused. These compurgators were not witnesses to fact, but only of their willingness to support the accused by testifying to their consent to his oath. If the number of compurgators was sufficient, the case stopped there with a dismissal of the charge. The oath was the strongest 'evidence' an accused party could wield, and for most charges it was more than adequate grounds for ceasing litigation.

In some cases, notably those against men whose reputation was bad, some charges, chiefly those of capital crimes, might entail the subjection of the accused to the ordeal, a process in which the judgement of God was invoked to determine an issue rendered insolvable by the limitations of human juridical procedure. Finally, in some cases, the two parties or parties designated by them might engage in judicial combat, which was also considered a form of ordeal, on the grounds that God would permit the victory only of the party in the right. Oath, ordeal and judicial combat constituted the 'irrational, primitive, barbarian' modes of proof before the mid-twelfth century. Archaic and unsatisfactory as they later appeared to be, they responded adequately to the fundamental premises of freeman-capacity and the procedural limitations it imposed upon courts. They also reflected the sense of what some historians have called 'immanent justice' during the period: the assumption that divine intervention in the material world was continuous in such a way as to refuse to permit wrongs to go unpunished, even to the extent of being invocable automatically against presumed wrong-doers. People accepted the judgements of ordeal, oath and judicial combat because they believed that they were judgements of God as well as ancient and accepted practices.

From the ninth century on, these procedures became part of the liturgical life of European society as well. Ecclesiastical rituals for the administering of the oath and the ordeal appeared regularly, and clergy participated in them – more, probably, because they could not deny the idea of immanent justice than because of the practices' antiquity and widespread use. Even in those areas in which some traces of Roman procedure survived, notably in Lombardy, little headway was made against them before the twelfth century, although the responsibility of the accused to furnish proof was sometimes modified to permit the plaintiff to do so as well, and ordeals seem to have been used less frequently; nevertheless, the system of the judgements of God remained in universal use throughout Europe.

In some courts, chiefly ecclesiastical, other traces of older Roman procedure were still prominent. The form of procedure known as *inquisitio* – the initiating of an action by an official, the collection of evidence of fact, the taking of testimony from witnesses, and the judgement issued by the investigating judge – was used in a limited number of kinds of cases. Charlemagne used this procedure, but not widely, and the tide of procedure and jurisdiction flowed away from *inquisitio* between the ninth and the twelfth centuries.

In order for the older system to be replaced, a number of distinct changes had to happen: an entire system of ancient and respected methods of procedure and the cultural assumptions they reflected had to be eliminated and replaced; the idea of immanent justice, or judgement of God, had to give way to a notion of effective human juridical competence and authority; and both clergy and laity had to concur in these changes. During the course of the twelfth century, except in a very small and specialized category of cases, these three changes did in fact occur. The older system of proofs gave way before two distinct but equally revolutionary procedures, those of the inquisitorial process and the jury; the ideal of a justice within reach of human determination came to be widely accepted, particularly with the creation of a legal profession and the spread of the new uniform procedures; churchmen and learned lay people both professed to find the idea of immanent justice repellent, stripped the earlier procedures of their liturgical dimension, and then built up a formidable theological denial of their efficacy.

The revolution did not take place simply in one area of social life or for one motive. It was not the revived study and application of Roman law in the twelfth century, nor a leaving off of earlier barbarian practices alone that caused these changes, but a complex combination of changes in society and political authority that influenced the new legal procedure in several different ways. The circles in which homogeneous legal practices were applied widened, as popes, kings and territorial princes centralized much of their authority; during this centralizing process, the administration of law fell more and more into the hands of specialists and, from the early twelfth century on, educated specialists who hunted out inconsistency and conflicting principles, and imposed a particular kind of rationality upon legal procedure. Specialists also wrote. The influence of literacy, from written instruments to specialized treatises on procedure, was enormous after the mid-twelfth century and seems to have played a key role in changing the nature and shape of social thought as well as specific details of procedure. Writing draws with it rationality. The schools and courts of the twelfth century were peopled by those who had studied formal logic and applied it to practical problems of conflicting sources and perceived paradox, and insisted that it guide legislation and the operation of the law.

The story of these changes has been told often and well; as they took place, a new system of Romano-Canonical legal procedure was erected in place of the older judgements of God. The inquisitorial procedure supplanted the accusatorial procedure. Whether the entire procedure was in the hands of a single judge, as in the inquisitorial system, or divided between a jury finding a verdict and a judge issuing a penalty, as in the jury system, the world of human experience required that proofs be sought, produced and examined, that witnesses be classified and interrogated under oath, and that the accused have some rational means of defence against the charges.

As each of the older procedures was abandoned, of course, a great deal of uncertainty remained about the new. As new procedures displaced older ones, themselves now under suspicion, the one kind of certainty that remained untouched was the value of confession. Indeed, and briefly, it may be said that the value accorded to confession offered a kind of protection to the new procedures that evolved. Confession ascended to the top of the hierarchy of proofs and remained there long after the Romano-Canonical inquisitorial procedure and the procedure of trial by jury had come to be firmly in place themselves. For jurists and lay people alike, confession was *regina probationum*: the queen of proofs. For all the uncertainties that attended the gathering and weighing of evidence, the testimony of witnesses, and the unpredictability of judges and juries, confession provided a remedy, and in some cases, chiefly capital ones, it came to be required. It is the importance of confession upon which hinges, if not the revival, then surely the spread and integration of torture into the legal systems of the thirteenth century.

The return of torture

From extremely slender roots in the ninth century, the procedure of *quaestio* (inquest) remained infrequently used until the twelfth century in lay courts, although it seems to have become generally used in ecclesiastical courts during the same period. One reason for this was the greater ability of church courts to accept the doctrine of *mala fama*, or 'bad reputation', which allowed an ecclesiastical judge to hale a suspect before him without the presence or fact of an accuser. Church courts also developed the doctrine of the notoriety of crimes, which also permitted the ecclesiastical judge to begin proceedings without an accuser. Such notions as these began to establish juridical distinctions among freemen, and the ecclesiastical alignment of Frankish and later ideas of *mala fama* with the older Roman legal doctrine of *infamia* created substantial inroads into the idea of the inviolability of the defendant. They were preserved in the influential canonical collection of Pseudo-Isidore from the mid-ninth century on. In church courts, at least, the man of ill fame, the Anglo-Saxon *tihtbysig* or *ungetreowe*, the Scandinavian *nithing*, would have a hard time making a case or testifying in one, particularly in church courts. He could not be ordained, and he found that ecclesiastical courts could diminish or consume his good reputation with greater effect than lay courts could. Precociously developed between the ninth and twelfth centuries in ecclesiastical usage, the notion of infamy was also enhanced by the renewed study of Roman law after the eleventh century. Roman *infamia* had entailed severe social disabilities; so too did the later medieval doctrine, including opening up a kind of hierarchy of defendants in place of the homogeneous assumption of freeman-capacity.

Among legal changes between the ninth and the thirteenth centuries, the development of a doctrine of infamy, more elaborate than that of the Romans, was particularly useful and versatile. Against it a defendant was less protected than before by conventional assumptions and even by the judgement of God. In 1166 in the Assize of Clarendon, the English king Henry II observed that even if those of bad reputation, evilly defamed by the testimony of many legal men, survived the favourable outcome of the ordeal, they were nevertheless to flee the kingdom and not return. With the inquisitorial process, the doctrine of infamy contributed to the overturning of one legal universe by another.

The legal revolution took more than a century to be accomplished. It appears that its new procedure was generally in place before torture became a part of it. Two other aspects need to be considered first: the role of confession and the problem of proof.

For all their shortcomings, more clearly denounced throughout the twelfth century, the archaic procedures – oaths, ordeals and judicial combats – produced definitive decisions. To secure equally definitive decisions from testimony, inquest, witnesses, juries and magistrates seemed, at least until the mid-thirteenth century, far less certain and far more risky for the defendant. Thus in some cases inquest could be used as a procedure only when the defendant agreed to it, as, at first, could the petty (or trial) jury in England. In capital cases, moreover, these were new standards by which to apportion life and death, and a convincing system of proofs took a long time to develop. Some jurists argued that decisions based upon inquest should only lead to lesser punishments. For a long time, the technical skills needed to pursue an inquest were hard to acquire and apply. Just as infamous or notorious defendants appeared, so too did reliable and unreliable witnesses, and judges, prosecutors and juries knew it.

Paradoxically, even though the various forms of the inquest produced entirely new pictures of defendants, cases and witnesses, vastly more information than had ever surfaced in a routine trial, they also increased the fear of error. Confession, once only one of several means of corroborating an accusation under older procedures, now loomed larger than ever as a means of overcoming that uncertainty. One could be caught red-handed, by the right officials and witnesses, only at the moment of the crime. But one could confess at any time. And in the course of the twelfth century, sacramental confession and doctrines of voluntary penance developed rapidly and elaborately. With sacramental confession (made an annual obligation on all Christians at the Fourth Lateran Council of 1215) already developed as one of the two principal arenas of canon law (the other being the canon law trial itself), the role of confession became central to many areas of twelfth-century life. It was not long before it became central in serious criminal cases as well.

Faced with the prospect of open testimony challenged by the defendant, or with secret testimony doubted by the judge, and by a series of proofs that had yet to be graded in terms of reliability and trustworthiness, late twelfth- and thirteenth-century jurists and teachers of law raised the confession of the accused to the highest level of value. Beneath it ranged, between 1150 and 1250, a hierarchy of proofs. Particularly for capital crimes, this hierarchy of proofs was to provide the essential background to the use of torture.

In the developed thirteenth century doctrine of proofs, only two stood alone. One could condemn the accused on the testimony of two eyewitnesses *or* upon confession. If confession was not forthcoming, and if there was only one or no eyewitness, a series of *indicia*, circumstantial evidences, might be invoked to constitute a partial proof. But without full proof, no condemnation could be made, and no combination of partial proofs could constitute a full proof. Without a confession and without two eyewitnesses, then, there was only a graded combination of partial proofs available to the judge and hence no chance of conviction. To overcome the lack of a second eyewitness and the presence of many but never sufficient *indicia*, the courts had to return to the one element that made full conviction and punishment possible: confession. And to obtain confession, torture was once again invoked, but on very different grounds from those of ancient Roman law.

But this has been to get ahead of the story a little. These events covered more than a century, and that century saw other concerns emerge that also touched questions of legal procedure. First came the renewed study of Roman law, dating from the work of Irnerius at Bologna around 1100. At first, indeed for half a century, scholars worked simply at reconstructing and explaining the *Corpus Iuris Civilis*. Roman law was held to be still binding in parts of Italy and southern France, although most of its provisions had long since fallen into disuse. And learned jurists still considered it an expression of supreme legal reasoning, whether it was specifically binding in a particular locale or not. Indeed, in many early commentaries from the twelfth century, the relevant sections of the *Digest* and *Code* that dealt with torture were simply not commented upon and probably not taught. But as the twelfth century went on and the changes described just above took place, Roman law began to influence all the laws of Europe, not merely those in France and Italy. First, it influenced the law of the Church, as Roman law came to be an introduction to canon law; second, it influenced all centralizing legal authorities, whether they adopted it entirely or not, even in those lands in which, as in England, another general system of law would eventually prevail. The doctrines regarding torture in Roman law were there when Europeans needed them, but they did not force themselves upon legal reformers, nor was anyone obliged to begin torturing defendants simply because Roman law contained a number of provisions for doing so.

The earliest mentions of torture in late eleventh- and early twelfth-century sources are explicit: it is reserved for known criminals and the 'lowest of men', *vilissimi homines*: 'Men living honestly who cannot be corrupted by grace, favour, or money, may be received as witnesses on the strength of their sworn oath alone. The lowest of men, however, those easily corrupted, may not be received [as witnesses] on their oath alone, but are to be subjected to tortures, that is, to the judgement of fire or of boiling water.' In this passage from the *Book of Tübingen*, around 1100, the familiar ordeals are referred to as 'torture' and reserved for a specific class of witnesses. The same text states elsewhere: 'A slave is not to be received as a witness, but is to be subjected to imprisonment or to torments, so that the truth may be made plain, just like thieves and robbers and others of the worst kind of malefactors.' Other instances of this ordeal-torture are to be found in the laws of the Latin Kingdom of Jerusalem. As Fiorelli and others have pointed out, the conceptualization of the judicial ordeal seems to have been changing from the late eleventh century on. But this was not without precedent. An addition to the law of the Visigoths states that a freeman accused of a crime had to undergo the ordeal of boiling water in order to see whether his interrogators ought to proceed to the torture. But the stream of legal literature that began to flow from the schools and teachers of Bologna early in the twelfth century began to distinguish among these confused aspects of criminal procedure and separated the legal definition of torture from the earlier ordeals, using the newly-read texts of the *Code* and the *Digest* for their definitions. Although not all commentators dealt with the sections *De quaestionibus*, and although it is sometimes difficult to tell the difference between teaching material and actual descriptions or prescriptions of judicial practice, by the early thirteenth century teaching and practice appear to have drawn very close together.

The most important text in this respect is the *Summa* of the great Roman lawyer Azo, written around 1210. The text is important, as Fiorelli points out (*La tortura*, I, 123–4), 'not only for its great quantity of data and citations, nor for the immense influence that the pages of this work exerted on the later doctrine, since it was reprinted and meditated upon and cited as if its author were still alive for four hundred years after his death, but because it is the unique surviving work from the period before the closing of the glosses.' Azo's mastery of his materials, his presentation, and his awareness of judicial practice of his own age mark his *Summa* as virtually the earliest surviving treatise to contain a discussion of torture as a legal incident in European history. Other Roman lawyers, from Roffredo of Benevento and Accursius to Thomas of Piperata and Albertus Gardinus later in the century, filled out and extensively developed the work of Azo.

In this respecct, the Roman lawyers went far beyond the scholars of ecclesiastical law in the twelfth century. The greatest of these, Gratian, whose *Concordia discordantium canonum*, or *Decretum*, written around 1140, became the basic textbook of canon law for nearly eight centuries, clearly stated that 'confession is not to be extorted by the instrumentality of torture', echoing centuries of ecclesiastical prohibition of torture. From the mid-twelfth century, however, canon lawyers considered the Roman law doctrines of torture and by the first half of the thirteenth century had approved its use in civil law procedure.

The first references to the practice of torture, however, occur entirely outside both the ecclesiastical and the academic legal frameworks. The *Liber iuris civilis* of the comune of Verona in 1228 empowered the ruler of the city to seek evidence in doubtful cases by the duel, any other judgement of God, or by torture. In some cases in the early thirteenth century, of course, torture must have seemed very like the ordeal: God would strengthen those who were just in order that they could resist it. It seems clear that those who are recorded as first using torture are local magistrates, like the *podesta* of Verona in 1228, or the officers of the Count of Flanders around 1260. Some of the earliest indications of the use of torture, then, indicate that it was introduced as a police procedure, perhaps even before any trial had taken place, and by lay officers. Some qualifications of the laws of Verona and other Italian city-republics and in Flanders itself in the course of the thirteenth century suggest further attitudes toward it. In Ghent in 1297, the count and his officers were forbidden to torture a citizen of the town without the approval of the town council. In Vercelli in 1241 no one was to be tortured 'unless he is a known criminal, a thief, or a man of ill fame'. As police powers broadened, informal torture was used from the early thirteenth century on, but originally as a *méthode policière*, and only much later assimilated into legal procedure. Citizens protested its use, at least against fellow citizens of good repute, but they approved it in the case of those generally of ill fame. Magistrates needed confessions and, as they found in the course of the thirteenth century, torture was often able to extract them. In the growing and crowded cities of thirteenth-century Flanders and Italy, the enforcement of a centralized criminal law often fell to the lot of legal officers who had much to do before a case came to trial.

In these early cases in lay courts, torture was probably used as a police method so that in the event of too few eyewitnesses, or insufficient other *indicia*, the case might begin with a confession. Once the confession became essential to the trial proper, however, methods used to achieve it had to be considered as part of legal procedure and therefore out of the hands of the count's or *podesta's* officers. In such cases, in the course of the thirteenth century, the kinds of privileges claimed for themselves by the citizens of Ghent and other towns disappeared. Once torture became part of legal procedure, fewer exemptions because of rank or status could be allowed. A man might be exempt at first because of his reputation as an upright citizen and a trustworthy person, but even this status did not long survive the routinizing of torture in court procedures. During that process there were indeed restrictions on torture, but they were not these restrictions.

As torture was introduced into legal procedure proper, it had to take its place within the framework of confession and the law of evidence. Both ecclesiastical and lay law asserted, for example, that no confession could be extorted. Hence, torture was not a means of proof, but a means of obtaining a confession. It did not intend to force a guilty plea, but a specific statement that contained details that 'none but the criminal could possibly know'. It could be expected to achieve these goals because of those events that triggered its use in the first place. First, there had to be at least one eyewitness or sufficient probable cause that the accused had committed the crime; the probable cause was measured by the number of specific *indicia* ranked and weighted according to accepted procedure. Second, when it was decided to apply torture, the court had to be reasonably convinced that a confession would be obtained. Third, the accused would be preached to and implored to make a confession, and to this end he was often shown the instruments of torture before the application itself.

R. C. van Caenegem ('La preuve', p.740) has summarized the procedure we have been describing:

> In the last analysis it was the needs of criminal practice and new principles for the pursuit of criminals that were responsible for the reappearance of torture in Europe, and not the revival

of Roman legal studies. It seems that the renewal of Roman law
and the reception of torture in ecclesiastical practice were the
result of the diffusion of the inquisitorial procedure in Europe.

Compared to the older forms of procedure, the new inquisitorial
process appeared far less repugnant to contemporaries than it may at
first seem to us. It was certainly more professional. The inquisitorial
procedure offered much that would seem familiar and acceptable to a
modern litigant: the avoidance of rigid, excessively formalized, and
ritually announced and answered charges; the open airing of
testimony and the weighing of evidence from both parties; the
presence of a trained judge who might also act equitably in weighing
intangibles. At its outset in the twelfth century at least, inquisitorial
procedure seemed to reflect precisely that reliance upon reason,
conscience, and a broadened concept of the social order that
historians have praised in other aspects of life in this period.

In addition to the new criminal, the new magistrate, and the new
procedure, the twelfth century also witnessed new (or apparently
new) forms of religious dissent. In some specific areas, notably the
schools and universities, an enormous leeway in discussion and
disputation was entirely permissable, but among those who were
thought to have no professional qualifications for dispute, and
indeed those who opposed the universally understood teaching
magisterium of the bishops and pastors, the appearance of religious
dissent, whether aimed at the structure and powers of the Church or
at actual dogma, was perceived by orthodox laity and clergy alike as
far more dangerous than any ordinary crime, no matter how
despicable. The apparent magnitude of dissent in society, the newly
articulated authority of the Church and clergy, and the unique
problems involved with the discovery of intellectual crime generated
considerable ecclesiastical and lay concern, and for several reasons
the new inquisitorial procedure (particularly in cases where accusers
were hard to find, or unwilling to testify) offered an appealing
approach to the problem.

The process itself, or rather an earlier form of it, had, of course
existed as a routine procedure in ecclesiastical courts for centuries.
In many cases there was hardly the need for a process at all, since a
number of dissidents were willing to announce their beliefs freely. In
the early eleventh and twelfth centuries, aside from sporadic acts of
mob violence, bishops generally used expulsion from the diocese or

excommunication as the treatment of self-pronounced or otherwise discovered heretics. Twelfth-century papal and conciliar legislation urged various other forms of ecclesiastical discipline, but none stronger than excommunication. Even the first papal decree against heretics everywhere in Europe, Lucius III's *Ad abolendam* of 1184, went no further than establishing the category of contumacy for practising heretics. Ecclesiastical discipline, in short, varied from time to time, from place to place, and from bishop to bishop. Preaching and conversion missions, episcopal visitations, the creation of the Mendicant Orders, all represent a generally neglected and probably effective response through the twelfth century. They represent the way of – *persuasio* 'persuasion'.

The steps taken against heretics by central ecclesiastical authorities after the middle of the twelfth century were based largely upon the increasingly sophisticated scholarship dealing with universal canon law. Canon law, generally diffused and regionally applied throughout most of western Europe between the sixth and the twelfth centuries, began to be considered as a single universally applicable law during the conflicts between popes and emperors at the end of the eleventh and the beginning of the twelfth centuries. Around 1140 a Bolognese scholar, Gratian, assembled a vast number of texts from earlier sources, arranged them analytically, and commented upon them as a body of law. Gratian's *Decretum*, as his collection came to be called, showed up the shortcomings of traditional law as well as its strengths, and his successors, including papal legislators and church councils, filled out the law and developed an ecclesiastical jurisprudence comparable – and in some cases superior – to that of twelfth-century Roman law.

Gratian and his successors naturally recognized Roman law, particularly since large parts of it dealt with ecclesiastical affairs, including imperial legislation against heresy and definitions of clerical status. In some respects, Gratian's remarks and texts concerning torture continued a long tradition of ecclesiastical rejection of the practice in church affairs. Gratian insisted that clerics could not apply torture (*Decretum* D.86 c.25), and he echoed the older papal prescription that such confessions were not to be extorted, but spontaneous (C.15 p.6 d.1). But Gratian recognized some exceptions to this rule, also traditional. He acknowledged that accusers of a bishop might be tortured (C.5 q.5 c.4), that in some cases people in the lowest ranks of society might also be tortured

(C.4 qq. 2–3), and that slaves might also be tortured (C.12 q.2 c.59). Gratian also noted the practice in Roman law; his successors, both scholars and prelates, similarly reconciled ecclesiastical law with contemporary Roman law practices. The next great collection of law, Gregory IX's *Liber Extra* of 1234, contained several papal letters from the twelfth century that recognize this (X.3.16.1; X.5.41.6). By the mid-thirteenth century, then, canon law became more universally known, studied and applied, and it drew closer to the precepts of Roman law, especially in areas of mixed interest like criminal sanctions and legal procedure.

It is in this context that the history of ecclesiastical legislation and procedure against heretics has to be considered. Lucius III's decretal *Ad abolendam* of 1184 has already been mentioned, and it should now be noted that the papal letter not only established the category of contumacy for heretics, but it also insisted that episcopal inquisitorial tribunals be established throughout Christendom. In the legislation of the Fourth Lateran Council in 1215 early condemnations of heresy were reiterated, and by the time of the council the legal doctrine of *infamia*, infamy, was inflicted upon heretics in both canon and secular law. In 1199 Pope Innocent III, building upon the relatively new laws of treason of the twelfth century, announced in his decretal *Vergentis in senium* that heretics were traitors to God, exactly comparable to traitors to Caesar in Roman law, thus opening up yet another broad avenue for new legal sanctions. During the early decades of the thirteenth century, the Albigensian Crusade against heretics in Languedoc and the constitutions of the Emperor Frederick II continued this emphasis. The decretal *Ille humani generis* of Pope Gregory IX in 1231, which for the first time charged a convent of the Dominican Order with the power to erect an inquisitorial tribunal with its authority derived directly from the pope, pursued the struggle with dissent and developed new procedures for dealing with it.

In some respects, it was the failure of the ordinary episcopal tribunals that intensified legislation after 1184 and led to the creation of the professional inquisitor. By the second quarter of the thirteenth century the crime of heresy had been aligned with the crimes of treason and contumacy in secular society, the heretic had been declared 'infamous', and therefore the category of heresy had come to be considered identical to those crimes which in secular law led to serious criminal penalties, required the application of the full hierarchy of proofs, and demanded confession for full conviction. The ecclesiastical inquisition did not create the inquisitorial process, with torture to secure confession, but adapted it well on in the process of discovering heresy and developing a number of different means to combat it. From the 1230s on, the Romano-Canonical procedure worked equally in ecclesiastical and lay criminal courts.

The jurisprudence of torture

From the second half of the thirteenth century to the end of the eighteenth, torture was part of the ordinary criminal procedure of the Latin Church and of most of the states of Europe. From its irregular appearances in the twelfth century and its apparent initial role as a police procedure, it entered the regular legal procedures of continental law, acquired its own jurisprudence and, indeed, became a learned specialty among jurists. One of the most striking features of torture, aside from its appearance and use in the first place, is its fascination as an object of study and academic exposition to generations of lawyers and jurists, from Azo and the anonymous author of the *Tractatus de tormentis* around 1263–86 to the French conservative jurist Pierre François Muyart de Vouglans on the eve of the French Revolution. The archives of European states record the first, and a voluminous and highly detailed literature records the second. Let us consider the nature and laws of torture first, and then the jurisprudence of torture.

In all legal systems there is always a greater or lesser degree of divergence between these two areas; in the case of the practice and theory of torture the divergence is more than a little perplexing. On the one hand, some scholars who study chiefly the theory see it as so dissimilar from the recorded practice that they regard it as little better than judicial hypocrisy; others regard the theory as a high standard never met by the actual courts. In the case of practice, social historians see little but unchecked brutality and sadism, while legal historians use a standard of measurement and judgement that often has little or no regard for the larger social questions involved.

In the Latin and vernacular sources the terms used are *tortura*, *quaestio*, *tormentum*, and occasionally *martyrium*, *cuestion*, *questione*, *question*. In German the latin form *Tortur* was used less frequently than the indigenous German word *Folter*, and other terms designated

Marter and *peinliche Frage* (from *quaestio*); in French, besides *la question*, the terms *gehine, or gene* (from *Gehenna*) were used. In addition, most European vernaculars developed specialized idioms to describe particular kinds of torture, many of them euphemisms. By the thirteenth century, when a specific juridical doctrine of torture had taken shape, specialists could address Ulpian's famous definition of *quaestio* as scholarly equals:

> By *quaestio* is to be understood the torment and suffering of [inflicted on] the body in order to elicit the truth. Therefore, simple interrogation or incidental threats do not pertain to this edict . . . Since, therefore, force and torment are the features of *quaestio*, the *quaestio* is to be understood in this way.

The ensuing sections of the *Code* and the *Digest* were then interpreted in this light, and subsequent definitions of torture echoed that of Ulpian. Azo called it 'the inquisition of truth by torment'; and the late thirteenth-century *Tractatus de tormentis* only slightly altered Ulpian's statement: 'an inquisition which is made to elicit the truth by torment and suffering of the body'. Some jurists, following the peculiar etymology of the seventh-century encyclopaedist Isidore of Seville, also spoke of the mental effects of torture, based upon the supposed derivation of *tormentum* from *torquens mentem*, 'the twisting of the mind: since, by the suffering of the body, the mind is therefore turned'.

Thirteenth-century jurists, once they had defined *quaestio*, turned to its legal nature, and some called it a method of proof. But the imprecision of this term, since torture was in fact a means, or an incident, of obtaining a confession, which *was* a method of proof, should not be overestimated. The literature on torture indicates that now magistrates knew exactly what torture was and why it was used.

In spite of the early confusion between torture, ordeals and punishments that prevailed in the twelfth century, the influence of such jurists as Azo, Tancred, Innocent IV and Hostiensis in the early and mid-thirteenth century erected a doctrine of Romano-Canonical procedure in criminal cases that endured until the end of the eighteenth century. The increasing professionalism of lawyers and judges, the role of the schools, and the proliferation of professional opportunities in cities empowered to appoint their own judges and establish their own municipal laws, all contributed to the clarity, common character, and definitiveness of the procedure.

Since later developments often obscure the early shape of the procedure, from the modifications of the Inquisition to the routinized practices of the period after 1450, it may be well to lay out first the doctrines that informed the judge of a crime and led through a complex process to a final declaration of innocence or guilt, and in the latter case to the infliction of the prescribed punishment. Given the great variety of particular applications of the law across Mediterranean and transalpine Europe and the different times at which different regions (including those areas like England that rejected large parts of it) adopted the procedure in its full form, the following description must be general, drawn from different legislations and different academic opinions alike. It constitutes merely a control for the consideration of torture in specific places and times.

A judge could discover the perpetration of a crime only in one of three ways: it might be reported to him by his own officials, who had sworn to seek out crimes and were protected by their oath of office from later accusations of calumny; he might hear of it through *fama*, notoriety, the oaths of respectable citizens who saw or heard of it; or he might know of it privately as an individual. In the last case, although there was some dispute on this point, the judge was generally considered to be one citizen aware of *fama*, and therefore absorbed into the second category.

Having been informed that an offence had taken place, the judge had to ascertain that in fact it had. His justification in doing this was the report of officials or common *fama*. 'It must first be proved', said the jurist Bartolus, 'that a crime has in fact been committed.' The crime had to be punishable. The judge might then call witnesses, hear testimony, and see if a *prima facie* case for anyone's likely guilt had emerged. This part was often called the *inquisitio generalis* or 'general inquiry', it followed the initial denunciations and might be compared to a modern inquest.

Once the accused was identified, the *inquisitio specialis* began: the 'special, or particular, inquiry' which would determine the accused's guilt or innocence – the trial proper. The accused had to be served a writ upon which were inscribed the substantial points of the accusation. The writ brought him to court and, in a residual resemblance to the old accusatorial procedure, either *fama* or the judge himself were said to stand in the place of the accuser. By the fourteenth century, however, the public prosecutor had emerged to take over this role and the management of the case against the accused as well. (Since torture could only be invoked in cases whose punishment entailed death or mutilation, we shall assume that the punishable crime was of sufficient seriousness.)

Once the *inquisitio specialis* had begun, the judge was required to use every means possible to discover the truth before the application of torture. This doctrine, that torture could only be used 'when the truth could not be illuminated by all other proofs', and the doctrine of the hierarchy of statutory proofs, from two eyewitnesses and confession down through the 'half-proofs' and the *indicia*, framed any decision to apply torture and, from the fourteenth century on, literally took the decision out of the judge's hands. Once torture was raised as a possible course of action, there had to be a great, although incomplete, body of evidence against the defendant, some of it circumstantial perhaps, but all of it presumptive. This evidence had to be tested itself: *fama* had to come from reputable people; eyewitnesses had to agree on every particular of their testimony; evidence had to be weighed according to a well-known set of criteria.

In addition, the defendant had to be given a written list of the *indicia* against him; he could cross-examine the witnesses against him; if the judge decreed torture, the defendant could appeal on the grounds that the *indicia* were insufficient or that he was an exempted person. Exempted people, a category drawn from Roman law but greatly modified in the Middle Ages, included children under a certain age, pregnant women, people over a certain age, knights, barons, aristocrats, kings, professors and, according to some, but not all, views, clergy. The appeal constituted an interlocutory decree and had to be answered before torture could proceed.

The torture itself was surrounded by protocols: it could not be savage or cause death or permanent injury; it should be of the ordinary kind, with new tortures frowned upon; a medical expert had to be present, and a notary had to make an official record of the procedure.

Even under such terms, the confession made under torture was not itself valid. It had to be repeated away from the place of torture. If the defendant recanted, torture might be repeated, because the original confession constituted another *indicium* against him. The combination of the presumptive evidence and the confirmed confession permitted the judge to announce the verdict and punishment to be carried out. If the judge had violated the guidelines for torture, he might later be sued under the *sindicatus* process (a formal review of a judge's actions) when his judicial term had ended.

This brief account of the European criminal procedure as it existed in most places between 1250 and 1750 derives from legislation and the opinions of the most influential legal scholars and constitutes a model against which actual practices and differences may be measured. As critics have long pointed out, the inquisitorial procedure has a built-in prosecutorial bias. No matter how restricted the judge is procedurally, such problems as his weighing the *indicia*, the suggestiveness of the interrogation under torture, the quick willingness to accept a confession without then checking its details, and the tendency to torture severely, to elicit a guilty plea instead of a confession, all stack the system against the defendant. The very caution expressed in the thousands of pages of discourse on the jurisprudence of torture between the thirteenth and the eighteenth centuries indicate that medieval and early modern jurists were very well aware of the dangers of the system. They too, spoke of Ulpian's *res fragilis et periculosa*, and they knew what they spoke of; but they worked in a system in which confession was the queen of proofs, and between the two, confession and its key role in the Romano-Canonical process seems to have carried much the heavier weight.

It is interesting to contrast the procedure of the Continental courts with that of other European regions that went through the same legal revolution but emerged without Romano-Canonical procedure and without torture. In twelfth-century England, the Assize of Clarendon stated that the king and his officials would put down certain categories of serious crime throughout the kingdom. England had emerged from more than a decade of civil war, and the subjects of Henry II, great and small, appear to have been more than willing to see the criminal consequences of the Anarchy repressed. The king's judgement and punishment were to fall on all those who were indicted by a local jury of respectable citizens. This, the origin of the grand jury, indicted defendants, who were then held over for trial by a travelling royal justice. The ordeal of water was used in the trial itself, until its abolition in 1215. At that time, after much uncertainty and speculation, King Henry III offered the petty jury, the actual trial jury, as a voluntary means of determining guilt or innocence.

Behind these developments there lay more than a century of

particular English history: under Henry I (1100–1135), powerful royal officials had undertaken prosecutions on their own. Between 1135 and 1166 great distaste was shown in England for the independent exercise of prosecutory powers by royal officials. In Church courts, in which historically a group of legitimate clergy, the *testes synodales*, or synodal witnesses, might accuse someone in a manner prescribed by certain scriptural texts, a similar growth of prosecution by officials had developed. When Henry II produced the Assize of Clarendon in 1166, he did not restore independent prosecution and accusation by royal officials, but created a kind of lay version of synodal witness in the jury of presentment, or the grand jury. The grand jury presented its accusations, not to a powerful local official, but to travelling royal justices, who could then go to trial by means of a petty jury. The kind of evidence that was acceptable in these circumstances was much broader than that acceptable in Romano-Canonical procedure. Circumstantial evidence could accumulate until a jury found it adequately convincing for conviction – as a Romano-Canonical judge could not. There was no state prosecutor who had to be controlled by a rigid system of limitations that demanded torture if played out to its formal conclusion. The English judge did not find guilt or innocence – the trial jury did. With the breadth of English rules of evidence, the absence of a state prosecutor, the different role of the judge, and the responsibility of the grand and trial juries, the place of confession in English law loomed far smaller than in continental law, and the problem of torture became generally irrelevant. Torture did not have a place in the law of England after 1166. Thus in spite of the growing accommodation with torture on the part of canon lawyers in the thirteenth century (and canon law ran in England as surely as it ran elsewhere), and in spite of the discussion of torture in the *Liber Pauperum* of Vacarius, a scholar of Roman law at Oxford in the 1140s, the reforms of Henry II gave a procedure to the law of England that eliminated the use of torture in the very centuries in which continental legal reforms were drawing closer and closer to it.

In a number of jurisdictions, of course, the accusatory process survived, even without the ordeals, and it did so too in the matter of lesser offences in areas where the Romano-Canonical process also existed for higher crime. The so-called 'feudal' courts proved to be reluctant to give up their traditional jurisdiction and their traditional forms of procedure, and they survived in many parts of Europe down to the end of the eighteenth century. Elsewhere, as in the Slavic lands and Russia, rational means of proof arrived late, sometimes under Italian influence, and they often co-existed with irrational means of proof in ways distinct from the rest of Europe. For example, in sixteenth-century Lithuanian law torture could be used only in the accusation of theft, and only at the insistence of an injured private party. It could be used only once, and then only within a year of the actual theft and in such a way as not to mutilate the body of the accused. If the torture failed to elicit a confession, the plaintiff had to compensate the tortured victim with a money payment.

In other parts of Europe the revival of torture took place during a period when, technically, torture had never ceased to be used in the laws of parts of Spain, notably Castile. Although the *Corpus Iuris Civilis* seems not to have influenced Visigothic Spain, the earlier *Codex Theodosianus* did, and its provisions for torture were extensive. Torture survived in Castilian law, figured prominently in the *Fuero Juzgo* of 1241, and occupied a prominent place in the seventh *partida* of *Las Siete Partidas* of Alfonso X in 1265. In Aragon, on the contrary, it was abolished in 1325.

In France, an *ordonnance* of Louis IX in 1254 permitted torture, but it forbade the torture of 'honest people of good reputations, even if they are poor' on the basis of the testimony of a single witness, the formal 'half-proof' of general Romano-Canonical procedure.

In Germany, torture is mentioned in the statutes of Vienna, around the middle of the thirteenth century, but in the form of a prohibition: it is forbidden to torture the accused by hunger, thirst, chains, heat or cold, or to force a confession to specific charges by blows. Any confession must be made freely, in full possession of mental faculties, before a judge. By the fourteenth century local regional legal codes had developed a fuller jurisprudence of torture, as did the regional laws of central and eastern Europe, generally under the influence of the revived Roman law. Torture appears not to have been part of any Scandinavian laws until the sixteenth century, when it was introduced under the influence of new and more ambitious and influential criminal legal codes from Germany.

The system described so far, whether in the realm of irrational or rational proofs, also possesses a social dimension. In the world of irrational proofs, those of the judicial combat and the compurgatorial oath seem particularly to have pertained to freemen, since only freemen could bear arms and only a freeman's word was considered worthy of belief. Fighting men tended to see in the judicial combat an appropriate form for their social status, and many courts recognized this throughout the Middle Ages. Indeed, the judicial combat, in the form of the duel, became one of the enduring signs of nobility long after the passing of the age of irrational proofs, and many courts prohibited serfs and very poor freemen this method of acquittal. For them was reserved the unilateral ordeal. This social apportionment of the means of irrational proof, as we have seen, was continued into the system of rational proofs. People who were considered 'honest', of good reputation, and perhaps important enough to merit it, were the ideal witnesses and, to a certain extent, privileged defendants. In many jurisdictions it took much more evidence to put a solid citizen to the torture than it took to put a known, or suspected, rogue in the same place.

But such divisions themselves were often unable to withstand the levelling effects of the professionalization of the Romano-Canonical procedure. Once torture had been admitted as a routine part of procedure, privilege tended to become weaker. This probably first occurred in the case of particularly heinous crimes, or crimes considered *crimina excepta* – those crimes whose importance was so great that they permitted the waiving of normal legal procedure in order to obtain a conviction. The history of the *crimen exceptum* has not yet been written, but it is arguable that it too is a development of thirteenth-century legal procedure, and that it was built around such offences as heresy, magical practices, counterfeiting, and certain kinds of homicide and treason. Those brought up on charges could count on much less protection from their social status. In the case of exempted persons, for example, later legislation concerning witchcraft and magic sustained most of the excepted categories of persons not subject to torture, but they specifically excluded old age as an exempting principle.

In short, the Romano-Canonical procedure itself contained levelling tendencies that the older system of irrational proofs did not; in addition, the development of a concept of infamy, or that of 'excepted crimes', tended to hasten that levelling process. This is a pronounced feature of the legal history of the fifteenth and sixteenth centuries. It is one of the paradoxes of the social history of early modern criminal law that, although some earlier social distinctions and privileges were lost, this levelling process also subjected larger numbers of people to procedures that originally were intended only for the lowest and most disreputable classes of society. By the fifteenth century every man might be tortured, as the groundwork of early modern criminal law was firmly and professionally laid out.

The inquisition

The treatment of torture in the preceding section of this chapter dealt with its description in the laws and in the jurisprudence of the period from the thirteenth century on. Such a focus has led some legal historians to praise the reason and restraint of the thirteenth and fourteenth centuries and to condemn later periods for the perversion of what had been a rational and protective legal system. Thus Walter Ullmann:

> This humanization of torture lasted as long as legal scholarship was destined to play a decisive role in the actual application of the law. The progressive decline of legal studies at the universities in later centuries brought forth a lower standard of the lawyers who were called upon to serve the cause of law. The authority of scholars diminished likewise, and their influence upon the practical administration of the law gradually faded away. The law itself was no longer regarded with the respect which was characteristic of previous centuries: lawlessness in social life and laxity in the application of the law went hand in hand.

Such a view seems to neglect unduly some conditions of actual practice in the thirteenth and fourteenth centuries and to attribute perhaps too great a practical role to the high standards of thirteenth- and fourteenth-century academic theory as well as too little a role to the academies of the fifteenth and sixteenth.

From its origins as a practical police tactic to its position as a recognized part of the Romano-Canonical legal procedure, torture was consistently employed in courts whose personnel were not always academically trained experts, and it is doubtful that the carefully guarded *consilia* and academic treatises ever had much of an influence except in offering a juridical ideal for actual magistrates and torturers.

The key element in the Romano-Canonical system was its rigid hierarchy of proofs, the place of confession in that hierarchy, and the frequent difficulty courts encountered either in finding the two required eyewitnesses or in obtaining a spontaneous confession from the accused. Two other elements appeared in the fourteenth century: the state prosecutor and the practice of concealing from the accused both the names and the testimony of witnesses against him. The appointment of a state prosecutor came about as a residuum of the old notion of the accusatorial process that there had to be an interested accuser if someone were to be haled before the court. In the twelfth and thirteenth centuries, as we have seen, some jurists said that *fama* took the place of an accuser, or that the judge himself did. In the latter case, however, there arose the objection that the judge could not be both prosecutor and judge, but this was circumvented by the role of the court officials or by the practice of anonymous denunciation, borrowed from ecclesiastical law. By the fourteenth century in France, we find the king's procurator stepping into the place of the old accuser, or the more recent *fama*, judge, or *denunciatio*. From the fourteenth century on, except in England, the state prosecutor plays a more and more prominent role in criminal jurisdiction and procedure. It is the result, not of a corruption of judges or law schools, but of the emergence historically of an official with a particular interest in the procedure, not only of accusation, but of active prosecution of the accused. The inherent prosecutorial bias of the Romano-Canonical sytem had been measurably strengthened.

At the same time, the old right of the accused to know the names of witnesses against him and to examine their testimony was no longer recognized. The roots of this denial of what had been a traditional right of the accused are obscure. As we will see below, they may lie in part with the practices of the ecclesiastical inquisitors, but there may be other reasons as well. First, French criminal justice, to take one example, distinguished between *ordinary* and *extraordinary* procedures in criminal jurisprudence. The *ordinary procedure* resembled the old accusatory process and included a kind of inquest, although one which did not permit the torture of the accused. The *extraordinary procedure* was inquisitorial and permitted torture. It could be invoked originally only for extraordinarily grave crimes, but it was tempting to use it also in cases where clear decisions could not be reached, and it appears to have been extended slowly to cover more and more categories of crime. The learned category of hierarchies of proof was especially felt in the extraordinary procedure, and its appeal to judges and prosecutors grew stronger. By the end of the fourteenth century in France it was the routine procedure for serious crimes. Because of the nature of the crime and the fear of danger to the witnesses or the flight of the accused upon learning the extent of the evidence against him, the concealing of witnesses' names and the substance of their testimony became the next step in the development of criminal procedure.

Another aspect of the increasing harshness of criminal procedure was the reciprocal influence of the ecclesiastical inquisition and the secular criminal courts. Since the Christianization of the Roman Empire in the fourth century, a number of crimes later considered purely ecclesiastical were made public offences. Among these were certain acts committed against churches and the clergy, most forms of religious backsliding and, most important, heresy. Thus, heresy was a crime 'on the books' of Roman law, and the emperor and his judges were obliged to act against it. Since secular courts had one power which church courts were for a long time denied, the power to shed blood, the Church consistently turned to lay defenders and rulers and courts in cases where clerical personnel were canonically prohibited from acting. When the crisis of religious dissent in the twelfth century became acute, many popes insisted that lay courts undertake the investigation of heresy. The most ambitious co-operation they received was that of Frederick II of Sicily, whose constitutions of 1231 against heretics constituted a landmark of secular statutory law. They were echoed in the laws of England, France, and Germany, and they enhanced the existing Roman law on the subject.

Yet, by the beginning of the thirteenth century, it seemed to popes and other churchmen that both routine episcopal courts and lay courts were failing in their duty. With the charge to the Dominican convent at Regensburg by Gregory IX in 1231, the popes created a new kind of official, an investigator deriving his authority directly from the pope alone, from whose decision no appeal lay, and who operated according to the traditional ecclesiastical mode of inquisitorial procedure. In addition, as we have seen, popes from Lucius III to Innocent III aligned heresy with other kinds of crime: contumacy, treason, and even theft, and they declared heretics infamous and prescribed other punishments common to the secular sphere, such as confiscation of goods and property, penitential exile and fines.

In addition, the most spectacular kinds of heresy, Waldensianism and Catharism, were discovered in those lands in which the influence of Roman law was particularly strong and in which magistrates had already spread widely the use of the inquisitorial process – in the cities of northern and central Italy and in the centre and south of France. The analogies between heretics and other types of criminals were pursued by a series of legally trained popes until the pontificate of the most able of the lawyer-popes, Innocent IV, drew the two even closer together. In his famous decretal *Ad extirpanda* of 1252, Innocent stated that heretics were thieves and murderers of souls, and that they ought to be treated no better than were literal thieves and murderers. A sixteenth-century commentator, Francisco Peña, introduces Innocent's text accurately:

> Originally, when the Inquisition was first constituted, it seems that it was not permitted to the Inquisitors to torture offenders under the danger (as I believe) of incurring irregularity, and so torture was used against heretics or those suspected of heresy by lay judges; however, in the constitution of Innocent IV, beginning *Ad extirpanda*, it is written: 'In addition, the official or Rector should obtain from all heretics he has captured a confession by torture without injuring the body or causing the danger of death, for they are indeed thieves and murderers of souls and apostates from the sacraments of God and of the Christian faith. They should confess to their own errors and accuse other heretics whom they know, as well as their accomplices, fellow-believers, receivers, and defenders, just as rogues and thieves of worldly goods are made to accuse their accomplices and confess the evils which they have committed.'
> (Lea, *Torture*, p.188)

Although Innocent's decretal permitted the introduction of torture into the process of investigating heretics, it still did not permit clerics themselves to inflict torture. But during the next pontificate, that of Alexander IV, the decretal *Ut negotium* in 1256 permitted inquisitors to absolve each other if they had incurred any canonical irregularities in their important work. After the mid-thirteenth century, torture had a secure place in ecclesiastical inquisitorial procedure.

Yet the crime of heresy, in spite of papal analogies, did not resemble ordinary grave crimes in ways that permitted the routine application even of extraordinary procedure. It was a difficult crime to prove; although heretics were said to behave in certain ways, it was essentially an intellectual and voluntary crime; it was rooted in places in which neighbours and families knew each other and people might be reluctant to testify, or might testify for other reasons than the disinterested respect for truth; witnesses to heresy might come from social ranks or have reputations which could have excluded their testimony in an ordinary criminal case; finally, heresy was a shared offence: heretics did not exist individually, and besides the salvation of the heretic's soul, inquisitors needed the names of fellow heretics. The end of the extract from Innocent IV's decretal *Ad extirpanda* cited above implies that torture to elicit the names of accomplices was a common practice in secular courts. In the fourteenth century, French jurisprudence distinguished between the *question préparatoire*, torture applied to obtain a confession, and the *question préalable*, torture applied after conviction to obtain the names of accomplices. Innocent may, then, have been referring to an early stage of this process, once again adapting an element of the procedure of secular courts in the hunt for heretics.

These circumstances, added to the fact that the early inquisitors seem not to have been particularly expert in legal procedure (the 'professional' inquisitor, with some training at least in the legal procedures of the inquisitions themselves and perhaps some formal legal training in canon law, appears only toward the end of the thirteenth century and the beginning of the fourteenth), appears to have led the new judges of heresy to employ the most drastic aspects of the inquisitorial procedure, often without understanding or appreciating its conventional safeguards for the defendant – indeed, perhaps, out of fear that those accused of heresy were far more dangerous to Christian society than ordinary thieves, murderers or traitors.

The early personnel of the inquisitions, then, mark one difference in ecclesiastical inquisitorial procedure. A second is their readiness to withhold the names and the substantial testimony of witnesses. A third is their customary restriction of the aid of counsel for the defendant. Fourth was the admission of the testimony of otherwise incompetent witnesses: interested parties, those declared infamous, those already convicted of perjury and so forth. A fifth was the relaxation of the rules of evidence and the greater weight given to some *indicia*, particularly in the area of facial expressions, behaviour, apparent nervousness, and so on. A sixth consisted of the policy of deceiving the accused by introducing spies into their cells, making promises of leniency, and developing a system of carefully designed forms of interrogation that were much broader than those prescribed in the ordinary inquisitorial procedure. A seventh was the category of degrees of suspicion in which accused heretics were held; these determined the intensity of the procedure used against them. In short, the ecclesiastical inquisitors had greatly altered the character of the inquisitorial process as they had found it in the mid-thirteenth century in use in Italy and France. In turn, the secular courts found themselves influenced by the ecclesiastical procedure in the four-teenth and fifteenth centuries. It is in these reciprocal relationships between ecclesiastical and lay inquisitorial procedures, the historical development of forms of criminal procedure, and the changing social and political status of subject and citizen in the fifteenth and sixteenth centuries that the place of torture in European law of the *ancien régime* must be located.

Torture in the ancien régime

Ulpian's response to the question 'What is *quaestio?*' and its variations among thirteenth- and fourteenth-century jurists shows the development of a jurisprudence of torture. Of what did torture consist? And how did it survive in the criminal procedure of the *ancien régime*? These questions must conclude our discussion of medieval and early torture.

Consider a case in progress, in which half-proof, such as one eyewitness, and several *indicia* have emerged in the testimony. The accused has been interrogated and has not confessed. The judge then orders torture. The accused appeals against the order, and the appeal is heard and denied.

The judge then must accompany the accused to the place of torture and will interrogate him under torture. A notary will be present, and a physician, in cases especially of severe torture. The torturer and his assistants are present, but no advocate for the accused. Generally, the accused might be shown the instruments of torture in order to obtain a confession quickly, particularly from the apprehensive or faint-hearted. The purpose of the torture is the confession of the accused, and the line of interrogation must be developed in such a way that at no time is the accused led on by suggestive questions.

The most generally used kind of torture was the strappado, *corda*, or *cola*, called by jurists the 'queen of torments'. The accused's hands were tied behind the back, attached to a rope which was thrown over a beam in the ceiling, and hauled into the air, there to hang for a period of time, then let down, then raised again. Sometimes weights were attached to the feet of the accused, therefore increasing the strain on the arm and back muscles once the process was begun. Perhaps the next most widely used form of torture, particularly in the seventeenth and eighteenth centuries, was that of the leg-brace, and later the leg-screw. The calves of the accused were placed between two concave pieces of metal, which were then pressed together, eventually by a leg screw, and the leg crushed. Later variants included a metal vice, which went around the leg and tightened by a screw device, with its inner edges serrated for greater effectiveness.

A third type, used in its less severe form chiefly for lesser offences and on children and women, was the tight tying of the hands; when the offense was greater, the cords would be tied extremely tightly, released, then tied again. In severe cases the feet of the accused would be covered with flammable substance and fire applied to the soles of the feet. Another torture was that of sleeplessness. The accused was kept awake for long periods of time (forty hours was the common length). Other tortures included stretching (and sometimes being burned while being stretched) on the rack, the torture of cold water, and a number of tortures designed to distend the joints and muscles. In the seventeenth century the thumbscrew was added to the repertoire of the instruments of torture.

The selection of a particular mode of torture was left to the judge, guided by the gravity of the charges against the accused and the customs of the region in which the trial took place. Most jurists urged that judges should not experiment with new modes of torture, and those listed above were the ones most commonly used. Although torture was not supposed to maim or kill, a number of these methods, particularly the most severe, surely resulted in permanent injury and disfigurement.

The judge and the law also regulated the duration of torture. A number of texts state, for example, that such and such a torment should be applied for the length of time it takes the judge to say a prayer, or the creed. In addition to time, the judge determined the degree of severity of the torture applied. Once a confession had been made, the accused was removed from the place of torture and was not usually interrogated for the space of one full day. The confession then had to be repeated in the courtroom in order to become official. If the accused recanted, torture might be applied again, since the confession, whether recanted or not, constituted another *indicium*.

Such, then, was the procedure that led to the regularizing of torture between 1250 and 1800, determined by legislators and jurists, applied by judges and torturers to an ever-widening circle, first of defendants, but later of witnesses as well. It was an incident of Romano-Canonical juridical procedure and, as more than one historian has pointed out, although it was possible to torture without using Romano-Canonical procedure, it was impossible to use Romano-Canonical procedure without using torture with it. Confession, the queen of proofs, required torture, the queen of torments. Precise, limited, and highly regulated in law and legal theory, torture became quickly roughened in the hard world of applied law among the hardened personnel of the court system. From the early sixteenth century to the mid-eighteenth, it had both critics and defenders, and during the same period it was the subject of an enormous legislation and an even vaster body of technical legal scholarship. The invention of print permitted not only the new legislation and scholarship to circulate, but older treatises as well, from that of Azo and the *Tractatus de Tormentis* awards. Print also helped circulate criticism of torture. It is in the light of these developments after 1500 that we must turn to the literature of torture during the *ancien régime*.

The inquisitory process and the criminal jurisprudence that it generated developed earliest in northern Italy, parts of southern France, and, within the wide circle of its jurisdiction, the courts of the Church. In some instances, of course, particularly the case of heresy, there were crimes that touched both ecclesiastical and lay jurisdiction, and here the procedure probably flowed freely between the two. The experience of the towns and the church courts shaped the jurisprudence of the universities, particularly Bologna, and the writings of the jurists circulated even more widely throughout Europe. Thus, in a number of places that did not formally recognize

Roman law and which indeed preserved older kinds of procedure and older or laxer means of proof, there was nevertheless the influence of and familiarity with the Romano-Canonical system. As we have seen, Hungary, Lithuania, Poland, Russia and the Scandinavian countries adopted some elements of this procedure in the fourteenth and fifteenth centuries, although most of their procedure remained traditional and accusatorial. As the legal historian Eberhard Schmidt showed in 1940, a similar process was at work in Germany.

Not all of this indirect influence carried the full Romano-Canonical procedure with it. In the trials of the Knights Templars in England in 1310, for example, papal inquisitors insisted upon the right to torture the accused. On occasion King Edward II seems to have given permission for them to do so, although no torture seems in fact to have taken place, partly, it seems, through the resistance of royal officers and the reluctance of those familiar with English common law to engage in it or support those who did, no matter how great their authority.

Still other instances suggest other channels of influence. The growing thirteenth- and fourteenth-century inclination of lay and ecclesiastical courts to prosecute not merely heretics, but magicians and later witches, generated procedures similar to those for the investigation of heretics, and were to a large extent based on them. In fourteenth-century Germany, the large-scale persecution of Jews for hidden crimes against Christians, particularly in connection with the Black Death of 1348 and later, performed the same service. No formal, wholesale reception of the Romano-Canonical process was required in a period when so many influences were pointing in the direction of the necessity of confession and the surest and time-tested means of obtaining it. Other systems besides the Romano-Canonical knew of the *crimen exceptum*, or at least something that approximated to it, and many turned to the one procedure that guaranteed its discovery.

Only the widespread, although often indirect influence of the Romano-Canonical procedure can explain the large amount of legislation and jurisprudence devoted to the problem of torture in the sixteenth and seventeenth centuries. The literature shows two features that may be taken as historically accurate: first, that those who teach, write or legislate are aware of the irregularities that the use of torture indiscriminately permits, and write or act in large measure to control these; second, that the extraordinarily detailed jurisprudence of torture does not foresee its end in any way, merely the end of its abuses.

Some of those abuses had been recorded in Roman law itself and were well-known to the thirteenth- and fourteenth-century jurists who commented on the jurisprudence of torture. That the application of torture depended heavily upon the character of the judge was known to all, and many of the most devout believers in torture nevertheless recount horror stories of judges vindictively torturing their victims. In Italy such judges were even known under the blanket term of *iudices malitiosi*, the medieval equivalent of our modern 'hanging judge'. In addition, although the judge was restricted in the inquisitorial procedure from using his own judgement, it was virtually impossible not to do so when so many things, including the weighing of evidence and *indicia*, offered a subjective dimension. Finally, the same judges who tried serious cases also tried *delicta levia*, lesser offences, in which the judge's own conviction determined guilt or innocence. It may have been difficult for a judge to shift from a trial in which his own convictions carried such great weight to a trial in which they were supposed to carry no weight at all.

Torture also measured, as all jurists agreed, the accused's ability to withstand physical pain. Most jurists warned that torture had to be conducted carefully, so that people would confess only the truth. Many jurists complained about confessions to murders that had never in fact taken place at all, or to crimes that could not possibly have been committed by the defendant. The early fourteenth-century jurist Bartolus was especially emphatic about the necessity of proving that a crime actually had been committed. One means of getting around this problem was the argument, related to the old magic of ordeals, that criminals who withstood torture might do so with the aid of the devil and, conversely, that weak people unjustly tortured might be given additional strength by God. As jurists noted, the first supposition was more acceptable than the second.

Further, skilful questioning was required to distinguish between a defendant who knew something about the crime and the defendant who had actually perpetrated it. The problem of verifying the confession was widely recognized, although many jurists felt that it was not often observed.

These and other shortcomings of the Romano-Canonical inquisitorial procedure were freely admitted even by its staunchest defenders. None of those defenders, and few of its early critics, envisaged doing without it entirely. As John Langbein has succinctly put it: 'The law of torture survived into the eighteenth century, not because its defects had been concealed, but rather in spite of their having been long revealed. European criminal procedure had no alternative: the law of proof was absolutely dependent upon coerced confessions' (*Torture and the Law of Proof*, p.9). Thus, much of the legislation and legal literature between 1500 and 1750 was aimed at correcting known abuses in the system, rarely and only exceptionally with abolishing the system itself. None of the arguments known to and used by later Enlightenment reformers was new in the eighteenth century.

Thus, the great criminal codes of the sixteenth century – the *Constitutio criminalis Carolina* of 1532 (explicitly for the Empire, but of enormous influence throughout Europe), the French *Ordonnance royale* of 1539, and the revised and reissued codes of the later sixteenth and seventeenth and eighteenth centuries sought to perfect the process that resulted from the momentous encounter of medieval legal needs and thought with the body of Roman law. The vast literature on criminal procedure and torture, raised to a great swell by the use of print, consisted of vast handbooks minutely regulating procedure and establishing and re-establishing principles of law, of which those of Marsili (1526–9), Farinaccius (1588), and Carpzov (1636), are the best known.

In spite of the ongoing criticism of the abuses of torture, and the beginnings of criticism of torture itself, the criminal procedure of the *ancien régime* refined and professionalized the doctrines of torture. As late as 1780, Pierre François Muyart de Vouglans, *Conseillier au Grand-Conseil* of France, dedicated to Louis XVI his massive treatise, *On the Criminal Laws of France in Their Natural Order*. In this work, Part II, Book II, Title, V, Chapter 2 takes up the question of the confession coerced by torture. Muyart begins by observing that many in his own age argue against torture, but he is unmoved by their arguments:

> I conclude that, however rigorous might be this manner of arriving at the discovery of crimes, it is without doubt that experience has made plain that one may use it with success in particular cases where it is authorized by this law, always in

conformity with the wise precautions which the law prescribes in this case.

He then goes on to reiterate the jurisprudence of torture exactly in the tradition developed since the thirteenth century. Perhaps not satisfied with his brief refutation of his opponents on the question of torture, Muyart appended to his large treatise a 'Refutation of the Treatise On Crimes and Punishments' which Cesare Beccaria had published in 1764 and which was perhaps the best-known attack on the use of torture in criminal cases. Muyart had originally written his 'Refutation' in 1766. After describing horrendous statements of Beccaria, Muyart leaves off this tack, hoping that the king 'will have seen enough to enable you to appreciate this work and to be aware of the great danger it represents and its consequences in the fields of government, morals, and religion.' The twenty folio pages of the 'Refutation' constitute the last learned defence of judicial torture in European history, and they reprise the arguments shaped over the preceding five centuries. But the treatise had no effect. In the same year as its publication, Louis XVI abolished the *question préparatoire* from French judicial procedure, and in 1788 the *question préalable*. Indeed, the eighteenth century saw not only a flood of literature concerning the abolition of torture, but a wave of reforming legislation that largely carried out this programme. The causes of that abolition and the sense of security which it instilled into European jurists and rulers are the subject of the next chapter.

3

The Sleep of Reason

Abolition, law and moral sensibility

The same period in the sixteenth and seventeenth centuries that saw the works of jurisprudence of Farinaccius, Damhouder and Carpzov also saw the compilation of the great systematic law codes of the *ancien régime*. The *Constitutio criminalis carolina* of 1532 for the Empire, the *Ordonnance royale* of 1537 for France, the *Nueva recopilacion* of 1567 for Spain, the ordinance of Philip II of 1570 for the Spanish Netherlands, and the *Grand ordonnance criminelle* of 1670 for France together constituted the largest body of legislation concerning torture the world had ever seen, enforced by the greatest powers of that world.

Yet within a century after the *Grande ordonnance criminelle* torture was everywhere under attack, and by the end of the eighteenth century that attack had nearly everywhere proved successful. In revision after revision from 1750 on, the provisions for torture in the criminal codes of Europe were rolled back, until by 1800 they were barely visible. Along with legislative revision, a large literature condemning torture on both legal and moral grounds grew up and was circulated widely. Its best-known example was Cesare Beccaria's immensely influential treatise *On Crimes and Punishments* of 1764, the work which had so outraged Muyart de Vouglans. Torture came to bear the brunt, and in many instances became the focal point, of much Enlightenment criticism of the *ancien régime*, and indeed of the legal and moral savagery and archaism of the early European world.

Although these changes had not occurred overnight, their substance was clear enough to trouble a number of people in the late eighteenth century, and to win the approval of many more, and of these certainly not all were in any sense revolutionaries. The rapid rate of these changes of both mind and institutions perplexed contemporaries, and they have since perplexed historians who tried to account for them. The most widely accepted and influential line of interpretation stemmed from the joining of moral outrage to judicial reforms. After the end of the eighteenth century torture acquired a universally pejorative association and came to be considered the institutional antithesis of human rights, the supreme enemy of humanitarian jurisprudence and of liberalism, and the greatest threat to law and reason that the nineteenth century could imagine. When the American historian of torture, Henry Charles Lea, described its history in his study *Superstition and Force* in 1866, his concluding paragraph summed up an entire line of humanitarian interpretation:

> In the general enlightenment which caused and accompanied the Reformation, there passed away gradually the passions which had created the rigid institutions of the Middle Ages . . . For the first time in the history of man the universal love and charity which lie at the foundation of Christianity are recognized as elements on which human society should be based. Weak and erring as we are, and still far distant from the ideal of the Saviour, yet are we approaching it, even if our steps are painful and hesitating. In the slow evolution of the centuries it is only by comparing distant periods that we can mark our progress; but progress nevertheless exists, and future generations, perhaps, may be able to emancipate themselves wholly from the cruel and arbitrary domination of superstition and force.

As an era of 'superstition and force' the period comprising the Middle Ages and the *ancien régime* was contrasted in the minds of its most learned and humanitarian critics with the law of progress that appeared to govern Europe and North America, at least, from the late eighteenth century on. The abolition of torture was regarded as one of the great landmarks of this change.

Yet several of Lea's 'future generations' have seen, not the permanent abolition of torture, nor the steady improvement of mankind, but more hideous manifestations of superstition and force than all of Lea's research had revealed in the past. Looking back on the late eighteenth- and nineteenth-century optimism we see it less as a quality of prophecy than as, in the title of one of Goya's *Caprichos* of 1799, a 'sleep of reason' in which humanitarian governments and humanitarian jurisprudence optimistically imagined that they prevented the return of superstition and force. As Goya noted, 'when reason sleeps, it produces monsters.'

The abolition of torture in the eighteenth century was surely related to Enlightenment thought, at least to those aspects of it that insisted upon the manifestation in criminal jurisprudence of a growing moral sense of human dignity and value. But that sense did not carry all before it, and moral sensibility did not become the constant in later history that the first historians of torture thought that it had. Therefore, the argument from moral sensibility must be considered in terms of other explanations for the abolition of torture. Among the most important of these are technical legal arguments concerning modes of proof and the legal standing of individuals and more general questions concerning the power and practices of the state and the individual's relation to it.

The argument from moral sensibility, however, did play a very important role in late eighteenth- and nineteenth-century views of the state and the law. It also coloured, as we have seen, a model historiography for the history of torture. And it subtly shaped twentieth-century attitudes, not only toward the history of torture but to the recurrence of torture in the twentieth century itself. These phenomena require discussion before a detailed analysis of the process of abolition itself.

From the isolated and diverse voices of the late Middle Ages and the sixteenth century to the writings of Christian Thomasius (1708), Montesquieu, Voltaire and Beccaria, the condemnation of torture took on a moral tone that justified demands for radical, even revolutionary legal and political reforms. In other areas of scholarship, historians of the Enlightenment have grown increasingly reluctant to take either reformers or their enemies at their own face value. And recent scholarship has more accurately understood the nature of what was lost as well as the character and worth of what was gained by the great cultural revolution of the late eighteenth century. In the case of criminal procedure alone, the initial judgements of the reformers held up for a long time. They satisfied the tendency of nineteenth-century jurists, legislators and historians to look upon themselves and their recent traditions as a triumph of humanitarianism and rationality over what Lea eloquently and passionately called superstition and force.

Such a model suited the temper of the nineteenth century, as it had suited the temper of the late eighteenth, and it gave to the historiography of torture a curious shape. Satisfied that the humanitarian-progressivist model accounted for the events of the period between 1670 and 1789, the nineteenth-century historians of torture (as of much else medieval and early modern) could write with a sense of freedom from the institutions and culture of the past and a sense of hope for the future that have since generally disappeared from modern historiography. Having identified, once and for all, the enemies of reason and humanity, having described and denounced them, they – and the society for which they wrote – were at last free of them. In the work of Lea, W. E. H. Lecky, Andrew Dickson White and others, torture, along with 'barbarism', 'superstition', despotism and theology, stand like gravestones over institutions and beliefs that meticulous scholarship and philosophical hostility had condemned once and for all to the buried wreckage of a hopelessly irrational past.

Spurred on by the humanitarian-progressivist model that Langbein accusingly dismisses as a fairy tale, Lea and others could write with confident assurance that torture, like the duel and the ordeal, had finally vanished from the rational European-American world. That certainty necessarily terminates in the juridical optimism of the late nineteenth and early twentieth centuries. For, by the end of the First World War, torture had returned, and since that time it has increased in frequency and intensity. The only explanation that the humanitarian-progressivist model can possibly offer is that in the twentieth century the world became noticeably less humanitarian and less progressive, less rational and more superstitious, although its superstition had different objects and the excesses of its force were often committed in the names of humanity and progress. Reason and humanitarianism are, however, difficult to quantify, and a model of history which sees them increasing and decreasing in intensity is a difficult model to grasp and use and, even more difficult, one it is impossible to agree upon.

When some modern historians face the question of the twentieth-century revival of torture, therefore, they tend to interpret it as the result of new 'religions', those of the secular authoritarian and totalitarian states, which exert a demand for total citizenship – that is, total subjection – upon their populations analogous to the spiritual discipline allegedly exerted upon Christians by the medieval and early modern churches. Regarded as new, secular, infinitely stronger, but no less intense 'religions', modern torture-using states thus assume the place in the old humanitarian-reformist model that was once occupied by the medieval and Spanish inquisitions and those secular courts that did their bidding. When torture appears in countries that have not yet been modernized, the same model accounts for these countries' 'primitivism' and thereby permits analogies to be drawn between Lea's old notion of superstition and force and the present state of underdeveloped political regimes and their use of what, to Europeans, seems an ancient and primitive tradition. The modern 'religious' state and the 'primitive' un-modernized state, then, simply replace in the old humanitarian-progressivist model the powers of the *ancien régime* and the allegedly primitive character of early European culture.

Philosophically, such a view of certain aspects of the modern world was supported by a long tradition of the criticism of post-eighteenth century society from all points of a broad philosophical spectrum. Karl Lowith's *Meaning in History* (1949), one of the most articulate of these polemics, attacked the very term 'progress' as being merely a misunderstood secularization of medieval Jewish and Christian religious ideas. With such support, the view that sees modern torture as a renewal of older practices and values, merely substituting certain kinds of state and a different geographical primitivism for older churches and an earlier European primitivism is able to extend the model of torture along lines laid down by its critics from the seventeenth to the nineteenth centuries. Even the idea of progress itself can be adapted to this view, as Lea long ago suggested that it could, simply by extending it through time and making it perceptible only in the comparison between periods quite distant in time. The argument then says that progress is indeed made, but not at an equal rate everywhere and not at a rapid rate anywhere. Such, it seems, is the governing premise in most modern histories of early European torture and most modern studies of torture in the twentieth century.

Within such a large conception, so large at its widest that it may be ultimately irrelevant in the explanation of particular changes, it is possible to arrive at both a denial of progress and an infinite extension of it. In either case, the humanitarian-progressivist model, by giving only general explanations for particular changes, must fail to satisfy those whose interest is in shorter spans of time and in particular places. Legal history may, in fact, work best when applied to particulars.

Abolition: the historians at work

Because of the enormous prestige and wide influence of eighteenth-century humanitarian reform literature, historians of torture have sometimes spoken of an 'abolition movement' in the case of torture which parallels abolition movements in the history of slavery or various suffrage movements of the past two centuries. In fact, the history of any institution touched by legal theory and practice is the history of a number of different forces, some technically legal, others more broadly social, operating sometimes simultaneously but more often independently. One approach to the problem of the abolition of torture is to sort out the different components identifiable in the process, to see less a concerted movement than a series of coincidental events, sometimes influencing each other and sometimes not.

In order to appreciate the work of the historians, it may be useful to highlight some of the central aspects of the practice of torture in the period between the late sixteenth and mid-eighteenth centuries. Torture was to be employed only in those cases in which full proof was lacking for the conviction of a defendant for a crime whose punishment was death or mutilation; lesser crimes, *delicta levia*, were not involved. For serious crimes there was no other punishment except death or mutilation: until the end of the sixteenth century imprisonment was very rare, and only the spread of imprisonment, and the institution of new sanctions like the galley or the workhouse, came to serve as an alternative to death. The category 'serious crime' varied from place to place, often including crimes no longer considered serious. Increasingly in the sixteenth century, from the publication of the *Malleus Maleficarum* in 1484 to the works of Jean Bodin, Nicholas Remy, and Martin Del Rio, the practice of magic and witchcraft were also included among the most serious of crimes, and much of the criticism of torture was part of the criticism of trials for these occult offences rather than criticism of torture for its own sake. As we have seen, there was a large and old literature on the abuses of torture, often part and parcel of criminal law handbooks, well known to and used by those who routinely condemned people to torture.

Even in areas where torture was not part of legal procedure, such as England and Scandinavia, torture appeared in the sixteenth and seventeenth centuries, partly from the influence of continental jurisprudence and partly from the needs of executive authority. In England, for example, although torture seems to have made little headway in common law, it made considerable headway during the sixteenth century in royal orders or orders in Council, particularly in the case of political crimes. The protests of Sir John Fortescue in the fifteenth century, Sir Thomas Smith in the sixteenth and Sir Edward Coke in the seventeenth that torture was unknown to English law were belied by the torture warrants of the sixteenth and seventeenth centuries, although chiefly in cases of treason, sedition, and similar offences, as recent scholarship has made abundantly clear. What seems to have prevented torture from becoming regularized in English law was its strict control by the Privy Council and its use primarily as an instrument for uncovering information rather than eliciting formal evidence, as on the Continent.

Finally, we return to the fundamental premise of the Romano-Canonical procedure: lacking full proof, a confession was the only means of conviction in the case of serious crime. Until the need for confession lessened, not all the humanitarian discourse in Europe would have been likely to have had much effect. In the light of these features of the period 1550–1750, it is possible to consider the gradual disappearance of torture less as the result of an abolition movement than as the concurrence of a number of distinct and different changes which took place independently of each other in the seventeenth and eighteenth centuries. The work of Piero Fiorelli and John Langbein throws considerable light on these changes.

Fiorelli suggests in *La Tortura Giudiziaria nel Diritto Comune* (1953–4) that the process of abolition be considered in terms of four aspects of the history of torture: the logical, moral, social and political. By these he means the sceptical rhetorical arguments against torture of the kind that had been present since the days of Greek law; the general Judeao-Christian (and later humanitarian) arguments against the immorality of torture; the place of the justification of torture in a universe which derived the very principles of its social existence from a tradition and from authorities which would be repudiated on all fronts if torture were to be repudiated; and the reluctance or willingness to deal with the question of the possibility of larger-scale political reform. The Calas affair in France (1763–5) had repercussions that touched the political as well as the judicial structure of France.

Fiorelli's category of logical criticism is the oldest in the literature. From Greek and Roman thinkers to seventeenth-century jurists, the logical flaws of a system which employed torture were widely recognized. Cicero, Quintilian and Ulpian all spoke of the problems apparent to anyone who studied torture, from persuasive language to the physiological accident of one's ability to resist pain. But these were not humanitarian motives and criticisms: 'One would search uselessly among the Greek and Roman writers for a condemnation of torture as inhuman and cruel.' Fiorelli's moral category focuses on the absence of torture from the Jewish and early Christian traditions, a remarkable example of which is the letter of Pope Nicholas I of 865 to the ruler of the Bulgars, forbidding the use of torture in criminal cases, although rather because it violates the principle that confessions are not to be extorted or coerced and is therefore forbidden to Christian laymen or churchmen. Beyond the strictures of Nicholas, however, there remained the prohibition against most churchmen's using torture or shedding blood. Of all currents of resistance to torture, the moral current is probably the most generally appealing and the least measurable in influence. It does not become a useful starting point for investigating the decline of torture until well into the eighteenth century.

Fiorelli's social category (*La tortura*, II, 218) places torture squarely in a cultural and social matrix from which it would be difficult to remove it:

> In an era in which all philosophy derived from Aristotle, astronomy from Ptolemy, medicine from Hippocrates and Galen, and the law was contained in those texts of Roman wisdom preserved in Justinian's compilation, to argue against torture, which these texts sanctioned, would have meant (unheard of temerity!) to undermine the common foundation of respect, of indisputable authority, of the thing speaking for itself, self-evident, upon which regulated itself in that epoch the entire ordering, not only of the laws, nor only of human wisdom, but of an entire human social structure.

Such a position of torture in a cultural and social context was reinforced, rather than checked, by the logical category of criticism of torture. Even the occasional sharp criticisms of a Vives or Montaigne, based on logical or moral principles, could have had little impact upon the institution of torture without a simultaneous loosening of its place in an interlocking social order.

It is perhaps in this light that the increasingly frequent late sixteenth- and seventeenth-century criticism of the use of torture in cases of magic and witchcraft may best be understood. From the polemics of Cornelius Loos (1546–95) through those of Adam Tanner (1572–1632) and Friedrick von Spee (1591–1635), the latter a Jesuit confessor of convicted witches, critics of the witchcraft persecutions raised bitter protests against the use of the routine practice of torture, which elicited confessions from people who, an increasing number of Europeans believed, could not possibly have done what they had confessed to. To this may be added an observation by John Langbein concerning the absence of any mention of torture in the English Petition of Right of 1628:

> The Parliamentarians who promoted the petition of Right had scant reason to fear the application of torture to themselves and their ilk. Even at its peak the use of torture [in England] had been confined to two sorts of victims, neither with any following in the House of Commons: suspected seditionists, especially Jesuits; and some suspected felons, mostly of the lower orders. (*Torture and the Law of Proof*, p. 139)

On the Continent, torture in cases of witchcraft and, even less equivocally, of religious dissent, increased the ire of those who might normally never have raised more than a logical or moral protest, like Langbein's Parliamentarians. One of the earliest and most articulate critics who based his attack on his own experience of religious persecution was Johannes Grevius, a Dutch Arminian, whose *Tribunal reformatum* of 1624, while professing great respect for Roman law itself, nevertheless condemned unequivocally the use of torture by Christians in any kind of case, for any reason, upon any person. Grevius' learning, his systematic and professional handling of legal sources and legal argument, and his relentless holding up of a standard of Christian charity as the only rule Christian magistrates may follow suggest that by the early seventeenth century some of the older but isolated kinds of argument against torture were beginning to become linked. This in itself might have achieved little, but once torture was applied to social orders not conventionally caught in the web of criminal procedure, such criticism was listened to and circulated outside professional or limitedly moralizing circles. The political category, in which an accumulating volume of technical and moral protest came to inform and put pressure on ruling assemblies and rulers themselves, may better be discussed in the next section. Fiorelli's logical, moral and social categories offer a much broader approach to the history of the abolition of torture than does the conventional notion of an 'abolition movement'. Even the general and indiscriminate collection of critics and protesters that Alec Mellor describes (*La Torture*, 1949) indicate less a movement than a broad and diffuse series of criticisms on widely differing grounds from the late sixteenth and seventeenth centuries. But the most incisive portrait of the decline of torture is that of John Langbein. Rejecting the humanitarian influence in the decline of torture, Langbein emphasizes two purely juridical forces at work in the early seventeenth century: the development of new criminal sanctions and the revolution in the law of proof.

In tracing those sanctions which arose in the sixteenth and seventeenth centuries, originally for entirely unrelated reasons, and which came slowly to enlarge the range of sanctions for serious crimes beyond death and disfigurement, Langbein notes another dimension of social change influencing legal procedure. The galley, the workhouse and the practice of transportation all offered immediately useful – and appealing – alternatives to death. They also bridged the chronological gap, as they influenced it, between an age of extremely limited imprisonment and the death penalty on the one hand, and a world of disciplining and reforming imprisonment on the other. Some aspects of this world and its transformation have been traced by Michel Foucault (1975; English tr. 1977) in his fascinating study *Discipline and Punish*, and by other scholars as well. By adding lesser sanctions than death as punishment for serious crimes, seventeenth- and eighteenth-century European society removed one of the underpinnings of torture, well outside the limits of conventional moral criticisms, and largely indifferent to them.

In terms of his second point, the revolution in the law of proof, Langbein points out the considerable discretion which judges possessed in many matters of deciding particular sanctions for the convicted, in contrast to the little or no discretion then possessed in the matter of preliminary procedure, specifically torture. The development of new criminal sanctions in the seventeenth century greatly increased judicial discretion in the matter of sentencing.

Discretion in sentencing and a wider range of possible punishments made the next step possible: in cases where sufficient *indicia* existed to warrant putting a suspect to torture, but the suspect successfully resisted, and in cases where there was some strong evidence against a suspect, but not enough to put him to the torture at all, the presence of penalties less severe than those which would have attended his conviction enabled courts to convict, not only without full proof, but without half-proof either. As Langbein points out, this practice, technically known as *Verdachtstrafe*, 'punishment upon suspicion', really meant punishment upon the court's private belief in a defendant's guilt, but without full Romano-Canonical proof: 'a new system of proof was appearing that did not require confession in order to punish crime.' An analogy may be seen here with some modern Anglo-American practices like plea-bargaining. Plea-bargaining often takes place in cases where there is too crowded a court calendar, where evidence is incomplete or uncertain, but also where there is reasonable cause to be convinced of the guilt of the accused. The accused pleads guilty to a lesser charge (and hence can expect lesser sanctions), even though in other circumstances he might be formally charged, tried and convicted of a more serious offence (and hence subject to more serious sanctions). The new sanctions and the application of kinds of proof formerly reserved for *delicta levia* offered to seventeenth-century magistrates and their eighteenth-century successors something comparable to plea-bargaining. In one sense at least, the revolution reminds us that, in theory, very considerable indications of an accused's guilt had always been necessary for torture in a world in which the only choice of sanction was between death or release. This formal requirement lies behind the theory of *Verdachtstrafe*, as it does modern plea-bargaining: it was indeed 'suspicion', but, as French jurists called it, *suspicion très violent*, very strong and well-based suspicion, based upon considerable, if not finally sufficient evidence. In the juridical world of the *ancien régime*, it took evidence to acquit as well as to convict, and when evidence for either was lacking, the new procedure and the new sanctions stepped in to fill the gap and resolve the dilemma. With the new range of sanctions, the revolution in the law of procedure, and the consequent diminishing of the central role of confession for conviction, the new professionally qualified and centrally controlled jurists of the eighteenth century no longer needed torture as an integral and unavoidable part of legal criminal procedure. With its technical and legal underpinnings gone, torture became at last vulnerable to those logical, moral and social criticisms to which it had for so long been virtually immune. It even fell victim to the most trivial of these, first announced by Grevius, but echoed even by the framers of the *Grande ordonnance criminelle* of 1670, that torture was *un usage ancien*, 'an archaic practice', identical with the old ordeals and other irrational practices of a remote and unsavoury past. When such criticism as this could be readily voiced, one aspect of the history of torture had come to an end.

Several other aspects of late eighteenth-century legal thought and culture may also illuminate the process of the abolition of torture. These are: the case of England, the doctrine of infamy, the movement to separate and define more sharply legislative and judicial powers, particularly on the Continent, and the increasing articulation and importance of theories of natural law.

As we have seen in the case of England, the relatively low place in the hierarchy of proofs occupied by confession, the virtual absence of extensive, indeed adequate, pre-trial investigatory institutions, and the remarkable liberty of the jury to convict on evidence that might barely constitute an *indicium* in the Romano-Canonical process, as well as the very slow and late development of the office of state prosecutor, all worked to keep torture out of English criminal procedure. Yet it can hardly be argued either that these aspects of English law reflect an inherently superior humanitarianism and rationality, or that in other aspects of the legal process they do not in fact represent real deficiencies in legal practice, compared to continental procedure.

Another aspect of the abolition of torture is the odd history of infamy. As we have seen in the case of Greece and Rome, *atimia* and *infamia* were two conditions that impinged upon the normal status of freemen before the law. From the twelfth century on, in both canon and Roman law, the medieval doctrine of infamy constituted a sanction that could offset the results of ordeal and constitute one of several *indicia* that also led to torture itself. So powerful a condition was it that its false imputation constituted one of the bases for later laws of defamation, slander and libel. Yet the loathsome doctrine of infamy also seems to have served in the revolution in criminal procedure which led to the abolition of torture. As sanctions became more numerous and less uniformly fatal, many of the *indicia* of the Romano-Canonical procedure acquired more weight in convictions and thus acted as another alternative to the need for confession and punishment. The disabilities imposed by legal infamy survived torture by many decades, and their survival may very well have indicated that they retained their appeal long after both legal reform and political revolution had had their effects on legal criminal procedure. The French Penal Code of 1791 contained a provision for civil degradation, according to which the convicted criminal was addressed publicly in the following terms: 'Your country has found you guilty of an infamous action: the law and the tribunal strips you of the quality of French citizen.' In 1842 Alessandro Manzoni published his epigonal indictment of the criminal procedure of the *ancien régime*, *The Story of the Column of Infamy*, an account of a famous trial in Milan in 1630, whose title referred to a column erected at the site of a demolished house of a criminal to remind the Milanese forever of the shame of the criminal. Although weakened by the criminal reforms of the late eighteenth and early nineteenth centuries, the legal doctrine of infamy survived that of torture, and its very survival may well have enabled the abolition of torture to come about a little faster.

The history of the abolition of torture, then, much like its beginning, should be read as the concatenation of a number of different changes in different areas of the law and of life. The question is more complex than simple moral satisfaction would like it to be, and more complex than Enlightenment historians and their successors, witting and unwitting, admitted it to be. A number of aspects of the abolition were shaped by doctrines and reforms that in other circumstances would be and have been condemned as sternly as torture itself.

In addition to the great drive to accommodate existing law to the principles of the Revolution, the revolutionary and post-revolutionary governments of France and, later, other countries, also adopted two other earlier eighteenth-century notions: that of the separation of powers and that of natural law. In the work of Montesquieu and later writers, fear of the arbitrariness of the judiciary of the *ancien régime* led to the argument that judicial and legislative powers should be separated, with the supremacy going to the legislative side, reducing the individual authority of the judge to that of a simple applier of statute law and depriving the judiciary of a review |power over the legality or applicability of statute. In the civil law tradition, such separation, which actually took place in the early nineteenth century, tended to diminish the stature of the judge and enhance that of the legislator. As the legal historian John Merryman has put it:

> When, with the rise of the modern nation-state, the administration of justice was taken out of ecclesiastical, local, and private hands and was nationalized, the ordinary courts became the principal instrument of the state's monopoly on the administration of justice. The [legislature] was given a monopoly on the nationalized process of lawmaking. The ordinary judiciary was given a monopoly on the nationalized process of adjudication. (*The Civil Law Tradition*, 1969, p.93)

Thus, procedure and the individual powers of the judge were both severely circumscribed and, given the intentions of legislative bodies, strictly limited and controlled in their ability to inflict unprescribed sanctions.

Beside their place in revolutionary or reformed constitutional structures, legislatures also reflected the other eighteenth-century idea of the universal value and the binding force of natural law. Seventeenth- and eighteenth-century theories of natural law focused often on torture as violating their most essential tenets, that of the natural dignity of humans and that of the individual natural right of humans to decide upon the means of preservation of their dignity. Paul Foriers has raised this question in connection with theories and practices of proof:

> Torture violates the natural right of the individual not to accuse himself and to be able to defend himself. This is a natural right which no treaty, no social contract can remove from the individual and which thus remains for the individual an essential prerogative, in the sense put upon it by Thomas Hobbes: 'whatever the criminal answers [under the effects of torture], whether true, false, or whether he remains silent, he has the right to do in this matter that which seems to him to be just.' Against natural law, torture was condemned by Natural Law theorists in the name of its uselessness and its inefficacity. (*La Preuve*, 1965, Pt.2, p.188)

Through natural law theories, much of the earlier criticism of torture on the basis of its illogical and unreliable evidence was strengthened and joined to earlier moral criticisms. From Montaigne, Thomasius and Bayle, it influenced Montesquieu and those of his successors who shaped late eighteenth-century legal reforms, whether in or out of revolutionary political movements.

This survey of historians at work has so far focused upon a generally agreed sequence of events and the problem of the complexity of their causes. However, a quite different and more ambitious approach is that of Michel Foucault, whose study *Discipline and Punish* deals not directly with torture but with the transformation of the abrupt, brutal and physically destructive forms of punishment under the *ancien régime* into the psychological reform of the nineteenth-century prison. Foucault, too, gives little credit to Enlightenment humanitarianism – although he does see, between the two extremes cited above, a temporary period of humanitarian dissuasion of crime by criminals' forced participation in public works. Far more than the humane moral sensibility of the Enlightenment, however, Foucault argues that the great transformation came about because of the reduced need for those in power to control the body of the criminal. In his view, power in the nineteenth and twentieth centuries was exercised far less through physical coercion than through 'carceral' institutions, which include not only the prison, but also the factory, the school, and the organized psychological discipline of military life. Foucault sees this process not as liberating and humane, but as creating an entirely new kind of human being:

> This book is intended as a correlative history of the modern soul and of a new power to judge; a genealogy of the present scientifico-legal complex from which the power to punish derives its bases, justifications, and rules, from which it extends its effects and by which it masks its exorbitant singularity.

What Foucault calls 'punitive reason' and 'disciplinary technology' mould passive human beings into objects of power. Disciplinary technology and normative social science combine in Foucault's world to create 'knowable man', the manipulated citizen of the modern world. Foucault's is a theory not without some truth, but also virtually without hope.

The work of legal historians like Fiorelli and Langbein, social historians like E. P. Thompson and archaeologists of culture like Foucault, offers a far wider and more ambiguous spectrum of explanations for the abolition of torture than the moral passion of Beccaria and the humane progressivism of Lea. Yet it is inviting to regard these very different approaches not as mutually exclusive, but as reflecting different facets of a single historical phenomenon. Foucault's approach has overarching implications for viewing both the archaic and the modern worlds; sceptical and hostile to the latter, Foucault forces us to regard the former with unaccustomed understanding. The other historians urge us not to place too great or too exclusive weight upon moral reawakenings, but to consider also such details as technical changes in the nature of legal sanctions and in the rules of evidence and proof, to look at areas of thought other than moral sensibility for important changes. These kinds of analysis avoid the trap into which Mellor's arguments draw him, his failure to explain why at a particular moment in the past a long and mixed line of criticism of torture came at last to push complex societies into positive action.

At the same time we yet must recognize the contribution made by the passions aroused and canalized by the work of Beccaria and recorded in that of Lea. The late eighteenth-century identification of torture with an entire rejected world-view was made on moral as well as legal grounds. Indeed, it has been primarily and properly on moral grounds that torture has been attacked ever since. Yet in the nineteenth and twentieth centuries there has also seemed to be a fatal divergence between moral sensibility on the one hand and law and state policy on the other. In the concluding sections of this chapter we will consider a brief period in history when the two were joined, apparently forever.

Statutory abolition

Against the background sketched by Langbein, the history of the legislative abolition of torture in most of the states of late eighteenth-century Europe may be understood in a historically more realistic way. Common to most of those states, the process of the abolition of torture was, first, part of a general revision of criminal law systems, and second, a process that occurred over marked periods of time, usually several decades, rather than instantly and categorically. Apparently the states of late eighteenth-century Europe, like their predecessors at the turn of the twelfth and thirteenth centuries, waited to see what statutory reform might produce before completing the process of abolition of torture on the one hand and general revision of criminal law on the other.

Sweden, technically the earliest country to abolish torture, provides a good example. Most forms of torture, which had arrived in Sweden only in the late sixteenth century as a result of the influence of the imperial German codes of criminal law, particularly the *Carolina*, were abolished in 1734, but torture in the case of a few exceptional crimes was not entirely abolished until 1722. Prussia reflects a similar, although briefer, process. In 1721 the Elector Frederick I insisted that torture could only be applied after the monarch had consented to each particular case. In 1740, when Frederick II came to the throne, he slightly revised this rule, establishing categories of cases in which torture could not be employed. In 1754, all torture was abolished in Prussia, the earliest date of complete abolition in European history. Between 1738 and 1789 the Kingdom of the Two Scilies accomplished a similar process, as did the Duchy of Baden between 1767 and 1831, the Austrian Netherlands between 1787 and 1794, Venice between 1787 and 1800, and Austria itself between 1769 and 1776. In a number of these cases, monarchs, legislatures and juristic experts worked together. In Prussia Frederick II had the advice of Coccejius, one of the foremost legal scholars of the century. Maria Theresa and Joseph II of Austria had the services of the great jurist Joseph von Sonnenfels. Even behind the polemics of Beccaria there lay the juristic expertise of the brothers Verri of Lombardy.

Other kingdoms and principalities abolished torture as a routine in the last quarter of the eighteenth and first quarter of the nineteenth centuries. Brunswick, Saxony and Denmark abolished it in 1770; Mecklenburg in 1769; Poland in 1776; France in 1780 and (in the case of the *question préalable*) in 1788, both measures confirmed by the revolutionary National Assembly in 1789; Tuscany in 1786; Lombardy in 1789; the Netherlands in 1798.

During the Napoleonic era French influence rapidly extended the reform of criminal law to areas conquered or influenced by France and its revolutionary or imperial principles. In one case, however, the export of judicial reform backfired. Switzerland abolished torture in 1798, but re-established it in 1815 at the fall of Napoleon. Only piecemeal revision, canton by canton, finally eliminated torture from Swiss law: Zurich in 1831, Freiburg in 1848, Basel in

1850 and Glarus in 1851. Bavaria abolished torture in 1806, Wurttemburg in 1809. Torture was abolished in Norway in 1819, in Hanover in 1822, in Portugal in 1826, in Greece in 1827, in Gotha in 1828. The Napoleonic conquest of Spain in 1808 ended the practice of torture, as it temporarily ended the Spanish Inquisition. But though the Inquisition was restored with the accession of Ferdinand VII in 1813, torture remained abolished.

This wave of judicial reform impressed its contemporaries as strongly as it impresses a modern reader. But its very speed and extent must recall the complex explanations of Fiorelli and Langbein; they describe many different reasons for opposing torture, including some pressing technical and social ones. Nor were the declarations of universal human rights enunciated by Tom Paine and the French *Declaration of the Rights of Man and Citizen* of 1789 universally accepted as the moral and juridical rationale for legal reforms. Edmund Burke, in his *Reflections on the Revolution in France* of 1790, denounced French revolutionary claims of moral righteousness. In England, Burke remarked, 'Atheists are not our preachers; madmen are not out lawgivers.' To be sure, Englishmen enjoyed the greatest liberties in the world, but those liberties sprang 'from within the nation', and were not derived from natural law or anything else. Jeremy Bentham, a more explicit admirer of positive law than Burke, was no less emphatic: 'Natural rights is simple nonsense, natural and imprescriptable rights is rhetorical nonsense, nonsense upon stilts.' But Bentham trusted less in the traditions of England and far more upon the power of utilitarian rationality to create a positive law which served the best purposes of mankind. In these instances and in others, the principles enunciated in 1789 and their moral imperatives encountered substantial resistance, although their opposition to torture did not. Robespierre, Burke and Bentham would all have agreed upon this point. And their agreement suggests that a process of universal statutory reforms like those described above must be considered in terms of a whole social and cultural complexity that prepares for and effects change. Although the linking of legal operation and moral judgement marks a monumental achievement, it does not define the entire process. Moral fervour does not create statutes, although it may colour those statutes in the eyes of those who look back at them and their symbolic achievement.

Some comparisons

It is tempting in the case of torture, as it occasionally used to be in the case of 'feudalism', to compare the experience of western Europe with those cultures either on Europe's fringes or outside the European orbit altogether. Such a practice, however, encourages a certain amount of reductionism and tends to neglect the profound (and, to echo Burke, usually crucial) differences in customs and experience that separate cultures. The comparison offered here is perforce generally superficial, for a truly comparative history of torture must await a truly comparative history of legal cultures, and that is a long way off. In spite of the great tradition from Max Weber to our own day, a comparative study of the place of law and legal institutions is still hardly conceivable. For this reason, the beginning of this book avoids any discussion of Egyptian and Persian practices, just as the end of the book refrains from speculating upon such topics as the alleged biophysical basis of aggressiveness in human nature. To make sense as history, history must reside somewhere between mere colourful anecdotalism and speculative philosophy and psychobiology.

One slender but measurable ground for comparison of very different societies and cultures is that of publicly recognized procedures, usually written procedures. For the use of written instruments in law, wherever they occur, distances the law, even if only to a certain extent, from the impenetrable matrix of unanalysed ritual and oral culture in which it first appears. The comparison of documented practices is certainly not the ultimate or the only kind, but for our purposes it may be adequate.

Torture in the Ottoman Empire offers striking differences and similarities to the case of Europe, at least to the European experience before the legal reforms of the eighteenth century. Islamic law, the *shari'a*, does not recognize the validity of a confession obtained by coercion or threat of coercion, and in spite of the frequent use of torture and its recognition by Ottoman imperial authorities, the *muftis* consistently opposed it and even went so far as to insist that if the torturer killed his victim he was obliged to pay blood-money for the act, even though the civil law did not demand that he do so. But the law of the Empire did provide for torture. Its doctrine stated that suspects with criminal records, with strong circumstantial evidence against them, or whose behaviour and answers in court were contradictory might be tortured, although mere accusation normally did not suffice for torture. The *muftis* also sharply condemned the person who accused someone falsely in a manner that led to torture. In practice, among the Ottomans as elsewhere, the doctrine did not describe what in fact happened. Beyond the official doctrine there is evidence of the wider application of torture, sometimes even before the beginning of a trial, so that the prosecutor arrived in court with a confession in hand which was then admitted as evidence and led to conviction.

The sharp distinction in the Ottoman world between the will of government and the resistance of the *muftis* is consistent with Islamic history and culture and offers sharp contrast to the place of the Latin Church in early European legal history.

The earliest evidence of the legal approval of torture in Japan occurs under the *Ritsuryo* system, derived from T'ang Chinese law. According to *Dangoku*, the Japanese equivalent of the Chinese *Ritsu*, or specifically criminal procedure, confession was required, and in the event that a confession was not forthcoming, the judge was empowered to have the defendant beaten on the back and buttocks with sticks. During the period between the tenth and the sixteenth centuries, these earlier rules of torture seem to have broadened to include archaic procedures, including that of *Yu-Gisho*, a form of the ordeal of boiling water, now used as interrogatory torture. In Tokugawa Japan, confessions were required in criminal cases, and the procedure of *Gomon*, a formal equivalent of the *quaestio* or *tortura*, was recognized. Yet *Gomon*, torture by suspension of the body by the hands tied behind the back, was permitted only in the cases of murder, arson, theft and robbery, unauthorized passage through a barrier, and the forgery of a document or seal. Japanese law also permitted the institution of *Romon*, a species of 'quasi-torture', which appears to have been used far more widely than *Gomon*, possibly because the resort to *Gomon* indicated an unskilful interrogator and because the failure of a formal application of *Gomon* to secure a confession may have proved an embarrassment to the court. *Romon* included whipping on the back, kneeling on triangular pieces of wood with 100-pound stone weights on the knees, and sitting crosslegged with a rope tied to each ankle and passing behind the neck, which, when tightened, bends the back painfully. *Romon* may seem hardly worth distinguishing from *Gomon*, but it was sharply distinguished in Japanese jurisprudence and used far more widely until the revision of 1876 and the definitive prohibition of 1879.

In the Constitution of the United States, in effect since 1789, the Fifth Amendment prohibits self-incrimination, and this right has been interpreted by European historians as the protective provision against torture in the United States law. The Fifth Amendment both echoes English legal history and anticipates some nineteenth- and twentieth-century problems of American law. First, it echoes a tradition in English common law which for several centuries prohibited any testimony at all from a defendant, and hence constituted one of the English safeguards against the institution of torture – if no testimony at all from the accused was admissable, torture to obtain a confession, or even other evidence, was pointless. The Fifth Amendment, somewhat earlier than English law, did, however, permit the defendant to testify voluntarily, but nevertheless prohibited his making any statement that touched upon his own possible involvement in the crime of which he was accused. In Great Britain, not until the Criminal Evidence Act of 1898 (S.I[b], 61 & 62 Vic. c.36) was the defendant given the option of testifying on his or her own behalf. The value of confession as evidence outside the actual act of sworn testimony, however, has had a long and rocky history in U.S. law, and, as we will see in the next chapter, may have constituted one of the back doors by which torture was readmitted in the juridical world of the nineteenth and twentieth centuries.

Perhaps the most interesting and useful comparisons, however, may be made between western Europe and Russia. The earliest Russian laws reveal many similarities with the archaic legal practices that we have observed earlier in Greece, Rome, and early medieval western Europe. From self-help to mediation, from the horizontal conflict between two parties to the appearance of the third party of public judicial specialists, the increasing role of public authority, usually the prince, and the development of elaborate sanctions all mark early Russian law as they do early law elsewhere.

The earliest instance of torture in Russian law occurs in the *Short Pravda*, around 1100, one of whose articles mentions that a peasant, tortured without the prince's command, may receive a fine in compensation. The expanded *Russkaia Pravda* of the thirteenth century repeats this article, but most of Russian law says little more about it. The Charter of the city of Pskov, with other town codes, deals extensively with fines and compositions as sanctions for criminal offences, permits the duel and the oath, but makes no mention of the ordeal or of torture. From the thirteenth century on, however, Russian law is marked by the increasingly prominent place given to the prince and his servants and to expanded categories of judicial personnel. As the legal historian Daniel Kaiser has summarized the process:

> In this way lateral legal relations and their primary regard for the litigants were essentially doomed. The plaintiff's concerns had become assuredly secondary to those of the society at large, whose interests were assumed by the state. This stance enlarged the role and conception of sanction, and at the same time diminished the rights of the victim to his compensation. (*The Growth of the Law in Medieval Russia*, 1980, p.91)

The emergence of the prince and his judicial apparatus is especially clear in Muscovy, and the code of Ivan III, the *Sudebnik* of 1497, reflects torture inflicted upon suspects of bad repute by princely judicial officials. The ordeal also appears in the *Sudebnik*, as do much more elaborate practices of inquest and interrogation. Torture is also documented about the same time, particularly in Lithuanian Russia. At the end of the sixteenth century Ivan IV created the short-lived Oprichnina, an order devoted to the protection of the monarch and the elimination of his enemies, which appears to have used torture indiscriminately, but well outside conventional Russian legal theory and practice.

The weakness of the monarchy during the first half of the seventeenth century, and the characteristic (which Russia shared with other states) of diversified and effectively autonomous centres of judicial authority, simply meant that torture by provincial governors (*voyevody*) was common. Indeed, the great diversity of judicial officials survived in Russia until 1880, and not all of them possess a sufficiently detailed history for any firm generalizations about the use of torture in their jurisdictions to be made.

The legal code of Alexis I in 1649 distinguished political from other kinds of crime and required the denunciation of political crimes as well. The czar's Secret Office, which functioned from 1653 to 1676, and the later Preobrazhensky Office (1697–1729) appear to have used torture as a matter of routine. Among the known techniques were the strappado, the knout for beatings, and fire, although there seems to have been a marked decline in the application of torture after 1718.

But Russia was not untouched by the judicial reforms in the rest of Europe, and Alexander I formally declared torture abolished by his Ukaz of 27 September 1801. Under the influence of the 'Commission for the Review of Formerly Criminal Cases', Alexander I had abolished the Secret Office. In 1801, he received word of a case of torture whose victim confessed, but was later proved to be innocent; upon investigating the case, Alexander issued the Ukaz of 27 September. The Governing Senate was:

> to ensure with all strictness throughout the whole Empire that nowhere in any shape or form . . . should anyone dare to permit or perform any torture, under pain of inevitable and severe punishment . . . that accused persons should personally declare before the Court that they had not been subjected to any unjust interrogation . . . that finally the very name of torture, bringing shame and reproach on mankind, should be forever erased from the public memory.

Three years later, Alexander had to issue a reminder of his decree, and P. S. Squire suggests that the Fourth Department of the Senate 'had long been inured to the established practice of torture not only by the Secret Office and its predecessors but also by local police headquarters, and it therefore distressed them considerably less than the youthful Alexander' (*The Third Department*, 1968, p.22). Squire also cites the case of a man tortured to death in 1827 in the context of General Benckendorff's 'Instruction' of that year, which complained still of considerable judicial independence throughout the Empire, '*Do Boga vysoko, do Tsarya dalyoko*' – 'God is high and the Czar far distant.' Although early nineteenth-century czars remained prepared to use extraordinary measures to protect state security, there is little evidence of their revival of earlier techniques of torture. The creation of the Third Section of the czar's Chancery in 1825 under Nicholas I and General Benckendorff constituted the chief political arm of government security throughout most of the century, although there is little evidence for torture under it. There is also, however, little evidence of its effectiveness, and in 1880 the Ukaz of 6 August abolished the Third Section, consolidating all Russian police functions into a single Department of Police under the Ministry of the Interior. A year later, however, separate branches of secret police were established in St Petersburg and Moscow charged with prosecuting political criminals. These were, to use the general and imprecise term most commonly designating them, the Okhrana, the 'protection' of the state and czar.

Although the reforms of the early nineteenth century appear to have effectively reduced the practice – and technically abolished the use of – torture, towards the end of the century, particularly in the climate of terrorism that surrounded the central authorities of the Russian state, the Okhrana appears to have used torture once more. At least some evidence from later successful revolutionaries after 1917 indicates strongly that in the area of political crime and its repression, torture had reappeared in Russia by the end of the nineteenth century. Its place in the twentieth century will be discussed below.

The case of Russia is particularly interesting, but in its widest outlines it is not entirely uncharacteristic of the rest of Europe. Confused, overlapping jurisdictions, a wide gap between jurisprudence and practice, autonomous local authorities, the perception of crime on the part of tzar and people, and precocious development of a doctrine of treason all suggest how difficult it is to find hard evidence for or against the use of torture on particular levels or in the particular areas of legal practice.

The freeing of the law

In the wake of the cultural and political revolutions that ended the eighteenth century and threatened the peace of the early centuries, the place of criminal law and the rights of citizens and subjects is sometimes difficult to regard as having the importance they genuinely possessed. In spite of the civil and military passions aroused by the revolutionary and Napoleonic wars and the intermittent bloodbaths of revolutionary terror, both Enlightenment thought and late eighteenth-century political and social reform saw in the law one of their chief instruments. Stripped of its ungainly accretions built up over centuries of privilege and tyranny, purged of its archaisms and ritual barbarity, and aligned with all that was best, noblest, and most compassionate in human reason and sentiment, the law of early nineteenth-century states professed to regulate and express the lives of citizens in harmony with those rights and

liberties that constitution after constitution categorically stated were
the natural right of all humans. Even early nineteenth-century
national sentiment, some aspects of which focused great interest on
ethnic legal history, failed to disown that harmony between universal
human rights and particular national systems of law. The key was
system. Apart from England, which had created – or had others
create for it – its own myths of the unique constitutional liberties of
unsystematic common law, most of the states of Europe in the early
nineteenth century would have agreed with the image used by the
French revolutionary Sieyès – that the key to the law was equality,
that the law was figuratively the centre of an immense globe from
which all citizens were equidistant, and that equidistance meant that
the law was at once the guarantor of reason, justice and equality. The
state no longer granted rights; it protected already-existing rights.
And its role was moral as well as political.

But that great dream of reason rested for a moment, at least, upon
solid institutional reforms with widespread social and political
acceptance. The England of Blackstone and Bentham, the France of
Nicholas, Dupaty and Périer (in spite of Muyart de Vouglans), the
Austria of Sonnenfels, and the Lombardy of the brothers Verri all
offer evidence that criminal law was on the broad track of reform
well before the political upheavals at the end of the century.

And behind both kinds of movements were the two great
problems of eighteenth-century criminal law: the reform of sanctions
and the problem of evidence. The English example, selectively
publicized to be sure, had long since showed that confession was not
necessary for conviction and that a system of criminal law that did
not so use confession – or even allow testimony of any kind from a
defendant – could nevertheless ornament a civilized and relatively
law-abiding society. In 1657 Frederich Keller had held up not only
ancient Israel, but modern Aragon and England as examples of
civilized nations that did not employ torture. In the late eighteenth
century other reformers used the example of Prussia in a similar
way. The development on the Continent of an alternative system of
sanctions and evidence and the emergence of psychological and
social theories that emphasized imprisonment and penitence over
execution and condemnation appeared successfully to account, in
the judicial sphere, for many of the values proclaimed by publicists
and philosophers in the moral sphere.

If the age of revolution did nothing else, it joined in the legal profession both general sentiment and technical reform, of which the profession itself was proud to become the guardian. In an age when constitutional and political change occupy the centre of most historical accounts, followed quickly by economic and social change, it is striking how many images of criminal law seem to dominate events. The storming of the Bastille, the guillotine, the focus upon torture as inhuman and irrational, the focus upon criminal law itself as a means of social repression, all these are among the most memorable images, not only of the French Revolution in particular, but of the revolutionary age in general. Criminal procedure seemed a conspicuous artifact of a bitterly resented past, a dramatic particular focus upon general injustice and inhumaneness, and a stirring symbol of an ideal just society. Whatever forces had moved the reform of criminal procedure a century before the revolution, the work of philosophers and publicists put the seal of revolutionary approbation and enlightened humanitarianism on those reforms and upon the profession that maintained them, the Bench and the Bar.

New criminal codes succeeded the wave of reform that abolished torture at the end of the eighteenth century, and however little Beccaria's *On Crimes and Punishments* of 1764 may have contributed to the legislative abolition of torture, it contributed enormously to the philosophy of the reform of criminal law and to the minds of those who administered it. Not only did prison now emerge among the chief criminal sanctions, but prison reform itself became a topic in which enlightened values might be expressed. John Howard's *The State of the Prisons*, published in 1777, compared prison conditions in England and France and had an enormous impact. The rise of utilitarianism, which contained a large dimension of concern over criminal law and punishment, further contributed to general concern over prison conditions. Jeremy Bentham, a learned lawyer himself, was particularly concerned with the relationship between utilitarian philosophy and legal institutions. Finally, prison reform became one of the chief objects of early nineteenth-century philanthropy, itself usually inspired by one form or another of Enlightenment humanitarianism.

At the other end of the process, the same period saw the development of regularized police forces and an equally intense concern for their training and their consideration of citizens' rights. The more efficient apprehension of criminals at one end of the process, and their humane reform at the other, constituted an ideal against which the old world of torture and brutal forms of execution came to be regarded as even more hideous than they in fact had been. They were part and parcel of a world not only overthrown, but utterly destroyed. In the light of reason and humanity they could not come again.

So powerful was this revulsion against torture as a symbol of the enormities of the *ancien régime* that not even the moral passions of the Revolution and the reaction that followed it inspired a return to torture. Neither the initial revolution itself, nor the terror, leaves a record of torture; neither the emigré nor, after 1814, the royalist press mentions it. The Vendée contains not a word. These aspects suggest the real influence of writers like Voltaire and Beccaria: their work simply made torture unthinkable, and it trusted in the reform of the law and the legal profession to make it unworkable.

The place of legal reform, whether as the particular embodiment of universal principles of human reason or as the manifestation of a collective national experience and character, placed a new, public face on the concept of legality, its relation to the rights of citizens, and the moral responsibilities of the legal profession. If the state existed in order to guarantee and protect rights – whether to property or liberty – then those rights were in some ways antecedent to and at least as sovereign as the state itself. Throughout the history of nineteenth-century France, for example, no ruler nor ruling assembly appears to have proposed seriously to interfere with the operations of the law. In the words of Alec Mellor:

> The tradition of Fouché [Napoleon's Minister of Police, who used spies and deception often enough but never torture and was the model for Balzac's Vautrin], continued [through the nineteenth century], and its indicators spread, even, and above all in the salons, but neither the opposition press nor the literature mentions any torturers.

> Neither Vidocq, in reality, nor Javert in novelistic fiction prefigures actual sinister figures. The most authoritarian ministers, Casimir Périer himself, remained liberals in principle, inflexibly attached to the idea of legality.

> The magistracy, recruited almost exclusively from the high bourgeoisie, educated, wealthy, allied to a natural gravity a constant concern for retaining its office. 'The police judiciary',

Duverger, a judge of instruction at Niort wrote in his *Manuel du juge d'instruction* in 1839, 'must never proceed until he is adequately informed by purely legal means; his premature involvement in a case will otherwise degenerate into espionage, inquisition, and will indelibly soil Justice.' (*La Torture*, 1949, p.173)

Throughout much of Europe, magistrates like Duverger may well have been conservative politically and socially, ruthless and ferocious in matters of penology, but they seem to have remained uniformly liberal in matters of procedure and legality. Their political rulers seem, on the whole, to have supported them in the stance, and, for a century, the law seemed to have become the greatest achievement of the new states, protected, isolated, free to protect liberties as well as to dispense, not merely justice, but Justice.

As Pierre-Henri Simon graphically put it:

> The nineteenth century was far from pure; in its civil wars, in its social struggles, in its repression of nationalist revolutions, it was covered with blood: the blood of the silk weavers of Lyons and the workers of Paris; the blood of the communards; the blood of Poles slaughtered by the armies of the czar; the blood of liberal Italians shot or hanged by their own petty princelings; the blood of the Kabyles and of the Boers. Nevertheless, the century had at least a kind of modesty which our own no longer possesses: even when its tribunals condemned the innocent, even when they pronounced judgement according to social class, they preserved at least enough of the humanist and Christian spirit implied in the *Declaration of the Rights of Man* and in the penal code which it inspired to spare those it indicted from torture . . . However hardened they might have been, neither Vautrin nor Javert ever imagined that they had the right to torture a suspect.

The first historians of torture, Henry Charles Lea and his successors, grew up precisely in this atmosphere, whether in the United States, England, or on the Continent. To them, as to their contemporaries, a long, grim and archaic story had come to an end in the late eighteenth century; moralizing publicists had given impetus and a direction to this achievement, and the nineteenth century was at last free of its consequences. It was a benchmark in the story of humanity, one which would remain forever unsullied, whose history, in the version accepted by nineteenth-century writers and thinkers, remained one of the greatest moral lessons for mankind, one real step up from the reign of superstition and force.

4

'Engines of the State, not of Law'

At the margins of the law

When William Blackstone briefly considered torture in his *Commentaries on the Laws of England* around 1769, he dismissed the subject as not being part of the province of English law; the rack was, said Blackstone, 'an engine of the state, not of law'. What Blackstone meant – and here he echoed legal literature, if not actual practice in England from Fortescue on – was that torture had no place in the Common Law, and its few and scattered uses had been solely by political authorities for political purposes. In general, Blackstone's judgement was proper and accurate, although, as the research of Langbein and Heath has shown, torture had not been entirely unknown to English criminal procedure in the sixteenth and seventeenth centuries. Blackstone's distinction, however, also serves to illuminate the nineteenth century when torture, now repugnant to virtually all continental criminal laws and systems, remained potentially an engine of the state, and the twentieth century when, still repugnant to most criminal codes, torture reappeared first in the hands of political authorities and, later, of legal authorities as well.

What Blackstone meant by 'state' was the monarch of England, royal servants and the Privy Council, a meaning that was safely made nearly a century after the Glorious Revolution and the tempered absolutism of the Hanoverian monarchy. Blackstone's 'state' was still largely a personal, privatized concept, and the concept of treason in the *ancien régime* was, by and large, still considered and described as a personal offence against the monarch, in his person, that of his family, or that of his servants. In this respect, eighteenth-century ideas of treason were not substantially different from those of the Roman Empire, reflected in Roman public law, which in turn had influenced most of the legal systems of Europe after the twelfth century. In Roman law, as we have seen, treason was a singular offence, the charge of which opened up one sure way of circumventing customary legal procedure and its attendant status- or class-based safeguards against torture. Even in the cases of free citizens and subjects who were otherwise immune from the most drastic of criminal sanctions, the charge of treason brought torture in its train, and the use of torture in treason cases opened the way for its use in other kinds of situations as well, some of them at or beyond the margins of the reformed law.

As in the case of criminal procedure and warfare, the eighteenth century seems to have witnessed a lessening of intensity in the concept of treason in terms of the person of the ruler, but at the end of the century it also witnessed the emergence of a concept of treason against the abstract state and people. In place of *lèse-majesté*, the French revolutionaries spoke of *lèse-nation*, injury to the nation rather than exclusively injury to the ruler who personally embodied the nation.

Throughout most of the nineteenth century the states of Europe became far more articulated and powerful than they had been in the days of Blackstone. Their strength derived from their ability to mobilize vast resources and from a broader-based concept of governmental legitimacy. Instrumental rationality and powerful regional-national solidarity made the state the vehicle of a people, *ethne*. The legal professional and state legislatures, secure in their professional liberalism and enlightened jurisprudence, could, for much of the nineteenth century, afford to believe that increasing state power actually enhanced the security of citizens, that the state, however powerful, was simply the watchdog and guardian of pre-existing and now publicly recognized human rights, perhaps a bigger and stronger guardian than it had ever been before. And those rights were recognized as belonging to more and more members of society.

Neither Blackstone nor anyone else – except for a few thinkers who regarded the extremes of the French Revolution as boding a newer and more ferocious kind of state – could imagine the extent of later nineteenth- and twentieth-century state power. But by the early twentieth century a number of states were strong enough virtually to abolish conventional courts and ignore their statutory laws, aided by a number of philosophical justifications for amending or ignoring the law at need or will.

Nor could Blackstone have foreseen that moment when the state itself might be subordinated to a merely instrumental role in the name or the service of an *ethne* or an ideology, and with it the law as well. Such a transformation of the state was foreseen neither by Blackstone nor by the first historians of torture under the *ancien régime*, Henry Charles Lea and his successors. For Lea's great fears, as indicated by his later masterpieces – histories of the medieval and Spanish inquisitions – lay in the direction of a re-institutionalized civil religion, not toward the excesses of the secular state. In the eyes of liberal nineteenth-century historians of legal procedure, the rational modern state was the great protective force that prevented the return of an autonomous, indiscriminate ecclesiastical power, and the law was its best weapon.

When, in the twentieth century, a number of states began to ignore the protective role of the law, first in political, extra-legal, and then in routine legal contexts, both the great power and the new idea of vulnerability of modern states stood out sharply. Under older ideas of treason, the person of the monarch might be in measurable danger, and the extraordinary character of earlier concepts of treason may be understood as attacks upon a particular kind of individual. In the twentieth century, however, to encompass the destruction of a people or a state was both a larger and less specific offence. To destroy a whole people or state was more imaginably monstrous than to plot against a single individual, no matter how exalted. But how did one destroy a people or state? How did one act against a people's revolution? As the intensity and degree of abstraction of treason or counter-revolutionary activity increased, the nature of the offences broadened and became more vague.

In the work of the extraordinary revolutionary commissions in the USSR between 1917 and 1922, then in fascist Italy and Spain, and finally in Germany under the Third Reich, torture reappeared under extraordinary revolutionary, party, or state authority and later, in some circumstances, under ordinary legal authority. For this process, early legal historians, from Blackstone to Lea, would have had no explanation. The history of torture has to be taken up from the other side of the watershed of 1917–45.

One of the first and most impassioned attempts to do this was that of the French jurist Alec Mellor, whose remarkable study *La Torture* appeared in a first edition in 1949, and, after the revelations of torture in French Algeria, in a second edition in 1961. What was in effect a third edition appeared under the title *Je dénonce la torture* in 1972, following the turmoil created by the publication of the memoirs of General Jacques Massu in 1971 (discussed in chapter 5 below). In a little over a decade, Mellor's history, which had originally focused upon the Cheka and the Gestapo in the twentieth century, had to be revised because torture had come home to France – and, in the decade following 1961, it seemed, virtually to the whole world.

Mellor's account of the nineteenth and twentieth centuries may be briefly and critically sketched, because it points out very effectively those areas of state activity which developed outside jurisprudence and where torture made its first reappearance under public authority. Mellor argues that the fundamental causes of the reappearance of torture were three: the appearance of the totalitarian state, of which the USSR was the end product; the necessity imposed by modern conditions of warfare of 'the seeking, at any cost, at every moment, always with the greatest urgency, of Intelligence, from which resulted the creation of special services and special methods of interrogation'; and a third, underlying cause, which Mellor calls 'Asianism', defined vaguely as state practice that exalts the occupation of the spy and recognizes no restraint upon the treatment of prisoners. The last of these Mellor dates in Europe from the Russo-Japanese war of 1905, brought to the west by 'the soviet canal'.

Mellor's work has never been translated into English, and it has met with harsh and often deserved historical criticism from legal specialists because of its author's impassioned and often undiscriminating anachronisms, its sweeping, ethno-centric condemnation of 'Asianism', its relentless anti-Marxist stance and its moralizing tone. Yet Mellor is a professional jurist, and his passion ruled his judgement as well as his admirable and exhaustive scholarship chiefly because he himself had witnessed the erosion of principles of jurisprudence and humanitarianism which had been forged in the Enlightenment and the early nineteenth century. In Mellor's own lifetime these principles seemed to be coming to an end in the most savage and grotesque way possible, by the revival, he thought, of that very world which was supposed to have disappeared forever by the middle of the nineteenth century. To Mellor, twentieth-century rulers of torture states were no different from later Roman emperors and medieval inquisitors. He regards twentieth-century states as mere revivals, technologically superior revivals, of earlier totalitarian empires and coercive churches, secularized, blasphemous, and therefore more hideously effective even than their predecessors.

Moreover, these modern states do not impose the wills of a ruling
elite upon an unwilling population, but they reflect the will of their
citizens, they speak a language common to rulers and ruled alike,
language that denounces the enemies of people, state, party or
revolution as guilty of sacrilege against the God-state of the
totalitarian age. France's experience in Algeria after 1954 did little to
modify Mellor's fears, and here he was echoed by a vast and articulate
chorus of French intellectuals, from Jean-Paul Sartre to Pierre
Vidal-Naquet. Indeed, much of the literature on torture produced
after 1945 reflects a similar tone.

Yet, for all the caution required, it is necessary to recapitulate
some of Mellor's arguments about the nineteenth and twentieth
centuries, for there is accuracy in many of them. In his treatment of
the first cause, the new totalitarian state, Mellor sketches the
transformation of the watchdog state of nineteenth-century political
theory into the instrumental state described concisely by Adolf
Hitler in *Mein Kampf* (II.2):

> The fundamental idea is that the state is not a goal, but a
> means. It is certainly the preliminary condition for the
> formation of a human civilization of superior worth, but it is
> not the direct cause of it. This resides solely and exclusively in
> a Race that is prepared for civilization.

The presence of a superior race, using the state as its instrument to
create a 'civilization' of superior value, then uses criminal law as a
'means of struggle against the vestiges of a past which must never be
reborn, and as a weapon which will necessarily assure, one day, the
arrival of a vastly superior order of humanity'. Mellor then argues
that the USSR became precisely that kind of instrumental state, its
most perfect representative. In his analysis, Mellor draws analogies
with the later Roman Empire, its divinized emperors, autocratic
administrative apparatus, thorough repression of dissent, and its
concept of the crime of sacrilege.

In his explanation of the second cause, the overwhelming and
urgent need for military political intelligence, Mellor cites the need
on the part of modern armies for speedy, detailed, and complex
information that must be extracted from prisoners in spite of
restrictive rules for the treatment of prisoners of war that a later
German general dismissed merely as relics of 'chivalric' notions of
warfare. Dating modern methods of military intelligence-gathering

from the Russo-Japanese War of 1905, Mellor then describes the development of espionage and counter-espionage techniques, the appearance of special cadres to carry out this work, and the changing perception of the place of the spy in international affairs. Mellor notes that, particularly during the period of the Russo-Turkish wars of 1877–8 and the Russo-Japanese War of 1905, the profession of spy began to lose its discreditable status and acquire some of the glamour that it has possessed until very recently. By 1914 even a son of Kaiser Wilhelm II could become a spy with his father's approval. Mellor also emphasizes the economic, industrial and cultural dimensions that espionage acquired in addition to its conventional military and diplomatic concerns. He then considers the response of late nineteenth-century states to the new phenomenon of espionage, as well as terrorism, culminating in France with the growth of the DST (*Direction de la Surveillance du Territoire*) in the later nineteenth century out of the *Deuxième Bureau* of the military world of the Second Empire.

Mellor then surveys the growth of torture under these new conditions of state power and state vulnerability in the USSR, fascist Italy and Nazi Germany, the appearance of 'police torture' in the USA, Argentina and France, and the development of intelligence services with 'special' techniques of interrogation in the rest of the world in the mid-twentieth century. The final chapters of his study deal with the social, medico-legal and moral problems of the resurgence of torture under these new conditions.

Any account of the revival of torture in the late nineteenth and twentieth centuries must certainly take some of Mellor's arguments into consideration, for several of them are virtually irrefutable. Much historical research has been done in many of these areas since Mellor first wrote, however, and some of his arguments need revision and reconsideration. There are traditional arguments to be made, anachronisms to be pruned, and passion to be postponed in the interests of accuracy. But Mellor's story remains important. For it is an account, in one sense, of how practices which began the nineteenth century as extra-legal began to become less repugnant to some branches of state authority, and when the law, which began the century as antecedent to and protected by the state, came to be, in a sense more thorough than Blackstone could ever have imagined, itself an 'engine of the state' and torture therefore an engine of the law.

Although any account of the nineteenth-century contributions to the revival of torture must necessarily consider Mellor's arguments, it need not do so with Mellor's emphasis or in Mellor's order. There is a certain logic in considering police practices first, since these were closer to the routine scope of ordinary juridical institutions. We may then consider military intelligence services and espionage, and subsequently, in areas where Mellor said little, the emergence of a doctrine which proposed new classifications of political crime, the subordination of the law to the sense of rightness held by the 'people', called in German *Volksgewissen*, and effected by transforming statute law and traditional procedure into administrative law and *ad hoc* procedure, and the parallel emergence of a similar doctrine that unfavourably contrasted statute law with the exigencies of a revolutionary ideology and movement. Finally we shall conclude with the initial appearance of torture in revolutionary and fascist states and with the shock to liberal democratic states when, as in Algeria after 1954, it was found to be more widespread than the experience of the USSR, Italy, Spain and Germany had at first hinted.

The police and the state

With the reform of criminal procedure in the late eighteenth century and the appearance of reformed legal codes in the early nineteenth, a third feature of modern criminal law appeared also: the police. Police and prison reform not only went hand in hand through the early nineteenth century, but were both the subjects of considerable international exchanges of practice and opinion, Alexis de Tocqueville's visit to the USA and John Howard's to France constituting only two visits out of a considerable series. Crime, prison, criminals and the police were on many early nineteenth-century minds, and the different development of responses to those marks the moden history of criminal justice. The historian Samuel Walker has summed up much of this development concisely:

> Three new institutions developed between 1820 and 1870; the police, the prison, and the first juvenile institutions. Each was designed to regulate, control and shape human behaviour. Regarding the police, Alan Silver points out that they represented an unprecedented social and political event: 'the

penetration and continual presence of central political authority throughout daily life.' Life was subjected to constant surveillance; 'unacceptable' behaviour was punished. In the same manner the prison subjected the life of each prisoner to constant observation and control. The French historian Michel Foucault, in his history of the prison [*Discipline and Punish*], argues that the factory, the school, the police and the prison had a common purpose: to control behavior, or to 'discipline and punish.' (*Popular Justice*, 1980, p.56).

Although some of these observations are distinctly exaggerated and can be said to have operated at best only intermittently and irregularly during the nineteenth century, the appearance of the prison and police does mark a turning point in the history of criminal justice, one not entirely consistent in practice with the reform ideals of the late eighteenth and nineteenth centuries.

Moreover, different societies developed different kinds of police. In England, where the police were the product of decades of research and political manoeuvring, from Henry Fielding's *Enquiry into the Causes of the Late Increase of Robbers* of 1754 to Sir Robert Peel's creation of a London police force in 1829, the resulting organization resembled far less the old parish-constable, voluntary and disorderly system of the English past than the contemporary English army. From the Gordon riots of 1780 to the Peterloo massacre of 1818, English politicians grew dissatisfied with the old parish-constable scheme while they remained apprehensive about the use of the army in quelling civil disturbances. This double concern gave great impetus to the creation of a police force which was conspicuously neither one nor the other. The unstinting efforts of Peel and other police officials overcame the twin fears of local authorities, who were displeased by the loss of parish-constables, and of liberal politicians, who feared that too strong a police force – especially of the *gendarmerie* type that had appeared in France during the Revolution – would dangerously increase government power and upset domestic policy. The English solution was the development of, in the words of the historian Eric Monkonnen,

> a new kind of bureaucracy, located in a social space midway between an outside military force and the group of people to be controlled. The semi-military uniform of the Metropolitan police carefully symbolized this position of the new police –

neither civilian nor military . . . The uniform symbolized the inherently ambiguous position of the new police, for by their very appearance, it was impossible to say which side they were on, the state's or the community's. (*Police in Urban America 1860–1920*, 1981, p.39)

Responsible to Parliament through the Home Secretary, the London police remained closely under judicial and parliamentary control, acted as representatives of the constitution, controlled their behaviour, manner, and demeanour in such a way as to be polite towards, but separated from the population whose activities they had been appointed to control.

Modelled in theory upon the English Metropolitan Police, American police forces developed in a different society and emerged by the early twentieth century as a very different institution. Circumstances and choice led to the creation of several thousand independent police forces in the USA; each was closely tied to local political forces, and therefore usually served the interests of only one part of the local population. The ensuing weakness of law-enforcement and investigative machinery was due, in the words of Charles Reith, 'to the fact that, as the people's choice, the police were allowed to become, corruptly, the instruments and servants, not of law, but of policy, and of local corrupt controllers of policy.' Besides the police, of course, local prosecuting attorneys also became closely entangled with local political forces and interests. Early nineteenth-century American laxity in regard to criminal activities, great latitude of American administrative and judicial discretion, the extraordinary latitude of the American jury compared even to the English jury, the admission of illegally obtained proofs by US courts, and the vagaries and inconsistency of sentencing and punishment kept the American police generally free to operate as they wished, often restrained less by principle and judicial supervision than by political and social pressure. One result was a mounting cry for police reform, echoing contemporary cries for prison reform. This movement, marked in different ways by Theodore Roosevelt's tenure as New York City Commissioner of Police and the professional careers of Richard Sylvester and August Vollmer at the turn of the twentieth century, resulted in the piecemeal reform of individual departments until 1931.

In that year, however, the immensely influential Wickersham

Report, technically the *Report of the National Commission on Law Observance and Enforcement*, recounted in enormous and grisly detail the arbitrary coercive character of police practices in the USA. It echoed earlier reports and highly specific criticism that had appeared in the preceding few years in such specialized journals as the *Harvard Law Review*, the *University of Pennsylvania Law Review* and the *University of Michigan Law Review*, and was itself followed by two remarkably comprehensive popularizations of its findings: Ernest Jerome Hopkins' *Our Lawless Police* (1931) and Emmanuel H. Lavine's *The Third Degree: American Police Methods* (1933). The slow pace of police reform picked up after the Wickersham Report, and after it police procedures became more closely aligned with the judiciary and the Constitution. The revelations of torture outside a loosely structured and insulated judicial system that had little or no control over, or interest in, the police illustrate one classic aspect of modern police history in relation to torture and other violations of civil rights. When information of evidence, or confessions themselves, could be coerced outside the purview of the judiciary and then were admissible as evidence before the judiciary – without judicial involvement in or official knowledge of torture itself – torture did not have to be an official incident of jurisprudence in order to occur and to influence the judiciary.

England had separated the police force from the public, nationalized it, and supervised it closely by the judiciary and by Parliament. The USA had separated the police from only some of the public, localized them, and supervised them only by local political authorities with little legal education or interest, and sometimes with a Bench and Bar in much the same condition. But other western countries developed yet different types of police forces and procedures. The great efficiency and universal presence of the Revolutionary Police in France that had so frightened the English opponents of Peel's police force seem to have been moderated under Napoleon and succeeding regimes. Alec Mellor, for example, finds no record of police torture until after the First World War in France. He sees it as beginning around 1929 and increasing until after the Second World War. From this period seems to date the infamous *passage à tabac*, the French equivalent of the American 'Third Degree', translatable approximately as 'rough handling', or beating. But the relative moderation of nineteenth-century French police tactics may be the result of the formidable intelligence network developed by the French police even before the revolution of 1789, improved upon by Fouché under Napoleon I, and maintained by Fouché's successors under the Second Republic and the Second Empire. Widespread police information systems, preventive detention, absence of bail, the double set of magistrates in French criminal procedure, the requirement of substantial evidence of probable cause in order to secure an indictment, and the right of the trial judge to find a verdict upon intimate conviction – all of these elements appear to have worked generally well in France before the First World War to prevent the occurrence of police torture, either in the older formal sense, or in the new police sense as in the USA.

Thus there is not a single history of the relationship between police forces and torture in the nineteenth century, but there is substantial evidence that police experience, in the USA and elsewhere, did contribute, however indirectly, to the resurgence of torture. The problem became more complex when police forces were used to deal with both criminal and political offences, when the police were closely or loosely supervised by other governmental branches, when police forces were controlled by governments rather than by independent judiciaries. The later history of police in Russia illustrates some of these points effectively. In spite of the adminis-trative reforms of the czars Alexander I and Nicholas I early in the nineteenth century which, as we have seen, formally abolished torture in Russia, Russia until 1880 still contained a number of different police forces, each with different responsibilities and powers, some of which, recent scholarship suggests, did use torture in the 1860s and 1870s. The Corps of Gendarmes, the local regional police forces of the governors-general, the Third Section of the czarist Chancery, and the city police forces under the Ministry of the Interior Affairs (MVD) were merged into a Department of State Police under the Interior Ministry in 1880 under the influence of M. T. Loris-Melikov. But even these substantial reforms seem not to have achieved the reformers' aims, because in 1881 secret police organizations were separately established in St Petersburg and Moscow. It would seem that chiefly after 1881, when the Okhrana became the chief instrument of Alexander III for the detection and repression of terrorism, did the use of police torture become widespread once again in czarist Russia.

The growth of an administrative bureaucracy in most of the states of Europe and North America in the late nineteenth century, coupled with police forces either under independent political control or with police forces charged specifically with political duties, offered considerable latitude for the re-emergence of torture, even in some states with a strong and independent judiciary and statutory prohibition of torture. The state had developed other officials besides judges to whom torture might be entrusted, and statutory prohibition meant little if it controlled only the judges and court magistrates and not state officials outside their purview.

The growth of state security police, political police proper, is perhaps the ultimate cause of the reappearance of torture in the twentieth century. But chronologically and institutionally it was preceded by the second of the extra-judicial organs of the modern state: the military.

Warfare, prisoners and military intelligence

In spite of the passions roused by the religious wars of the sixteenth and seventeenth centuries, and by the dynastic wars of the early eighteenth, older notions of the rules of warfare, at least those applying to command-level personnel, were still recognized into the nineteenth century and occasionally observed. When an age of limited warfare arrived in the second quarter of the eighteenth century, it coincided with some of the other political and moral changes considered earlier. Like the operation of the law, the practice of warfare also came under Enlightenment scrutiny, and once more rules governing combatants and non-combatants alike came to be discussed, elaborated, and also occasionally observed. After 1792, however, new passions were infused into warfare, and these transformed among other things the treatment of prisoners and the acquisition of military intelligence.

First, the uniformity of severe military discipline created a kind of life in military service that brutalized even as it regulated and homogenized the conduct of soldiers. The appeal of the French revolutionaries for citizen-soldiers began the process of identifying the cause of state and soldier as one. The armies of Napoleon became the forerunners of large-scale citizen armies. Like treason, warfare was no longer purely an affair of kings and their ministers, but of whole peoples, of their morality, and of their sentiments as well. These new, larger, complexly organized, technologically superior citizen-armies required their own rules and their own governors. These rulers wielded internal legal authority as surely as they wielded the technological knowledge that enabled them better to arm and equip their forces. The kind of information that might now be provided by prisoners or captured spies could also prove to be crucial and was needed quickly. The interrogation of prisoners of war, carried out in the heat of battle, guided only by the least enforceable rules against an enemy unprotected by a common law, marks the conduct of warfare in the modern world. Even the existence of a series of international conventions and a substantial literature and diplomatic agreement about the rights of prisoners, seems not to have prevented an autonomous military from developing its own rules for dealing with potentially informative prisoners.

In the matter of captured spies, of course, there was even less protection and less consideration of rights. Until the First World War, the spy performed a *métier vil* – a shameful occupation in which he received no mercy if caught. By the third quarter of the nineteenth century, espionage was also a very well-populated occupation. It has been estimated that in 1870 Prussia had 30,000 agents of various kinds in her service. From the mid-nineteenth century on, more and more nations recognized the value of military intelligence and at the same time dealt severely with those spies from the other side who fell into their hands.

The cases of the prisoner of war and the captured spy reflect both military autonomy and the expanded need for military intelligence. These rest in part on the increased vulnerability of industrialized urban societies. The composition of military forces and the new demand for military intelligence placed considerable strain upon the traditional and the new ideals of regulated warfare, from residual chivalry to nineteenth-century diplomatic instruments. Although most states professed to recognize the humane responsibilities of warring enemies, few states possessed the capacity to regulate minutely the conduct of those participants. The growing independence of military commanders and staffs and the growing destructive capabilities of modern armies put great strain upon doctrines of respect for prisoners' and non-combatants' rights and did little to improve the lot of the captured spy.

Just as citizens became soldiers and military targets, they also in some cases became combatants, either as partisans or revolutionaries, guerilla forces in either case. And, as Raymond Aron once observed, 'the discipline of clandestine war requires more brutality and terror than that of regular troops.' So too does that type of industrialized warfare that requires the control and discipline of enemy civilians, an army of occupation.

Perhaps it was not indeed, as Mellor argues, until the beginning of the twentieth century that all these new aspects of military activity became sufficiently systematically used in concert to reveal the military forces of modern states as, in one crucial sense, 'concealing behind the Laws of War a formidable quasi-jurisprudence which possessed not only its own practices, but its own rules'. Even before the Russo-Japanese War and the First World War, however, the free hand of the military constituted a second area relatively uncontrolled by the judiciary and hence ultimately unanswerable to the rules of civilian jurisprudence.

Before those dates too, particularly during the late nineteenth century, there emerged civilian terrorism, which was widely reported in the press and later depicted graphically in novels, memoirs and films. Not only the spy, but the terrorist too became a hero of fiction – and of reality. The excesses committed by the police and military forces outside the authority of civilian jurisprudence often found an echo in a civilian population more widely, if not more accurately, informed about the dangers to their state and the needs and opportunities of taking extraordinary measures to defend it and destroy its enemies.

The vulnerability of the state itself may be measured in part at least by changing attitudes toward political crime.

Political crime

Like Blackstone's concept of treason, early European designations of political crime generally dealt with the person of the ruler and his immediate officials. As Pierre Padadatos has pointed out (*Le délit politique*, 1955), one of the most striking changes of the French Criminal Code of 1791 consists of a new definition of political crime as being an offence against the State, *lèse nation* rather than the more personalized offence of *lèse majesté*. From this date on, more slowly in some European countries than in others, the larger and more abstract State, nation, or people was posited as the object of political crime, rather than, or rather than exclusively, the person of the ruler, his family and servants. Initially, the great horizon of political crime became much wider and many of the earlier categories indeed carried over into the new legislation which stemmed from new political theory. Yet, in spite of the Terror of 1793 and the decades of imperialism and reaction that followed until 1830 in France, the horizon itself remained narrow. The first chapters in the modern history of political crime are marked by roughness indeed, but also and more consistently by liberal principles and, as far as can be seen, liberal practices.

As Mellor has shown, neither the Girondins nor the Jacobins, Napoleon nor Louis XVIII, the July Monarchy nor the Second Republic appear to have reinstated torture into the laws or police practice of France, in either the criminal or the political area. Considering the other steps in political control most of these regimes practised, and considering the even less savoury reputation of the Second Republic and the Second Empire as 'police states', it is remarkable that the European nation which experienced most acutely the birth-pangs of modern political experience, and which underwent much wider and more dramatic swings between revolution and reaction more consistently than any other, never took up torture for any purpose during that period. The *ordonnance* of Louis XVI of 1788 survived into the revolutionary Code of 1791, the *Code des délits et des peines* of 1795, the *Code d'instruction criminelle* of 1808, and the *Code pénal* of 1810, and it has stood in French law ever since.

Some aspects of political crime, of course, have altered much more dramatically, from penal policy to transportation and exile, but this is not the place to offer even an abbreviated history of that vast subject. On occasion, too, some offences were reinstated and redefined in state codes throughout the nineteenth and twentieth centuries. Misprision of treason, for example, the failure to report knowledge of plots or political crimes to the authorities, was instituted in the French *Code* of 1810, abolished in 1832, but reinstated in 1939. In Russia it was instituted in 1649, and in Hesse in 1795 and Prussia in 1798, although it was abolished in the new German code of 1871. In England it was embodied in a statute in 1797. It is also true that as offences deemed political increased, punishments for them often became more lenient. The history of political crime is a far larger subject than can adequately be dealt with here.

Some aspects of political crime, however, play crucial roles in measuring the judicial temperament of nineteenth-century and early twentieth-century states. One conclusion that a number of government officials and legal philosophers drew from the European experience of 1789–1830, as we have seen elsewhere, was the ideal and the necessity of an independent judiciary. François Guizot, for example, argued that political offences were beyond the competence of judicial systems and constituted a danger to them, because they stretched legal definitions beyond the limits foreseen by the jurists and legislators who had created them, they tended to force acts to be considered in terms of the persons accused of them, they invited judgement on intentions rather than acts, they allowed presumptions to supplant proofs, courts were too extensively informed about defendants, in political trials individual persons were tried on the basis of general political ideas rather than particular offences, testimony often came from spies, informers and *agents provocateurs*, political trials often saw the Attorney-General as prosecutor, and the press was often excluded from courtrooms. Such criticism of the judiciary's problem with political crimes was echoed in other quarters as well. The influence of the doctrines of Jeremy Bentham, particularly on the French *Code* of 1810, brought the balanced principles of utilitarian jurisprudence to bear in addition to humanitarianism. In short, in France and England and, as we have seen, in Russia as well, the period between 1830 and the early twentieth century was what Barton L. Ingraham has called (*Political Crime in Europe*, 1979) the 'spring and summer of leniency' in the matter of political crime.

Although many governments advised a number of new punishments for political criminals and kept revising the definition of political crime, and although a number of governments became expert in placing informers, spies and *agents provocateurs* inside suspected groups, they did not torture. Even the tendency after 1848 to distinguish anarchists from 'opposition' political criminals had as its chief result the exclusion of a few categories of criminal anarchists in particular from the protection of the new and more liberal laws concerning political crime. This practice seems to have become even more common after 1886, particularly in cases of espionage and the trials of anarchists. The chief lesson to be drawn from this experience is probably that the abolition of torture in fact and in theory did not necessarily abolish the tendency of some states to be in practice more authoritarian than liberals would wish.

But the generally liberal treatment of political crime throughout most of the nineteenth and early twentieth centuries did achieve two matters of importance for the history of torture. It led to a detailed and prolonged consideration of the nature and authority of the state, from many diverse points of view. It also laid down a history of lenient treatment of political crime that could be reacted against when attitudes toward some kinds of political criminals changed at the end of the century. The first of these to be affected were the anarchists, but besides anarchy and terror there occurred a transformation in attitudes toward political crime and the state itself.

As historians of political crime have often pointed out, nineteenth-century thought on the subject recognized two kinds: internal and external. It is the former, committed by people who were generally admitted to be high-minded, noble of principle, and idealist reformers, which received the lightest treatment during most of the nineteenth century. When, after 1870, many European states once more turned to threats that were external, particularly after the first spreading of intense feelings of nationalism, and the mobilization of these by the franchise and propaganda, the political criminal then ran the risk of appearing as a betrayer of national unity, of a people (of which a state was a mere expression), rather than as an idealistic reformer. The most dramatic of these changes were probably the French *lois scélerates*, the 'shameful laws' of the 1890s. England, notoriously hospitable to political fugitives and exiles during most of the century, turned anti-anarchist itself after 1894.

The great transformation in attitudes and legislation toward political crime dates from the years immediately before and after the First World War. As Ingraham has succinctly put it in *Political Crime in Europe*, external political crime became more reprehensible, and internal political crime came to be seen as equivalent to external. One reason for this change was, of course, the renewed outbreak of diplomatic tensions and real wars after the 1870s, heralded by the Russo-Turkish and Russo-Japanese conflicts of 1878 and 1905, and the looming of the First World War over the first two decades of the new century. States that had seemed to satisfy the demands of those with the greatest political voices now satisfied fewer people; criticized by particular rival states, international movements and vociferous internal oppositions, early twentieth-century states perceived themselves much more vulnerable to political enmity than they had done throughout most of the nineteenth century.

In addition to this new and measurable enmity and vulnerability, the state had acquired other characteristics during the latter part of the century. Those aspects of national community that had begun the century by seeming so abstract in the thought of Hegel and so non-political in that of Herder had become by the end of the century far more concrete and political. Indeed, organic nationalism was a product of the end of the century when, in Eugen Weber's phrase, peasants turned into Frenchmen, as did petit-bourgeois and others, and in other states passions turned many more English people into Englishmen, Rhinelanders, Saxons, Prussians, and Bavarians into Germans. The identification of the state with the ethnic national community, supported by other propaganda and legislation, constituted in the early twentieth-century state a very different organism from the abstract State of the Enlightenment and its nineteenth-century successors, the eclectics, classicists, utilitarians and positivists. Now, the state, like the law, represented, indeed personified, a people, and it was operated according to the people's will; those who opposed it, whether ordinary criminals or political criminals, opposed the will of the people, and gradually the political criminal came to be regarded as more dangerous – and more repulsive – than the ordinary criminal. For the people-state, spying became honourable, as did other acts hitherto suspect or scorned.

In addition to the new conception of the National State, there emerged after 1917 the new revolutionary marxism, which used particular existing states merely as interim political organizations designed to further the aims of an international philosophy. Not only did the defence of the national state entail the defence of a people, but it now had to be defended from enemy national states as well as from international revolutionary movements that in themselves scorned ethnic states as un- or counter-revolutionary. Thus political crime itself changed after the turn of the twentieth century. The conditions under which it was committed also changed, and the former lenient conception of the political criminal, legislated into existence earlier in the century by many governments whose members had themselves once been political criminals, disappeared before the twin powers of the nation-state and revolutionary philosophy. In its place there emerged a heightened idea of political crime and an extension of the concept 'political' itself. In terms of both law and other engines of the state the new image of political crime reflected both a conceptual and actual vulnerability of the twentieth-century nation-state. For beside the new concept of political crime there also appeared in greater numbers real political criminals, as well as others who, for reasons far removed from conventional definitions, became political criminals by arbitrary state definition.

To a great extent the most extreme positions of nineteenth-century anarchism corresponded to the state's vulnerability. J. L. Talmon has effectively paraphrased much anarchist debate upon the rights of the revolutionary:

> Theirs was a mission to rebel, to act against the law, against a legality which was evil incarnate. This invited, necessitated, and justified unconventional and lawless acts, ruse, deceit and violence. As only fanatical determination and ruthless action could be effective and succeed, the ability to command them became the test not merely of efficiency, but also of the strength and depth of conviction and devotion. The loathing for the existing kingdom of evil and the courage not to shrink from anything in the process of destroying it, demanded an equally deep and passionate belief in the absolute goodness, purity and salvationist quality of the world which the revolutionaries were destined to bring into being. (*The Origins of Totalitarian Democracy*, 1970, p.315)

At its most extreme positions, nineteenth-century anarchism concedes nothing to any similar rhetoric of the twentieth century. In its own age it was even more effective than the latter is now, because it was more original and less routinized.

States without revolutions thus developed categories of political crime out of their experience of intensified internal political dissent and intensified external opposition, whether from rival powers or revolutionary movements. Revolutionary states, on the other hand, had their own rationales for revising the law and redefining political crime. They became the first states to use torture in a more visible and routine way.

Law and the state in revolutionary societies

In a number of states during the early twentieth century the traditional separation of law and politics was sometimes abolished in the interests of stronger and more ruthless regimes and in the name of a magnified or diminished idea of the state. The earliest European nation-state in which such regimes and ideas assumed power was Russia after October 1917, but a number of states generally grouped under the label 'fascist' offer a wider variety of examples. When a revolutionary government gained power in Italy in 1922, it was led by Benito Mussolini, himself a recently converted socialist revolutionary. Alec Mellor cites the definition of the new Fascist state contributed by Mussolini himself to the *New Italian Encyclopedia* of 1932 (*La Torture*, 1949): 'Man is nothing. Fascism raises itself up against the individual abstraction which is based upon materialistic foundations and utopias. Beyond the state, nothing that is human or spiritual has any value whatsoever.' In Italian Fascism, the state was the representative and agent of a much larger and more important entity, the nation of people. Nothing outside it – and nothing else inside it – had any legitimate authority. In spite of the resistance of parts of the Italian army and some of the judiciary to these claims and to the changes in legal procedure which followed in their train, the Italian government and party functionaries wielded extraordinary authority in their assertion and maintenance of power. After 1929 the OVRA – The Voluntary Organization for the Repression of Antifascism – the secret political police, used torture regularly upon suspected enemies of state, party and people (Finer, *Mussolini's Italy*, 1969).

In Germany after 1932 similar doctrines were carried several steps further. The German state itself became simply the administrative vehicle of the National Socialist Party. The party leader, Adolf Hitler, personified – according to party propaganda – the will and community of the people, the *Volk*, and the *Volk* itself was construed to be radically exclusive as a national historical community. Even the party in this case became something quite different from conventional parties, as Hitler himself pointedly observed: 'Political parties are inclined to compromise; philosophical doctrines, never. Political parties arrive at agreement even with their enemies; philosophical doctrines proclaim themselves infallible' (Mellor, *La Torture*, p.207). The National Socialist Party was, therefore, not a political party at all in the conventional sense, but rather the active embodiment of an infallible 'philosophy' of a people, the *Volk*, to which state and law were themselves both necessarily subordinated. In this world, the old Enlightenment doctrines of the abstract state, as well as the originally quite diverse thought of Herder, Hegel and Fichte, found a popular and powerful force in which to express themselves.

The party used the state on behalf of the newly and exclusively defined *Volk*. To the community of the *Volk*, the *Volksgemeinschaft*, or *Volksgenosse*, was thus imputed a single supreme wisdom and a single will. It was ostensibly the validating element of both state and party. Folkness, *Volkstum*, represented the highest and most exclusive values, the preserve of all honour, and the ultimate meaning for individual selves. The individual had no identity or worth outside membership in the *Volk*.

Just as older concepts of party and state had been subordinated to the grander vision and dedicated agency of the National Socialist Party, so was the older idea of the law. As Otto Kirchheimer remarked,

> The separation of law from morality, an axiom in the period of competitive capitalism, has [in 1939] been replaced by a moral conviction derived immediately from the 'racial conscience,' *Volksgeswissen* . . . The 'racial conscience' has been introduced into the criminal law through the elevation of concepts like 'welfare of the people' and 'healthy national sentiment' to official normative standards. (*Punishment and Social Structure*, 1939, pp.179–80)

The juridical consequences of National Socialist theory and practice included the creation of special tribunals, the widening definition of political crimes, and the intensification of methods of interrogation and punishment. After 1933 a series of special courts, *Sondergerichte*, handled cases thought too important by the party to be left to the surviving judicial system, whose judges could not be trusted to find a politically acceptable verdict. In 1934 the *Volksgerichtshof* was created, a tribunal in charge of cases of treason and composed only partially of professional jurists, the remainder of its members being drawn from party organizations and lacking all judicial training and experience. There was no appeal from the *Volksgerichtshof*, and rarely was any favour shown to the accused. As Kirchheimer acidly stated elsewhere:

> The system of technical rationality as the foundation of law and legal practice has [in 1941] superseded any system for the preservation of individual rights and thus has definitely made

law and legal practice an instrument of ruthless domination
and oppression in the interest of those who control the main
economic and political levers of social power. Never has the
process of alienation between law and morality gone so far as in
the society which allegedly has perfected the integration of
these very conceptions. (*Politics, Law and Social Change*,
1969, p.109)

Like the State itself, the law entered the service of Party and *Führer*
in the name of the *Volk*. The 'People's sound sense of justice', the
gesundes Volksempfindung, became the only norm against which
individual rights and legal procedure were to be measured – and
found always wanting. Mellor (*La Torture*, p.211) cites the definition
of Friedrich Frick, German Minister of the Interior, in 1933: 'Law is
what serves the German people. Injustice is what injures it.'

Historians have often pointed out that revolutionary societies,
medieval or modern, are generally led by 'new men' – individuals of
uncertain social status, lacking ties to traditional social structures,
and therefore not controlled by the moral and institutional restraints
that operate in traditional societies. Although traditional elites might
co-operate with them at first, the difference in revolutionary and
traditional views soon disaffected these supporters, and the revolutionaries were left alone to redefine goals and eliminate restraints. In
the Third Reich not merely the routine structures of the law were
modified or eliminated in the name of state and *Volk*, but other
traditional sanctions, including those against generally recognized
political crimes like treason and espionage, suffered similarly.
Mellor cites the response of General Keitel in 1941 to a protest over
his improper treatment of Soviet prisoners made by Admiral Canaris
(*La Torture*, p.212): 'One raises these objections which are inspired
by a chivalric conception of war, but we are dealing here with an
ideology. Therefore, I approve and will continue to use these
methods.' State, law and the rules of war themselves had now
become anachronistic relics of another age.

In June of 1942, a year in which the creation and authorization of
special services reached unaccustomed heights, Heinrich Himmler
issued an order authorizing the use of what he specifically called 'the
Third degree' in interrogations, clearly intending by that term to
indicate torture. The Third Degree was to be used to elicit
confessions from prisoners in all cases in which preliminary

investigation indicated knowledge of useful information, particularly concerning the Resistance:

> The Third Degree in this case may be used only against communists, Marxists, Jehovah's Witnesses, saboteurs, terrorists, members of resistance movements, antisocial elements, refractory elements, or Polish or Soviet vagabonds. In all other cases, preliminary authorization is necessary.

The Third Degree was to include a diet of bread and water, close confinement, extraordinary exercises, hidden cells, deprivation of sleep, and beatings. Although physicians were to be consulted after more than twenty strokes, Mellor is surely correct in regarding this qualification as stemming from the need to prevent prisoners from being killed under torture, that is, preserving them for further interrogation. He points out the extraordinary role played by the medical profession elsewhere in the Third Reich, notably in the concentration and death camps. As the next chapter will suggest, not only did the Third Reich bring back torture, but it transformed it into a medical speciality, a transformation which was to have great consequences in the second half of the twentieth century.

The nation-state and the *Volk* constitute one of the routes by which torture returned to the world of the twentieth century. Another lies in the history of the revolutionary ideology. When Hitler spoke of 'philosophical doctrines', he was merely using an intellectually pretentious term for *Volk* and blood. Beyond these, his mind did – and could – not go. But, whether from the Russian revolution of 1917 or from the remoter seeds of Enlightenment political inventiveness, there did emerge a genuine set of philosophical doctrines which did indeed in its turn lead to practices that its originators probably did not imagine and would not have acknowledged.

The attitudes of modern revolutionary regimes toward jurisprudence, statutory law and the legal profession has generally been one of two kinds. Sometimes, as in the case of the United States and Revolutionary France, much of the law as it existed prior to the revolution may seem worth preserving with relatively few changes. Sometimes revolutionary regimes in fact preserve more of the jurisprudence of the past than they, in the heat and fury of their gestation, might once have wished. At other times, a dual system of jurisprudence has emerged in which, at least in the twentieth century, 'normal' offences and routine litigation have operated in ways that remain traditional, however modified in form by the new philosophical or ideological principles of justice; certain categories of crime, however, perceived by the revolutionaries to be particularly sensitive, have been handled by special tribunals according to novel procedures.

The second set of attitudes generally regards the law of the older regime as a signal instance of its error or corruption, a basic defect which needs to be utterly obliterated in order to create a totally new society. Robespierre urged that in the perfect revolutionary state law need not even exist, when the concord of popular will and the alignment of the government to it ruled society. Until 1794, Robespierre's doctrines received a favourable hearing in Revolutionary France. Robespierre's successor, Claude de Saint-Simon, also foresaw a revolutionary society in which, political structures again aligned to the popular will, there would be minimal, if indeed any, formal mechanisms of law enforcement. Still later, other revolutionary thinkers urged the abolition of present law in favour of a 'living law' created by a revolutionary artist, rejecting the dead weight of the old law in favour of the progressive law which reflected a progressing society and therefore could not be codified beforehand.

Of all modern political philosophies, socialism has perhaps been the harshest toward existing legal systems, not only because they represent a hated power structure, but also because they represent what socialism considered fundamental error – the error of the bourgeoisie which erects law as a superstructure to conceal the bourgeois conservation of power, privilege and wealth. Much of the strength of Marx and Engels' ideas of law and crime lies in their acute perception of the inconsistencies between bourgeois statements about the law and the criminal and the actual practice, even on the part of liberal democratic states, in applying the law.

Thus, a line of utopian criticism of traditional legal structures may be traced from Robespierre through Marx and Engels towards a number of revolutionary states of the twentieth century. Lenin, after a long career among the vicissitudes of socialist legal theories, ultimately came to a similar position:

> In a classless society in which all citizens served in the people's militia, the need for a special police would almost cease, since the people as a whole would do the watching, judging and

punishing. There would be active participation by all citizens in legislation by rotation, as well as in the administration of community affairs, and superimposed officialdom would become superfluous. (Talmon, *Origins of Totalitarian Democracy* (1970), pp. 424–5)

In Communist terms, law, as the bourgeois state had known it, would virtually cease to exist, and in its place would be the communist version of *Volksgewissen*, the people's constant and voluntary awareness and application of revolutionary principles. A generation before Lenin, the revolutionary socialist Lavrov had envisaged something similar, 'direct people's summary justice'.

As revolutionary societies have become more evident during the past half century, much criticism of their jurisprudence has been focused upon the second of these responses, that which reclassifies offences from a philosophical (ideological) perspective. In doing so, much of the rest of their jurisprudence, including in most cases, its bulk, has been neglected, and entire revolutionary systems stamped with the stigma of only a part of their legal and administrative practice. In the following discussion, it is worth marking now and remembering later that, except for 'political' offences, however defined, much of their jurisprudence and juridical practice has survived from earlier regimes and does not enter into this account.

However much modern revolutionaries have proclaimed the death of earlier judicial systems, and to whatever extent systems like that of the Third Reich in fact and deed transformed all jurisprudence into their own image, it was not until the Russian Revolution of 1917 that the doctrine effectively appeared that insisted upon the right of a revolutionary government to take measures to protect itself and the revolution in general as had already been taken to protect a nation, state, or *Volk*.

Even in the best-known case, that of the transformation of czarist Russia into the Union of Soviet Socialist Republics, the defence of the Revolution was not immediately, nor for some months after October 1917, erected into a governing principle in determining political crime and in that determination willing to inflict torture and other extraordinary sanctions for political reasons. In spite of the bitter, and nearly universal resentment of the czarist system of jurisprudence among the revolutionary bodies of 1917, much of the reform principles of justice of 1881 were retained by the new government, in much the same manner as many of the recent jurisprudential reforms of the *ancien régime* were retained by the Revolutionary government in France after 1789.

Although it is not possible to trace the transformations of socialist theories of justice and jurisprudence here, a number of their features should be emphasized, if only in relation to events in the Soviet Union between 1917 and 1922, and from 1936 to 1938. The disappearance of the law has remained a principle of Soviet theory, but it has been removed far into the future.

The series of circumstances that turned Lenin first into a proponent of the dictatorship of the revolutionary section of the proletariat, and second into the leader of the Revolution of 1917, led to spectacular changes in Russian legal structures. Although initially some earlier jurisprudence was preserved, in the Soviet Union two developments virtually marked and prophesied its extinction: the use of special revolutionary tribunals and the formation of the Cheka from 1917 and 1922, and the rejection of Pashukanis' ideas of the withering away of the law in 1936 and 1937, and in their place the erection of several subsequent codes of Soviet law, from the Constitution of 1936 to the Criminal Code and the Code of Criminal Procedure of 1965.

In the revolutionary justice defined and practised by the Cheka under its first director Feliks Edmundovich Dzerzhinsky, torture seems to have been routinely used, at least in that wide variety of cases deemed to touch upon counter-revolutionary activity. Under Dzerzhinsky the Cheka became the instrument for the defence of the Revolution, an instrument upon which few restraints could, even in theory, be put: 'We have nothing in common with the military-revolutionary tribunal . . . We stand for organized terror – this should be frankly stated – terror being absolutely indispensable in current revolutionary conditions. Our task is to fight against the enemies of the Soviet Government and the new order of life' (Leggett, *The Cheka* (1981), p.68). Such a mission had little use for conventional legal safeguards, certainly not in its operation in discovering suspects and maintaining even minimum levels of prison conditions, let alone refraining from harsh forms of interrogation. Suspects might be arrested late at night, verbally and physically abused, rushed into a prison, threatened with death (and even led to a place of execution several times, only to be returned to prison), and were tried by no regular procedure, with no defence permitted.

Aside from the conditions of the prisons themselves and the horrifying physical conditions under which prisoners were routinely kept, interrogation itself was often accompanied by beatings, but the different Chekas developed particular kinds of torture. One 'went in for scalping and hand-flaying; some of the Voronezh Cheka's victims were thrust naked into an internally nail-studded barrel and were rolled around in it; others had their forehead branded with a five-pointed star, whilst members of the clergy were "crowned" with barbed wire' (ibid.). Alexander Solzhenitsyn (*Gulag Archipelago*) points out that the standard form of torture for hoarders of gold in the 1920s was the forced feeding of salt herring.

The Kiev Cheka was said to have devised a method of interrogation which consisted of placing one open end of a metal cylinder against the prisoner's chest, placing a rat in the other end and sealing the outer end with wire mesh. When the tube was heated, the rat, in a frenzy to escape, ate its way into the prisoner's flesh.

Although a number of official statements from the Cheka's leadership denied the use of torture, individual Cheka offices and publications seem to have admitted to it freely. In light of the superior morality of defending the Revolution, lesser moral concerns (or, rather, other moral concerns which automatically seemed lesser) could have no claim, nor could the routine judicial procedures of the Soviet State.

The Code of Criminal Procedure of 1923–4 took the further step of abolishing the distinctions between police interrogation and pre-trial investigation and placing both, and much of the trial itself, under the supervision of Public Prosecutors. Although the Code itself (Section 136) states: 'the investigator shall not have the right to seek testimony or confession by the use of violence, threats, or other similar methods', such reservations historically seem to have been applied in cases with no political dimension, if they existed. In other cases, the evidence is abundant, even after the demise of the Cheka, of widespread use of torture, particularly after 1936. Nikita Kruschev himself cited a telegram from Stalin to the People's Commissariat for the Interior in January 1939, which stated that:

It is known that all bourgeois intelligence services use methods of physical influence against the representatives of the Socialist proletariat and that they use them in their most scandalous forms. The question arises as to why the Socialist intelligence service should be more humanitarian toward the mad agents of the bourgeoisie . . . The Central Committee of the All-Union Communist Party considers that physical pressure should still be used obligatorily, as an exception applicable to known and obstinate enemies of the people, as a method both justifiable and appropriate.

Other sources, of course, testify to the growing practice which made procedures that were extraordinary from 1917 to 1922 routine after 1936–7. In those countries that came under Soviet influence after the Second World War, similar instances of torture also occurred, notably in Poland in 1956 by the State Security Police.

The point of discussing these changes in the USSR after 1917 has not been to suggest that torture is routinely and indiscriminately applied, even in all political cases, in Eastern Europe. It has been rather to suggest the role of a particularly successful revolutionary ideology in creating categories of state authority in which torture may be and has been used. The present Soviet Criminal Code of the RFSFR in fact makes the element of torture (on the part of a criminal) an exacerbating offence which lengthens the normal sentence (Arts.108.2, 109.2).

In spite of very different approaches to other issues, the experience of the Third Reich and the Soviet Union with the legitimation of torture in what was technically an extra-judicial setting constituted the first breach of the principles which had been laid down in the eighteenth century and enshrined in the first modern revolutionary constitutions, that of the US and the French Declaration of the Rights of Man and Citizen. The events and ideas of the period between which those two sets of revolutions took place may account for the differences between them. On the other hand, besides the way in which the nineteenth and early twentieth centuries were perceived by National Socialists and Bolsheviks, the consequences of twentieth-century revolutionary justice also reflect the precarious place of the judiciary in the face of a vastly more energized state whose administrative powers overshadow both legislature and judiciary. Blackstone's observation that in England torture was the engine of the state, not of law, was indeed true as far as it went. But the revolutionary state of the twentieth century was something that Blackstone could not have imagined. Infinitely more wealthy and powerful, moved by ideologies that excited more and more of its citizens, possessed of organs and intelligence that could dispense with traditional divisions of authority, the coercive revolutionary state of the twentieth century could reintroduce torture into any or all of its procedures, for it had developed not only new powers, but a new anthropology. In place of the rights of man and citizen, there was substituted the exclusive right of the *Volk* or Revolution. Against these, the fragile barriers in which late eighteenth- and nineteenth-century thinkers and jurists had misplaced so much faith began to crumble more quickly than they had ever dreamed possible.

The events described so far in this chapter provide a description of the great watershed that lies between nineteenth- and early twentieth-century accounts of the history of torture and accounts produced after 1945. Even the final sections of Piero Fiorelli's great history *La tortura giudiziaria nel diritto commune* (1953–4), fail adequately to come to grips with the twentieth-century experience. They also help to explain some of the passion and inaccuracies in the work of Mellor. Mellor is a Christian humanist and a professional jurist, and he saw what had happened to that professionally liberal and high-minded judiciary when non- or extra-judicial elements seized control of the law and thus of much of the fate of human beings. Mellor, of course, was not alone. In a remarkable memoir of Russian prison life published in New York in 1951, two former political prisoners, F. Beck and W. Godin, devoted a perceptive and grimly witty chapter to the 'theories' constructed by their fellow prisoners, most of them perfectly orthodox marxists, to explain the horrifying circumstances in which they found themselves in a marxist state and the horrifying ways in which they had been treated. The 'theories' run the gamut of twentieth-century political paranoia: some argued that 'fascists' had infiltrated the communist government and legal administration of the USSR and that torture was therefore a 'fascist' import. Others argued a version of Mellor's 'Asiatic' theory – Russia possesses a character that is fundamentally 'Asiatic' and therefore naturally violent and barbaric, and that it was this character, rather than the administration of the communist system, to which torture must be attributed. Beck and Godin describe many other 'theories', none of them different in character from the two cited here.

Other thinkers and writers besides Mellor, Beck and Godin also took up twentieth-century torture. Arthur Koestler, in his novel

Darkness at Noon (1941), and George Orwell in *Nineteen Eighty-Four* (1949) both echoed information concerning torture in fascist and communist states before and during the Second World War. Hans von Hentig, an accomplished and prolific legal historian, also expressed pointed awareness of the fact that the optimism of earlier legal historians was no longer available to similar scholars in the second half of the twentieth century. By 1950 scholars and journalists both admitted that the history of torture was still open and unfinished, and that earlier accounts of that history would have to be revised. The final section of Fiorelli's *La tortura giudiziaria* was entitled 'Senza una fine?' – 'Without an end?' In that section, after an extensive catalogue of statutory prohibition of many different forms of torture by nineteenth- and twentieth-century states, Fiorelli briefly noted its return, or, as he openly wondered, the signs of its undocumented continuation. He notes its newer forms, its new technology, and its psychological dimension, the last topic already having been the subject of the remarkably perceptive final chapter of Rudolf Quanter's study *Torture in German Customary Law* (1900). Quanter's title, 'Die Seelenfolter im heutigen Strafprozess' – 'the torture of the spirit in contemporary criminal procedure' – was an odd anticipation of Foucault's argument many decades later. Quanter raised the question of whether or not modern impersonal judicial procedure and forms of incarceration exert more illegitimate force upon the human spirit than the older bodily sanctions.

Yet all of these concerns also presupposed that the twentieth-century revival of torture had been restricted to certain 'aberrant' societies in certain extraordinary circumstances, that is, to Nazi Germany and the early and insecure stages of the rule of Lenin and Stalin in the Soviet Union. Events in Algeria after 1954, however, and their slow but relentless exposition in the French Press, raised an even more troubling aspect: that twentieth-century torture was not exclusively a product of the Third Reich nor of the early USSR and their dependent client states. Between the first edition of Mellor's *La Torture* in 1949 and the second in 1961 there occurred the discovery of Algeria.

The discovery of Algeria

Most liberal-democratic states took a long time to appreciate the juridical inventiveness of both the Third Reich and the USSR. Once they had perceived, among other things, the reappearance and justification of torture, their first response was to dismiss it as an aberration of psychotic or degenerate governments, lacking popular support, and in clear violation of all universally recognized principles of justice and public law. In 1957 and 1958, however, slowly and hesitantly at first, rumour, then news, began to circulate in France that the French army and colonial police forces had begun to use torture in dealing with Algerian rebels, at least since the launching of the Algerian revolt in 1954. After 1957 the news became a flood that eventually contributed substantially to the demise of the Fourth Republic, the creation of the Fifth Republic, and the independence of Algeria in 1962. Nothing in French law had changed, the French army had been given no extraordinary powers, and the French public, if anything, prided itself upon the humaneness of its institutions, even in the colonies, especially in the light of France's own experience under German occupation and the Vichy government that had occurred so recently. As Jean-Paul Sartre bluntly put it,

> In 1943, in the Rue Lauriston [the Gestapo headquarters in Paris], Frenchmen were screaming in agony and pain; all France could hear them. In those days the outcome of the war was uncertain and we did not want to think about the future. Only one thing seemed impossible in any circumstances: that one day men should be made to scream by those acting in our name. (Alleg, *The Question*, 1958, p.3)

Once again, as in the case of Beck and Godin, there appeared a number of rationalizing 'theories': the torture was an aberration carried out by the Foreign Legion, and hence by non-Frenchmen (a modernized variant of the 'fascist' infiltration theory); that the torture was exaggerated; that, according to the notorious Wuillaume Report of 1955, duress was indeed being used, but it was 'not quite torture'.

In the following several years all of the rationalizations collapsed except those of the torturers, and these were eventually repudiated by a vast majority of French citizens. With the rationalizations dispersed, much of the world had to face the question put by Sartre: how had France come to do this, so recently after her own political agony and with a legal tradition aligned more closely and more explicitly to doctrines of human dignity and civil protection than any other country? Everyone understood perfectly by 1957 how torture had come to be used in the Third Reich, and even (Krushchev had delivered his speech to the Twentieth Party Congress in 1956) in the USSR during the Revolution and the period of Stalin's solidification of his own rule. But that French officials should practice torture upon Algerians and French citizens, that it was not merely the military, but the police who used it (Henry Alleg in *The Question* (1958), notes the first questions asked of new detainees by fellow prisoners: 'Have you been tortured? By the Paras or the detectives?'), and that, as Sartre reported in 1957, there were denials of its use in the National Assembly at the same time as there were rumours spreading 'that the Question is applied in certain civil prisons of the Metropolis' – these observations stunned not only France but the whole world. The publicity attendant upon the revelations of 1957 and after brought the question of torture out of the arm's-length land of despised and sub-human enemies into the streets of Paris and the prisons of Algiers. Even the democratic West was no longer immune from what Sartre called the plague of the twentieth century.

The news of torture in Algeria, brought first to France by those returning from military service – particularly, as Sartre notes, by returning priests, and later by scholars and political officers like Germaine Tillion and François Mitterand – was widely circulated in several key books, most strikingly in Henri Alleg's *La Question*, with an anguished essay by Sartre in 1958. The work was quickly published in the United States, also in 1950. The impact of the work of Alleg, or rather his testimony, along with that of Pierre-Henri Simon, Pierre Vidal-Naquet, Mellor and others after 1957, focused at last upon the return of torture under conditions few were prepared intellectually or emotionally to accept. As Sartre stated in his preface to *La Question*: 'Torture is neither civilian nor military, nor is it specifically French; it is a plague infecting our whole era.'

Sartre's remark raises another important point: to what extent had the Nazi and Soviet – and now Algerian – experience simply been the earliest indications of a worldwide twentieth-century phenomenon: Sartre's 'plague infecting our whole era'? The case of Algeria clearly struck the consciousness of a part of the world that had believed itself immune at least to torture. Yet it also raises another issue, hinted at obliquely by Mellor among others: to what extent were the practices described in Algeria the result, not of any sequence whose first two members were Germany and the Soviet Union, but the appearance of yet a third area in which, under special circumstances, torture could once more be practised? Specifically, to what extent did the history of European powers' relation with colonized peoples (as was so in Algeria) constitute a third modification of traditional civil government restrictions against torture, after the Nazi exaltation of the *Volksgewissen* and the Soviet exaltation of the defence of the Revolution?

Immediately, the case of Algeria takes on a powerful role in the colonial question. The first victims of torture in Algeria were Arabs, less-than-human 'others' not inside the territory of the nation (as it had been with the Jews in Germany), but indigenous to the colonialized territory. Many of the military personnel in Algeria, and many of the police, had experience elsewhere in French colonies, most conspicuously and most recently in Indo-China. Pierre-Henri Simon and Henri Alleg both note earlier cases of torture in French Indo-China. It is necessary, therefore, to consider the general problem of European colonization policies, in which legal safeguards well entrenched in the homeland turned out to be less well entrenched in the colonies, and not merely in Indo-China and Algeria, nor exclusively among the French.

The first European settlers of the world outside Europe brought with them in the sixteenth and seventeenth centuries the legal procedures of the lands they had left. Among these at that date was procedural torture, and in most cases this seems to have been routinely used in the colonies of countries that used torture at home, not merely upon white Europeans, but upon natives as well, and eventually upon natives exclusively. In Dutch South Africa, for example, torture was routinely used on both blacks and whites from 1652 on, 'not primarily to get information or to punish the prisoner, but to get him to confess his crime out of his own mouth', that is, in a manner generally consistent with Dutch legal procedure, which did not abolish torture until 1798. A mid-seventeenth century statute even fixed the fee for the torturer at one shilling and fourpence. Torture was first abolished in South Africa with the English conquest of 1795.

Even after the independence of South Africa from Britain in 1961, there is considerable evidence that methods of torture were not reintroduced immediately, and that the judiciary, at least, maintained a relatively tolerant attitude toward blacks accused of crime, even of political crime. In 1964, however, at the trial of three constables and a clerk of the court of the community of Bulfontein, testimony emerged from one of the constables that torture had been used in the interrogation of one of the accused, Izak Magaise, who died from the ordeal. Three other defendants had also been tortured and survived: they had been beaten, subjected to electric shocks, struck with a *sjambok* (a dreaded whip made of rhinoceros hide), and partially suffocated by plastic bags. The constable who made the most extensive confession, Jacob Barend Maree, also gratuitously remarked that in virtually every police station in South Africa the same practices were used. Maree and the other defendants were sentenced to prison terms of from three to nine years, and questions raised in Parliament about police brutality elicited further information indicating the truth of many of Maree's generalizations. Public orders were issued by the commissioner of police to cease torture during interrogation. The date of the Bulfontein case is important, because the legal historian Albie Sachs regards the 1960s as a period in South African history in which 'the law began to lose much of its more tolerant liberal aspect' (*Justice in South Africa*, 1973). Counter-charges of terrorism and torture were exchanged by African revolutionaries and whites, and indeed since the 1960s reports of torture have become routine. But with the case of an independent South Africa we have reached the extreme of colonialism, an independent colonial state with a dominant population of colonizers who re-introduced a practice that had, in the law and in general report, ended during an earlier state of colonization.

From the early attacks upon European colonial policies by John Atkinson Hobson in 1902 through the criticisms of revolutionaries of the 1960s, charges of European officials using or permitting the use of torture, especially upon native populations, have occurred with great frequency during the twentieth century. Even earlier than Hobson, however, there is evidence of torture in colonies even committed by native police upon natives. Fitzjames Stephen observed that during the preparation of the Indian code of Criminal Procedure in 1872, there was some discussion about the Indian Police's habit of torturing prisoners: during the discussion a colonial civil servant remarked: 'There is a great deal of laziness in it. It is far pleasanter to sit comfortably in the shade rubbing red pepper into a poor devil's eyes than to go about in the sun hunting up evidence.'

But Stephen's civil servant had had other evidence available to him than simply his own estimation of the energy of Indian police officers. Seventeen years before, in 1855, there had appeared in Madras the *Report of the Commissioners for the Investigation of Alleged Cases of Torture in the Madras Presidency*. That voluminous report noted that:

> Among the principal tortures in vogue in police cases we find the following – twisting a rope tightly around the entire arm or leg so as to impede circulation; lifting up by the moustache; suspending by the arms while tied behind the back; searing with hot irons; placing scratching insects, such as the carpenter beetle, on the navel, scrotum, and other sensitive parts; dipping in wells, and rivers, till the party is half-suffocated; squeezing the testicles; beating with sticks; prevention of sleep; nipping the flesh with pinchers; putting pepper or red chillies in the eyes, or introducing them into the private parts of men and women; these cruelties occasionally persevered in until death sooner or later ensues.

The police officers here described are native police acting, so the Report states, in defiance of commands issued by European superiors. But was it the 'laziness' of native police alone that permitted these acts? Was it that 'Asiatic' brutality which, for many twentieth-century westerners, appears to have become a universal explanation for anything un-European and unpleasant? In many cases, the colonial experience appears to have created novel kinds of power relationships, not only between colonizers and colonized, but among colonized peoples themselves. Some traditional forms of local authority were abolished and others were transformed by being placed in the service of colonial authorities. Novel forms of authority, like native police forces, were also introduced, and it may well have been the existence of new forms of power among native peoples that permitted such practices as were reported in the Madras Report. Police, normally under conventional restraints in Britain, were less strictly bound to those restraints when they were members of a society whose traditional power relationships had been transformed by the colonial experience. Not necessarily European colonizers themselves, but the institutions of power among colonized peoples that they created, may have been behind the discoveries at Madras in 1855 and the concerns attending the preparation of the Indian Code of Criminal Procedure in 1872.

One of the standard explanations that accounts for the reappearance of torture in the twentieth century, as we have seen in the case of Beck and Godin, and later in Mellor's work, has been that a peculiarly non-European form of violent treatment of other human beings was imported into Europe, according to Mellor after the Russo-Japanese War of 1905 by the *canal soviètique*, and according to other writers via the network of colonial administration. The question is thus raised: were practices used by non-Europeans on each other adapted by colonial administrators and returned with them to home countries? Does this explain Algeria?

Early on in South Africa, torture was clearly brought by the Dutch and applied according to European standards and procedures. Evidence is slight for the colonial administrators of other areas, but it seems clear that whatever practices non-Europeans employed upon each other, nothing in local repertoires matched the kind of authority and the disregard for non-European populations that colonial administrators, particularly low- and middle-grade administrators, found themselves empowered and inclined to use. The argument from 'Asianism', in short, does not hold up well. As the works of George Orwell reveal, the relationship between colonial administrator and native was full of dissonance, just as was the relationship between legal authorities and criminals in Europe. But the colonial circumstances offered none of the controls that the legal practice and theory of European countries offered. The colonial experience indeed seems to have contributed to the reappearance of torture, but not because colonial administrators and police learned such practices from the populations they governed; rather, the very circumstances in which they governed populations which became increasingly restive during the twentieth century led to the abuse of authority that included torture and later became routine in places like Algeria. Additional circumstances – racial differences, ethnocentrism, the violence of revolutionary movements and actions, and the legal powerlessness of colonialized populations – coloured and intensified a problem whose root cause was the unique circumstances and personnel of colonial rule.

Many of the 'paras' of Algeria had been in service in Indo-China, and many former colonial police and military personnel returned to service in other colonies or in France and other European countries themselves. Rough handling of those in their power was hard to stop, particularly when the judiciary was unaware it was happening and the public and legislators hard to convince. In the case of

Algeria, the history of early accounts of torture took a long time to find a place in the French Press and to be discussed in the National Assembly. The government itself prevented the printing of Alleg's *La Question*, and the American edition of that book has as an appendix an open letter to the president of the Republic signed by Andre Malraux, Roger Martin du Gard, François Mauriac and Jean-Paul Sartre, asking that the government investigate the case of Alleg and openly condemn the use of torture, 'in the name of the Declaration of Man and of the Citizen'.

The news from Algeria had indeed taken a long time to come home to France. In 1949 the Governor-General had explicitly forbidden torture. In 1955, Premier Mendès-France reiterated the prohibition, as did the new Governor-General Jacques Soustelle. Among the advisers to Jacques Soustelle in 1955 were Germaine Tillion, the sociologist of Algeria, who had survived torture by the Gestapo and worked on a war crimes commission in New York, and Vincent Monteil, who violently objected to the strict reprisals undertaken by the French army in Algeria after 1954. In 1955, Monteil resigned after having found himself unable to prevent the continued persecution and torture of several Algerian rebels from Ighil-Ilef. In the same year appeared the Wuillaume Report, which admitted that some violence had been done to prisoners suspected of political connections with the *Front Libération Nationale*, but that this was 'not quite torture', and that some of the violence might even be institutionalized under the present extraordinary circumstances:

> The water and the electricity methods, provided they are carefully used, are said to produce a shock which is more psychological than physical and therefore *do not constitute excessive cruelty* . . . According to certain medical opinion which I was given, the water-pipe method, if used as outlined above, involves no risk to the health of the victim.

Although Soustelle rejected the Wuillaume Report, torture continued in Algeria, and beginning in 1957 enough word of it had got back to France for a number of very diverse writers to take up the issue.

The Roman Catholic writer Pierre-Henri Simon published his own diatribe *Contre la torture* in 1957. In 1958, besides the devastating effect of Alleg's book with its essay by Sartre, the classical scholar Pierre Vidal-Naquet published *L'Affaire Audin*, the account of a mathematics professor at the University of Algiers who had died under army interrogation. Vidal-Naquet in particular among French intellectuals relentlessly pursued his investigations. In 1962 he published *Raison d'ètat*, a carefully research account of systematic army torture. In 1963 he published in English the influential work *Torture: Cancer of Democracy*, a work that examined for the first time the civil consequences of such evidence as he had discovered in Algeria. The cancer was not the torture itself, but the public indifference to it that eroded and rendered meaningless even the most explicit protections afforded by civil rights and public law. In 1972 this book was published for the first time in French, and it was followed in 1977 by *Les Crimes de l'armee française*, a documentary account of the horrors of French repression of the Algerian revolution.

The discovery of Algeria completed a lesson that finally had to be learned by the world of the late twentieth century: torture had not died with the Enlightenment legislative and judicial reforms and their optimistic view of human nature. Nor was it exclusively the eccentric practice of deranged and psychotic governments. It was no longer likely to turn up only in the fragile circumstances of marxist revolutions, and it was not an importation from barbarous non-European peoples. It was practised by Europeans upon Europeans and non-Europeans alike, in spite of legislation forbidding it and reformers intent upon exposing it. It could no longer be dismissed, written off, or ignored. The lesson was sobering, and the answer to its questions have not yet been found. Among the most articulate and pressing of those questions is one asked by Sartre himself in his preface to *La Question*:

Suddenly, stupor turns to despair: if patriotism has to precipitate us into dishonour; if there is no precipice of inhumanity over which nations and men will not throw themselves, then, why in fact do we go to so much trouble to become, or to remain, human?

5

'To become, or to remain, human . . .'

A new Enlightenment?

In that brief and hopeful interlude between the end of the Second World War and the revelations at the Twentieth Party Congress in Moscow in 1956 and the events in Algeria of 1954–62, a number of international organizations and congresses undertook in all serious- ness and with a genuine optimism to ensure that the horrors of the previous two decades should never recur. In doing so, they invoked the most inspired and universal claims of the political revolutions of 1776 and 1789, which, although they had legislated for individual nations, had claimed that their legislation had a valid universal basis. The subsequent influence of these universalist claims had been great, and they seemed never so great as in the years immediately following 1945, when internationalist thought, in obscurity since the failure of the League of Nations and the International Court, once again claimed its place in the sun.

In spite of the increasing coldness of the Cold War, such optimism had ample cause. The history of universal protection for human rights had not had unremitting triumphs, but it did provide grounds, particularly in the wake of the Nuremberg trials and the world's reaction to the internal history of the Axis states during the Second World War, for a real hope that international agreements, democratically reached and ratified, might prevent those horrors from happening again.

In 1864, the year following the establishment of the International Red Cross, the first Geneva Convention had attempted to carve out a small area of universal agreement on certain rights of personnel in wartime – specifically, the rights of medical attendants to be considered as neutrals in order to treat the wounded. This convention, revised in 1906 and embodied in a new treaty in 1924 which was itself revised and implemented in 1949 and 1977, was dependent upon informal bodies without power to impose sanctions.

The International Red Cross, the International Labour Organization, and the League Mandates Commission and Anti-Slavery League represent the early twentieth-century attempts to create a universally recognized convention of basic human rights that might be placed, by states themselves, ahead of individual state policy. Such ambitions, promoted, when they were promoted at all, by what one historian called 'humanitarian diplomacy', were thrown into sharp relief by the revelations of the internal history of the Third Reich and other Axis powers as the Second World War drew to a close.

The Charter of the United Nations of 1945 attempted to restore concern for universal rights to the forefront of the post-war world. Article 55 of the UN Charter of 1945 contains the first post-war assertion of 'a universal respect for, and observance of, human rights and fundamental freedoms for all without distinction as to race, language, or religion'. In 1948 the Universal Declaration of Human Rights expanded upon Article 55 of the Charter and produced thirty articles, of which Article 5 stated that: 'No one shall be subjected to torture or to cruel, inhuman, or degrading treatment or punishment.' Like the Charter, the Universal Declaration has been criticized because it is at best a UN recommendation without binding force within individual states; it remains general in terminology, and the Declaration depends upon the goodwill of individual states for its implementation, if any. But, aside from the eight nations which abstained from signing the Declaration, the forty-eight nations which did clearly intended, on 10 December 1948, in United Nations Document A/811, to recognize a set of universal human rights, among which the right not to be subject to torture was emphatically included. Almost exactly twenty-seven years later, on 9 December 1975, the United Nations General Assembly adopted Resolution 3452 (XXX), the 'Declaration of the Protection of All Persons from being Subjected to Torture and other Cruel, Inhuman or Degrading Treatment or Punishment', based upon the assumption that 'recognition of the inherent dignity and of the equal and inalienable rights of all members of the human family is the foundation of freedom, justice and peace in the world.'

In an Annex to the new Declaration, twelve articles spelled out in specific detail the nature of torture and of cruel and inhuman punishment. According to Article 1 of the Annex, torture is:

any act by which severe pain or suffering, whether physical or mental, is intentionally inflicted by or at the instigation of a public official on a person for such purposes as obtaining from him or a third person information or confession, punishing him for an act he has committed or is suspected of having committed, or intimidating him or other persons.

The Annex stated that torture constituted an aggravated and deliberate form of cruel, inhuman or degrading treatment or punishment (Article 2). The Annex also denied states the right to claim exceptional circumstances, even war, as justification for torture (Article 3); required individual states to take appropriate steps to see that their officials shall not practice nor permit torture (Article 4); specified that states shall train police and other public officials not to employ torture (Article 5); required that all states systematically review methods of interrogation (Article 6); required that all states incorporate into their criminal law the provisions of Article 1 (Article 7); assured those who claim to be victims of torture that competent authorities within their own states will examine such charges (Article 8); stated that upon information offered without formal complaint, state officials must investigate alleged violations of the provisions of Article 1 (Article 9); required that upon such investigation as specified in Articles 8 and 9, persons found to have been guilty of torture be appropriately punished under the state's criminal code (Article 10); assured redress and compensation to the victim of such a public official, duly convicted (Article 11); and denied the evidentiary character of any information or statement made under torture (Article 12).

Further, on 16 December 1966, the General Assembly of the United Nations adopted for ratification Resolution 2200 A (XXI), the International Covenant on Civil and Political Rights, which took effect on 26 March 1976. Article 7 states: 'No one shall be subjected to torture or to cruel, inhuman or degrading treatment of punishment. In particular, no one shall be subjected without his free consent to medical or scientific experimentation.' Finally, on 1 August 1975, thirty-five nations signed the diplomatic agreement known as the Final Act of the Conference on Security and Co-operation in Europe, commonly called the 'Helsinki Agreement', which contained the 'Questions Relating to Security in Europe'. Section VII of the 'Questions' states that: 'In the field of human rights and fundamental freedoms, the participating States will act in conformity with the purposes and principles of the Charter of the United Nations and with the Universal Declaration of Human Rights.'

Thus far went the ambitious, optimistic and uncharacteristically explicit condemnation of torture in the three decades that followed the end of the Second World War. To some extent, these declarations represented what people hoped would be a new Enlightenment, one with universal civil and political (as well as social and economic) consequences for all people, not only the initial forty-eight signatories of the Declaration of 1948, but of the hundred-odd nations that have joined the UN since. In addition to the several UN statements on human rights, particularly those concerning torture, several regional assemblies, most thoroughly the Council of Europe, also provided guarantees and definitions of human rights, notably in the European Convention on Human Rights, created from its first draft of 12 July 1949, and signed at Rome on 4 November 1950. Its third article prohibits torture and inhuman or degrading punishment. The publication in 1973 of the *Travaux préparatoires* of the Preparatory Commission of the Council of Europe, Committee of Ministers, Consultative Assembly, offers considerable insight into the minds and public stances of the participants as they created the Convention during a year and a half's work.

The efforts of the Council of Europe formed part of the great groundswell of concern for human rights that was represented by the UN on the international, global scale, and by a number of regional movements, specifically the unofficial European Movement, whose 'Congress of Europe' adopted at The Hague in May 1948 a 'Message to Europeans'. The message included the demand for 'a Charter of Human Rights guaranteeing liberty of thought, assembly and expression as well as the right to form a political opposition'. In addition, the message demanded the creation of a Court of Justice armed with adequate sanctions to implement the Charter. In February 1949, the International Council of the European Movement approved a Declaration of Principles of European Union and established an International Juridical Section, under the chairmanship of Pierre-Henri Teitgen, which set to work on a Draft European convention on Human Rights. The results of the Teitgen Committee's work were submitted to the Committee of Ministers of the

Council of Europe, an official body, on 12 July 1949. The latter body had been created in May 1949, committing itself and its member nations, in Article 3 of its own Statute, to the acceptance of 'the principles of the rule of law and the enjoyment by all persons within its jurisdiction of human rights and fundamental freedoms'. A new Committee under the chairmanship of Sir David Maxwell-Fyfe was commissioned in August, with Teitgen as *rapporteur*, and the Teitgen report was submitted for discussion on 5 September 1949. Its treatment of torture is recorded in the first two volumes of the *Travaux préparatoires*, covering discussions held between 5 and 8 September 1949. Subsequent history of the European Convention may be traced through Volumes III–VII, including the final draft of the instrument itself.

More than the UN Declaration, the preliminary discussions of the Consultative Assembly reflect the attitudes of Europeans towards torture in this heady and optimistic period. In his initial report, Teitgen laid out as eloquently as anyone before or since the need for such a Convention and the detailed difficulties facing any body which proposed to legislate one. He cited the UN Declaration of 1948, the evidence from the Nuremberg trials, and the Permanent Court of International Justice as precedents, and listed, among the rights and freedoms to be guaranteed,

> a collective guarantee, not only of freedom to express convictions, but also of thought, conscience, religion and opinion[.] The Committee wished to protect all nationals of any Member State, not only from 'confessions' imposed for reasons of State, but also from those abominable methods of police inquiry or judicial process which rob the suspected or accused person of control of his intellectual faculties and of his conscience.

In the draft itself, Section I, Article 1 and Article 2.1 specifically echoed the UN Declaration of Human Rights, and an Appendix to the draft specifically listed the relevant texts of the UN articles, including Article 5.

In September the delegate F. S. Cocks proposed the following amendment to Section I, Article 2.1:

> In particular no person shall be subjected to any form of mutilation or sterilisation, nor to any form of torture or

beating. Nor shall he be forced to take drugs nor shall they be administered to him without his knowledge and consent. Nor shall he be subjected to imprisonment with such an excess of light, darkness, noise or silence as to cause mental suffering.

And to Article 1 Cocks suggested adding:

The Consultative Assembly takes this opportunity of declaring that all forms of physical torture, whether inflicted by the policy, military authorities, members of private organisations or any other persons are inconsistent with civilised society, are offences against heaven and humanity and must be prohibited. They declare that this prohibition must be absolute and that torture cannot be permitted by any purpose whatsoever, neither by extracting evidence for saving life nor even for the safety of the State. They believe that it would be better even for Society to perish than for it to permit this relic of barbarism to remain.

In his long reply to this and a number of other suggested amendments, Teitgen echoed the sentiments of Cocks and others, and urged the Assembly to consider also the real danger of the recurrence of recent events:

Many of our colleagues have pointed out that our countries are democratic and are deeply impregnated with a sense of freedom; they believe in morality and in a natural law. We are protected from such attempts and ordeals. Why is it necessary to build such a system? Other countries, great, beautiful and noble countries, were also subjected to a sense of ethics and morality and civilization. And then one day evil fell upon them. They suffered the ordeal. All our countries might be liable one day to suffer severe constraint for reasons of State. Perhaps our system of guarantee will protect us from that peril.

There is irony in these words. Nearly a decade later, another M. Teitgen, Maître Paul Teitgen, was secretary-general of the Algiers Prefecture in 1956–7. A hero of the Resistance and a survivor of Dachau, Teitgen submitted to the 'Safeguard Committee' a report which contained the following observations:

Even a legitimate action . . . can nevertheless lead to improvisations and excesses. Very rapidly, if this is not remedied, efficacity becomes the sole justification. In default of a legal basis, it seeks to justify itself at any price, and, with a certain bad conscience, it demands the privilege of exceptional legitimacy. In the name of efficacity, illegality has become justified.

The report of the second Teitgen proved precisely how prophetic the words of the first Teitgen in fact had been. By way of furthering the irony, France did not ratify the Convention on Human Rights until 1973.

Pierre-Henri Teitgen also remarked that his report and draft had not attempted to define the principles of natural law, because:

> It has a history as old as the world and as our civilisation; it is the natural law of Antigone; it is also that of Cicero: *recta ratio, diffusa in omnes, constans, sempiterna*, if my memory is correct. Then there is the natural law of Christianity and of humanism. These are the principles and ideals upon which our Statute is based. It is a question of whether, above human laws, there are immutable principles which the State cannot overlook, and on which human laws are based.

In the Assembly's discussion of the Cocks amendment, the generous eloquence of Teitgen was echoed again and again, not least by Cocks himself, who was obsessed with torture and the events of the preceding two decades: 'The most terrible event in my lifetime in this century has been that torture and violence have returned – returned fortified by many discoveries of modern science – and that in some countries people are even becoming accustomed to it.' He concluded:

> I say that to take the straight beautiful bodies of men and women and to maim and mutilate them by torture is a crime against high heaven and the holy spirit of man. I say that it is a sin against the Holy Ghost for which there is no forgiveness. I declare that it is incompatible with civilization.

For reasons of efficiency and existing adequate language, Maxwell-Fyfe urged Cocks to withdraw his amendment, reminding the Assembly that nevertheless Cocks 'has underlined the eternal truth which we must all remember; that barbarism is never behind us, it is underneath us. It is our task to see that it does not come to the surface.' In the final version, Article 3 did not contain Cocks' amendment, but the texts of the *Travaux préparatoires* make clear as day the temper and concerns of the assembled delegates. Deferring to the legal wisdom of Teitgen and Maxwell-Fyfe, they nevertheless echoed the sentiments of Cocks, and their language, like the language of the legal philosophers of the first Enlightenment, rang with the highest of human sentiments. To read their discussions a quarter of a century later is to admire the hope, and perceive, almost against one's will, the irony in its deceptive optimism.

The language of Eden

One of the significant achievements of eighteenth-century political and legal thinkers was to have influenced legislation in such a way as to place a moral framework around the operations of laws and states, measuring every act of the law or the government by the moral standards of traditional European and Enlightenment humanitarianism. To a great extent, governments and judiciaries acceded to this policy well into the next century. In spite of the scepticism of critics like Burke and Bentham on the one hand, and the cynicism of Robespierre and Saint-Simon on the other, most nineteenth-century states professed adherence to an idea of inherent human rights and dignity against which the operations of states and judiciaries might be measured. Even historians like Henry Charles Lea shared these sentiments, and Lea wrote his history of torture with a strong view towards preventing its recurrence.

Yet historians have perceived a certain ambivalence about such respect for human rights, even in the very century that most eloquently professed it. In a devastating and impassioned section of her long and important study *The Origins of Totalitarianism* (1951), Hannah Arendt briefly traced the nineteenth- and twentieth-century history of the idea of inalienable rights. After pointing out the failure of any body, national or international, to guarantee the rights of stateless persons in the nineteenth century, and the preference, even on the part of stateless persons, to seek security among the positive laws of a nation-state rather than appeal to an international body or set of laws, Arendt goes on to point out that

> Even worse was that all societies formed for the protection of
> the Rights of Man, all attempts to arrive at a new bill of human

rights, were sponsored by marginal figures – by a few international jurists without political experience or professional philanthropists supported by the uncertain sentiments of professional idealists. The groups they formed, the declarations they issued, showed an uncanny similarity in language and composition to that of societies for the prevention of cruelty to animals. . . . The victims shared the disdain and indifference of the powers that be for any attempt of the marginal societies to enforce human rights in any elementary or general sense.

Arendt's original and troubling book appeared in 1951, and it launched a number of ideas about modern politics, many of which were then, and some of which have since become, unpalatable to many readers. But no reader of the 1949 UN Declaration or the Convention on Human Rights is likely to be surprised by Arendt's contentions. Indeed, those instruments have been most effectively criticized on the grounds that they carried no enforcing authority and that they had been produced by 'marginal' people, unaware of the realities of political life in the second half of the twentieth century.

One cause of the problem perceived by Arendt and other critics has been, as the work of Ernest Gellner and others has pointed out, the enormous strength and influence in the areas of law, morality, and sentiment, of the nation-state, a fact that would not have entirely surprised Burke and Bentham. The moral republic of Europe lasted but a short time, and its constituent parts claimed an increasingly stronger hegemony over both morality and sentiment, as well as an increasingly exclusive claim to define the rights of the state, to assert the identity of citizen and state in more and more restrictive terms. This process, as the last chapter indicated, led to the development of extra-judicial procedures on the part of the state that ultimately weakened the judiciary and helped to return extraordinary measures into the routinized vocabulary of political life.

But there are other causes as well, and some of them bear upon the case of torture. The association of torture with the moral evils of the *ancien régime*, not entirely fairly, shifted the grounds for the condemnation of torture from the specifically legal to the more generally moral. Torture was then condemned – by Voltaire, Beccaria and others – because it was incompatible with a new idea of human dignity. Any government that wished to be associated with that view of human dignity had to dissociate itself, constitutionally and institutionally, from all of the manifestations of the old. The work of Enlightenment thinkers and their successors, even if they had not been instrumental in abolishing torture in their own age, so discredited the vocabulary of the *ancien régime* that it could not be revived in direct usage and so was rarely revived even in polemical usage. The expression 'torture' slipped from a specifically legal vocabulary – in which it had possessed specific meanings – into a general vocabulary of moral invective.

At the same time, 'torture' also slipped into a vocabulary of sentiment. From the first denunciations of ecclesiastical procedures during the Reformation, through the growing – and increasingly picturesque – literature of religious polemic of the sixteenth and seventeenth centuries, the practice of torture on the parts of the medieval and later Spanish Inquisitions constituted one of the focal points of Reformation and Counter-Reformation polemic. In a series of widely circulated polemics, from Foxe's *Book of Martyrs* and Montanus' account of the Spanish Inquisition's tortures, in 1587, polemical accounts of medieval and early modern church practices rarely failed to portray the incidence of torture luridly and lingeringly. This literature, much of it far from accurate, appealed to sentiment as well as to morality (or rather to sentiment as an enhancement of moral judgement), and it became a legacy available, not only to moral reformers, but to novelists and painters alike. Beginning in the late eighteenth century, novels, fictitious accounts of 'memoirs', travel literature and serious histories of the medieval and Spanish Inquisitions used incidences and scenes of torture regularly to pique the interests of their readers. A glance at the character and sources of a well-known story like Poe's 'The Pit and the Pendulum' of 1843 suggests the appeal based upon sentiment and only marginally associated with legal or moral outrage. The story was in fact partly derived from Poe's reading of a popular history of the Spanish Inquisition – although the particular device mentioned by Poe seems never to have been used, or indeed thought of, by the Spanish inquisitors – and many other works of fiction, particularly those dealing with specialized forms of eroticism and some varieties of the Gothic novel, also borrowed heavily, and also for reasons of sentiment, from that earlier pool of lurid description.

This third, sentimental, dimension of torture suited well the nineteenth-century concern with human cruelty in general. Beyond

Arendt's sharp criticism, reformers, philanthropists and idealists felt the seriousness of their causes no less intensely because they sentimentalized some of the objects of their concern. Having removed torture from a specific place in a legal vocabulary and indicted it as a general moral outrage, nineteenth-century thinkers further widened its definition by including it in a sentimental vocabulary. The very humanitarian morality that had relegated torture to the general vocabulary of shame then applied it to all the other manifestations of that particular kind of shame for which it had come to stand. And besides its legal and moral associations, torture also came to acquire sentimental associations which widened its applicability, even as they lessened its precision. It came to designate, not a specific practice, but, as Malise Ruthven has termed it, the 'threshold of outrage' of a particular society.

The nineteenth-century language of morality and sentiment, expanded and applied to increasing kinds and numbers of human relationships, widened the applicability of the term to all areas of human brutality, from the workplace to the home. Owners now tortured workers, husbands wives, parents children, criminals victims. All oppressors tortured all the oppressed. And torture thus entered a general vocabulary with sentimental and moral meaning.

One example of the semantic shift can be documented. The English Criminal Law Procedure Act of 1853 (16 and 17 Vic. c.30) was designed in part to deal with the widely perceived problem of wife-beating and, shortly after its passage, was seen not to have been particularly effective. The moral outrage generated over this question during the next twenty-five years led to the somewhat more effective Matrimonial Causes Act of 1878 (41 and 42 Vic. c.19) which offered more substantial protection to abused wives, as indeed has subsequent legislation. One of the pieces of persuasion that influenced the passage of the 1878 Act was the pamphlet of Frances Power Cobbe, *Wife Torture*, also published in 1878. The title speaks for itself. The word *torture* was arresting and unambiguous. It was astutely chosen and created a perspective upon the problem that must have focused a great deal of hitherto diffused attention upon the central aspect of the problem by linking it to a term which, by the later nineteenth century, was one of virtually universal opprobrium and therefore potentially effective in harnessing what had until then been a scattered opposition. Torture was acquiring its semantic expansion, as always, in an honourable and important cause.

The entry for *torture* in the *Oxford English Dictionary* suggests that in its sense of 'Severe or excruciating pain or suffering (of body or mind); anguish, agony, torment; the infliction of such', the term had become figurative as early as the seventeenth century, referring to generalized emotion and suffering of any particularly extreme kind, from whatever cause. This figurative and generalized use seems to have occurred somewhat earlier in English than in other European languages, perhaps because torture was not as technical an aspect of law in England as it was on the Continent. Cobbe's *Wife Torture*, then, is part of an important semantic history.

Nor was 'torture' the only term to undergo such a metamorphosis. In a brilliant essay of 1946 entitled 'Politics and the English Language', George Orwell identified the process by which the political manipulation of language became one of the strongest forces of twentieth-century life, producing a mass – and largely meaningless – language in the service of political sentimentality. Although he did not specifically note the thinning out of certain terms as a result of their having been casually taken up in earlier moral and sentimental contexts, Orwell was concerned with the despecification of language and its restriction to the stirring of political sentiments instead of being used as the vehicle for ideas and argument. Once political language is defined by an ideology it becomes applicable to that ideology and its enemies only according to certain terms. And moral language, being universal, may be applicable to particular things and cases at will, and therefore may become nothing in particular. Everyone may now be accused of torturing everyone else, and therefore no one tortures anyone.

The term torture now exists almost wholly in a generalized vocabulary. And because it does, it is easy for torturers to deny that what they do is torture (witness the genuine ambivalence of the Wuillaume Report); on the other hand, it is difficult for people who use the term for anything that seems synonymous with cruelty to carry much conviction when they use it for something close to its original meaning.

A good example of the dilemma may be found in V. S. Naipaul's account of his interview with an Argentinian trade unionist on the eve of Juan Perón's return from exile:

'There are no internal enemies,' the trade union leader said, with a smile. But at the same time he thought that torture would continue in Argentina. 'A world without torture is an ideal world.' And there was torture and torture. '*Depende de quien sea torturado.*' It depends on who is tortured. An evildoer, that's all right. But a man who's trying to save the country, that's something else. Torture isn't only the electric prod, you know, poverty is torture, frustration is torture.'

Indeed, in the moral and sentimental universe, nothing may be torture, and, with a slight shift of perspective, everything may be torture: the electric prod, poverty, frustration, perhaps even boredom or vague dissatisfaction. Semantic entropy does not serve very well to keep distinctions sharp. Another good example occurs in one of the reviews of John Langbein's *Torture and the Law of Proof* (1977). Langbein himself had admitted that he 'left it for others to draw the implications for European political, administrative, and intellectual history'. This is fair enough, and Langbein did the history of torture a great service by so doing. But one reviewer called Langbein's approach 'narrowly legal', because 'to define torture in legal terms is perhaps too limited, as the coercion of prisoners can indeed run the gamut from bullying to brainwashing'. The coercion of prisoners can indeed run that – and many other – gamuts, but torture, if it is to be specifically defined, cannot. It may be suggesting too much to suggest that those offences that *can* be defined upon specific grounds in fact *be* so defined. Such definition may deprive them of moral standing, but it makes them more identifiable and makes evasion of precision more difficult for those who wish to do so. Legal historians have consistently identified the moment of creation of law as a particular science with the moment when legal reasoning was separated from morality. Although such a position places great weight upon jurisprudence and legal institutions, it suggests the specifically legal context in which torture may be identified. When journalists, and occasionally legislators (as well as international jurists and legal philosophers), use the term 'torture' to designate activities that may be (and usually are) already adequately and technically defined as assault and battery, or trespass, the term 'torture' itself becomes simply picturesque, its legal definition is gutted and in its place is substituted a vague idea of moral sentiment. It is then easy to argue torture away simply by applying to a higher moral sentiment than that of one's opponents or critics.

The humanitarianism of the New Enlightenment and the generalization of the terminology of moral sentiment constitute two influences of the language of Eden upon modern definitions of torture. A third has already been mentioned: the inherently imprecise character of political language in the late twentieth century, a characteristic noted by George Orwell and other political writers. 'Politics and the English Language' is one of Orwell's first, but by no means his only, instances of concern with the *discourse* of politics. Although by the end of his life, with the publication of *Nineteen Eighty-Four* in 1949, Orwell increasingly emphasized the deliberate falsification of language and its relation to thought, his letters and essays show a number of other concerns, including the potential of political language for purely inadvertent slovenliness: '[The English language] becomes ugly and inaccurate because our thoughts are foolish, but the slovenliness of our language makes it easier for us to have foolish thoughts.' But as Orwell concerned himself more and more with the deliberate misuse of language, other passages of 'Politics and the English Language' became more and more prophetic: 'The word *Fascism* has now [in 1946] no meaning except in so far as it signifies "something not desirable." The words *democracy, socialism, freedom, patriotic, realistic, justice,* have each of them several different meanings which cannot be reconciled with one another.' Although Orwell does not include *torture* on his list, it certainly belongs there. His great contribution in this case was his identification of both effects of politicizing and sentimentalizing language, their restriction of its ability to clarify thought and their own inherently imprecise and misleading character.

The language of the moralists and sentimentalists of the eighteenth and nineteenth centuries was a language of Eden, a language whose meanings were fixed and put to the service of a great cause. In the light of the history of the language of Eden in the late twentieth century, it becomes possible to understand the real uncertainty in the terminology of a civil servant like M. Wuillaume concerning whether or not what he saw in Algeria in 1955 was really 'torture'. It is also possible to see the denials of torture on the part of many governments as something more than mere hypocrisy or blatant public relations mania. Because it has been so variously defined, torture is now, without extremely precise language, virtually impossible to define. The journalist who reports that a criminal has abducted and 'tortured' his victim; the 'torture' of a battered wife by a brutal husband; the ambitious righteousness of Naipaul's Argentinian trade unionist: 'Poverty is torture, frustration is torture'; all of these have thinned out the meaning of torture to the point at which, covering everything, it covers nothing. And it is as easy to avoid acknowledging its use as it is to accuse another of using it. In spite of the heroic moral sentiments of the delegates to the United Nations in 1948, the relentless attempts at precision of those to the Constituent Assembly of the Council of Europe in 1950, and the meticulous detail of Resolution 3452 of the UN in 1975, the history of the language of Eden has constituted a formidable, if inadvertent barrier, not only to a universally acceptable definition of torture, but to most attempts at effective action against it. Orwell may have been the most acute pathologist of modern political discourse after all; intended as a commentary upon Europe in the 1930s and 1940s, his strictures have turned out to apply as well, if not better, to the world of the 1970s and 1980s.

After Algeria

Torture was a first-order word and a first-order fact to the framers of human rights legislation after the Second World War. Its semantic history since then indicates that it became a second-order word and fact in many parts of the world. In some cases, the practice of torture was deliberately and consciously spread into areas dominated or strongly influenced by both the Third Reich and the Soviet Union; that is, into Greece and Hungary and later into Yugoslavia and some Eastern Bloc countries. Elsewhere, as in Algeria, the etiology is more difficult to trace, and in countries very recently made independent, revolutionized, or controlled by strong and authoritarian governments, it is hardly possible even to guess at an etiology.

But it is possible to construct a geography of torture – and a calendar. Alec Mellor (*La Torture*, 1949 and 1961) made one such attempt in the case of Argentina, as we have seen above, but he himself despaired of giving a fuller account even of Latin America. What was difficult for Mellor in 1949 is somewhat less difficult now, chiefly because the flow of information, largely through journalism and private organizations. The Bulfontein case in South Africa in 1964 brought a world of police torture relentlessly to light, and the spotlight has not been off South Africa since. Private memoirs have also provided information on particular places and times, as, for

example, Nicholas Gage's moving memoir of the torture and
execution of his mother in his book, *Eleni* (1983), an account of some
obscure events in northern Greece in 1948 and Gage's personal
investigation of them.

One way of approaching the subject is to consider for a moment
the differences between 1949 and 1961 editions of Mellor's *La
Torture*. This work, followed in 1952 by Mellor's *Les Grands
Problèmes contemporains de l'instruction criminelle*, which Mellor
considered to be a 'completion' of the study of torture, appears to
have raised considerable criticism, but was awarded the Prix de Joest
by the French Academy and praised by Pope Pius XII in a letter to
the author over the signature of Giovanni Battista Montini, then
Secretary of State, later Pope Paul VI. Pius XII later made an
elaborate denunciation of torture in an address to the Sixth
International Congress of Penal Law in 1953, as did the Second
Vatican Council in *Gaudium et spes*, 27.3, in 1965. As might be
expected, most of Mellor's book was reprinted without significant
change in the second edition. The two significant additions dealt
with the revelations of Krushchev's speech to the Twentieth Party
Congress in 1956 and with Krushchev's repetition of these charges to
the Twenty-Second Party Congress in 1961. Mellor considered
his earlier accusations against the Soviet Union vindicated by
Krushchev's revelations. The second major addition, also as might
be expected, was an account, not complete, of the revelations that
had emerged from Algeria between 1954 and 1962. Both additions
seemed to Mellor to warrant the truth of his earlier thesis and to
suggest that little had happened to change the world he had
described in the final chapters of the first edition of 1949. Yet Mellor
also expressed some hope for real change. He took pride in the
denunciation of torture in Algeria by the French bishops in 1960 and
1961, and he also cited the case of the Paraguayan journalist Eliseo
Sosa Constantini, arrested and tortured in Paraguay by the
government of Alfredo Stroessner in 1960, but later freed after a
protest by the Paraguayan bishops, the Press Association, and liberal
journalists. These seemed admittedly to be small triumphs, but they
permitted Mellor to end the book on at least a slight note of hope.

In spite of the United Nations Resolutions of 1975 and 1966/76
and the later inclusion of specific policies on human rights in the
administrations of a number of governments, notably that of the
United States between 1976 and 1980, the most effective source of

information concerning the use of torture after Algeria has been private organizations, initially the International Red Cross, but after 1961 also Amnesty International.

Founded as a private association dedicated to ministering to the lot of political prisoners, or 'prisoners of conscience', by the London attorney Peter Benenson in 1961, Amnesty International stated that its policy was aimed at mobilizing:

> public opinion quickly and widely before a government is caught up in the vicious spiral caused by its own repression . . . . The force of opinion, to be effective, should be broadly based, international, non-sectarian, and all-party. Campaigns in favour of freedom brought by one country, or party, against another, often achieve nothing but an intensification of persecution. (Larson, *A Flame in Barbed Wire*, 1979)

Benenson had been inspired to take this kind of action by reading in 1960 a newspaper account of two Portuguese students who had been arrested and imprisoned by the government for having raised a toast to freedom. Despairing of the inefficacy of both individual and national protest, Benenson, with his colleagues Louis Blom-Cooper and Eric Baker, as well as the members of the lawyers' group Justice, which had been founded in 1957 to urge compliance with the 1948 United Nations Declaration, decided to form an organization whose members as individuals would seek the release of those imprisoned for their opinions, to see that such prisoners received a fair trial, to elaborate the right of asylum and to aid refugees to find work, and to urge effective international machinery to guarantee freedom of opinion and expression. Benenson and his associates decided that the most effective means of achieving these goals was publicity:

> The most rapid way of beginning relief to prisoners of conscience is publicity, especially publicity among their fellow-citizens. With the pressure of emergent nationalism and the tensions of the Cold War, there are bound to be situations where governments are led to take emergency measures to protect their existence. It is vital that public opinion should insist that these measures should not be excessive, nor prolonged after the moment of danger. If the emergency is to last a long time, then a government should be induced to allow its opponents out of prison to seek asylum abroad. (Ibid.)

Publicity depended upon Amnesty's membership rolls and its access to Press coverage. Both expanded very quickly, and in spite of some internal dissension in 1966, Amnesty International not only achieved considerable success in ameliorating the treatment of many political prisoners, but also created a network of information resources probably greater than that of any other world body. Its sources of information flooded its London office with stories of individual cases, meticulously checked by a research staff and then assigned to one of the many small groups of members in dozens of different nations. These groups then 'adopted' individual prisoners and managed the publicity campaign that might eventually lead to release.

In 1965 Amnesty published its first formal report, an account of prison conditions in South Africa. Coming within a year of the Bulfontein case, the report outraged South Africa, but increased Amnesty's international visibility. In the same year Amnesty was recognized by the UN itself, the European Court at Strasbourg, the International Red Cross, the International Commission of Jurists and other human rights associations, and was awarded consultative status with the Council of Europe. Also in 1965, two further reports were issued, on Portugal and Romania, and in 1966 one on Rhodesia. The revelations of South Africa and Portugal in particular revealed the extensive use of torture on political prisoners, and in the next few years, torture became one of the most prominent of Amnesty International's objectives.

Under the direction of Martin Ennals, the International Assembly of Amnesty International which met at Stockholm in 1968 adopted as one of the organization's major aims Article Five of the Universal Declaration of Human Rights of 1948: 'No one shall be subjected to torture or to cruel, inhuman, or degrading treatment or punishment.' The action was precipitated by the concern of the Swedish section of Amnesty over reports of torture emerging from the revolutionary regime in Greece, which had taken power in 1967. In 1968 Amnesty published two first-hand reports on the use of torture by the Greek government. As a result, Greece was expelled from the Council of Europe in 1968 for having violated nine of the articles of the 1950 European Convention on Human Rights. After the overthrow of the colonels' regime in 1975, Amnesty published its extraordinarily detailed and documented study *Torture in Greece*, one of the classic works on the documentation and techniques of torture in the late twentieth century.

What makes *Torture in Greece: The First Torturer's Trial 1975* an important work, with implications extending far beyond the regime of the Greek colonels, is the fact that it describes a governmental investigation by a subsequent government, possessing access to records and personnel, unconnected to the actions of its predecessor government. It is free of partisanship and casts unrelenting light upon the process of torture in a twentieth-century state. Few other cases of torture in this century have been so thoroughly and publicly examined, documented and described. Following the amnesty of 1974, people who had had to flee the country were able to return, and the evidence against the torturers proved to be vast and conclusive.

On the other hand, the regime of the colonels was not the first modern regime in Greece to use torture. In spite of a number of partisan revisions of Greek history from the pre-war Metaxas dictatorship to the overthrow of the colonels, it is also clear that the German occupation of Greece played a distinctive role in creating climates and practices of terror, and that the bitter feuds between the Communist (ELAS) partisans and the 'Nationalist' (EDES) partisans of Napoleon Zervas between 1941 and 1949 also produced instances of torture on both sides. It is in its circumstances and extensive documentation alone, rather than in its uniqueness in history, that the *Torture in Greece* study is important. What preceded it, because it is less easily documented and the subject of intensely partisan historiography, remains, except for particular cases, inaccessible. But *Torture in Greece* is also a model study for later investigations. In the light of personal testimony difficult to verify, partisan reporting, the absence of records, and a frequent weariness with rehearsing the past, only such a thorough, governmentally sponsored and conducted investigation as this is likely to carry the conviction and description necessary to reveal modern torture as it is. In June of 1984, for example, the Associated Press carried a story dealing with the growing revelations of torture having been used by the regime of Sekou Touré in Guinea. In this and similar cases, other reports similar to *Torture in Greece* might be undertaken.

In 1972 Amnesty International had officially begun its Campaign for the Abolition of Torture, which resulted in the publication in 1973 of the international survey on torture which covered the preceding decade. A second edition appeared in 1975. The problems encountered by Amnesty's campaign against torture can be ironically illustrated by a *New York Times* story dated 4 December 1973. The *Times* reported that UNESCO had denied Amnesty International the use of UNESCO facilities in Paris for its planned conference on torture in the wake of the 1973 Report, because many countries represented in UNESCO were unfavourably mentioned in the Report, and UNESCO had a general rule that 'an outside conference at UNESCO not use material unfavourable to any member state'. In fact, Amnesty had named more than sixty countries, from democracies to police states, that used torture systematically.

In 1973 Amnesty reported on the overthrow of the Allende government in Chile and the use of torture by the new government's police. In 1972 it published a similar account of torture in Brazil, and the 1973 report included Turkey. In 1976 Amnesty reported on torture in Iran and Nicaragua; in 1980 Argentina; in 1981 Iraq. In twenty years, through the unremitting efforts of private individuals and a skeleton organization, Amnesty International had succeeded in publicizing the widespread use of torture more thoroughly than any individual or organization in history. And its publicity did not easily disappear. In 1977 it received the Nobel Peace Prize.

The Amnesty procedure of private reporting, checked and researched by professionals, and publicized by reports was much more elaborate than, but in some ways reminiscent of, the earlier work of writers like Alleg, Simon, and Vidal-Naquet in France. The dedication of organized private individuals had achieved considerable success in a world in which the largest international organization was prevented by its own rules from observing its own Declaration of Human Rights. In the decade since it had begun its Campaign to Abolish Torture, Amnesty International had revealed a world more full of systematic torture than even Mellor had dreamed, in democratic states as well as authoritarian ones, and it had made much of the world uncomfortable, not merely UNESCO members and torturers.

An example of that discomfort may be seen in the case of Jacopo Timerman, an Argentine journalist who was imprisoned and tortured in Argentina between 1977 and 1979. Timerman, freed and moved to Israel, published in 1981 his account of his experiences in the remarkable book *Prisoner Without a Name, Cell Without a Number*. Timerman's revelations received an extremely mixed reception. Many reviewers, of course, condemned Timerman's treatment outright and unqualifiedly. Others, however, both wrote milder criticism of the regime that tortured Timerman and focused their concern upon Timerman himself, suggesting that he may somehow have invited and perhaps even deserved what in any case was necessary, exceptional and uncharacteristic treatment – in effect, that Timerman had brought his own troubles, including his own torture, upon himself. Timerman returned much of his critics' fire eloquently and vigorously, and a number of reviewers, notably Michael Walzer, raised the broader question of the motives and world-views of Timerman's critics in response to events for which a decade of reports from Amnesty International ought long since surely to have prepared them.

Between 1956 and 1981, then, an enormous amount of reportage and investigation concerning the nature and extent of modern torture appeared, most of it unchallenged, some of it denied, much of it ignored. In the wake of these revelations, extended and brought up to date by the Amnesty International 1984 publication *Torture in the Eighties*, even the fears of Orwell, Mellor and Arendt now seem inadequate. And Algeria has now come to seem, as Sartre said of the Third Reich and the USSR, routine rather than exceptional. Against its backdrop, medieval and early modern torture appears considerably more restricted in its application, purpose and technology. For torture has appeared in many other arms of state authority besides the judiciary (and has sometimes deliberately been kept out of the purview of the judiciary). Its purpose and character have changed as well. It is time to give some account of them. What does this revelation tell about torture? What is torture in the late twentieth century?

Room 101 – and other rooms

When Winston Smith, the protagonist of George Orwell's *Nineteen Eighty-Four*, is finally arrested by state officials, he is first subjected to isolation and sensory deprivation and then tortured by a complex technical device that appears to produce a series of sophisticated electrical assaults upon his nervous system. The information which the device invariably extracts, however, is already known to Smith's interrogators; what the torture sessions seem to be designed to do, in fact, is simply to establish Smith's co-operation. The final and greatest torture is designed to transform forced co-operation into broken-willed assent to the principles of the party. In Room 101 each victim is threatened with a torture that consists of the single thing in the world which he or she fears most. In Smith's case it is an attack on his body by rats (a device which Orwell may have taken from reports on Cheka tortures); each victim may avoid the actual torture application only by betraying the last remaining human ties and assenting to the supremacy of party and state. In the world of Room 101 this sequence of torture always works, and it is designed to break the will of its victims, not primarily to extract information. The discussion of Smith's torture and experience in Room 101 echoes a remark made by another fictitious torturer, Gletkin, in Arthur Koestler's *Darkness at Noon*: 'Human beings able to resist any amount of physical pressure do not exist. I have never seen one. Experience shows me that the resistance of the human nerve system is limited by Nature.' Tolerance also varies individually.

Orwell is purposely vague about the machine which first tortures Smith. Nothing like it existed in 1948, but for Orwell it was a solid and predictable piece of the future; since pain could achieve the conversion of recalcitrant individuals, the dismantling and re-creation of personalities, then a device for producing adequate volumes of pain for this purpose would have to be invented. O'Brien, Smith's torturer and teacher, abruptly dismisses earlier forms of physical and psychological coercion that had been designed merely to elicit information or confession. The Inquisition, the Third Reich, and the early Soviet Union are to him crude institutions whose limited and primitive techniques were used for trivial purposes. Herbert Radtke, an honorary member of the Federal German Council of Amnesty International, has observed a similar quality in many late twentieth-century uses of torture:

> One way of assessing the real purpose of torture is to examine the areas in which it is most frequently used. From this it is clear that the torturers' main aim is to spread a climate of terror. The procuring of information is only of secondary importance . . . Torture is becoming increasingly scientific. Alongside physical brutality and mutilations, the use of sophisticated mechanised equipment is becoming more and more common. A particular cause for concern is the growth of psychological and pharmacological methods of torture. While once doctors present at an interrogation were generally there to

prevent the victim's death, today medical science plays an active role in improving the torturer's techniques. (Böckle and Pohier, *The Death Penalty and Torture*, 1979, p.10)

The 'inventiveness' of Orwell and Koestler appears to have become routine for the torturers of 1984. Not only the traditional institutions, but the traditional methods of torture have been generally discarded; the strappado, the rack, thumbscrews, legsplints and fire now belong to an age whose technology, even whose technology of inflicting pain, has been surpassed by modernity.

The problem of the technology of late twentieth-century torture and the participation in it by medical and technical experts has attracted an enormous amount of research and testimony, especially since 1974. Some of the results of these investigations remain vague and unconvincing. Accusations of 'Asiatic' torture techniques secretly passed along a torture communications network running from Asia to western Europe are difficult to verify; so too are the more elaborate claims for the existence of 'schools' of torture, along the lines of one described in a broadcast over London radio in 1943: 'The future specialists of the Gestapo learned their trade there, generally in a four-week period, taking courses in physiology, practical training sessions, and a final examination.' Although the Third Reich certainly developed new techniques of torture and permitted these to be used by the officials of collaborating regimes, there is little evidence of formal training schools and not a great deal more for contemporary accusations of the existence of similar schools in Latin America or North Africa. The USA too has been accused of training torturers in the process of training officers of Latin American countries in maintaining public order.

Every ideology presupposes an anthropology – an idea of what human beings are and how they are to be treated in order to create the society that each ideology requires. The legal anthropology of the *ancien régime*, for example, presupposed a group of stubborn, intractable criminals, capable of resisting pain to an extraordinary degree, requiring pain to speak the truth, but invariably truthful when tortured. What Foucault calls the 'control of the body' of the criminal entailed not only physically painful and destructive punishments, but also imprecise and painful methods of interrogation. The neurology of early European torture depended chiefly upon the pain of distended muscles and dislocated joints, the relentless pressure of clamping devices upon highly innervated tissue and musculoskeletal systems, the searing of large areas of nerve endings by fire, and the suffocating and viscera-distending effects of water. The first of these is ischaemic pain. The dislocation of joints produces reflex neurological activity – slowing of the heart, hypotension, and syncope. Such methods, considering the kinds of pain they used, can have been at best approximate and uncertain – a point recognized by most writers on the reliability of evidence extracted by torture.

The technology of torture in the late twentieth century is in part the result of a new anthropology, and its attendant technology. It is not primarily the victim's information, but the victim, that torture needs to win – or reduce to powerlessness. By expanding the types and frequency of torture, by acquiring and exploiting a more exact knowledge· of psychology and neurology, torture in the late twentieth century has become able to inflict an immense variety of relatively graded degrees of pain upon anyone, for any amount of time, with, as Orwell and Gletkin once suggested, invariable success. The new anthropology subordinates individual human beings to a new transcendent good. As Koestler once observed, the human capacity for intra-specific violence and murder seems to derive less from a hypothetical biophysical aggressive drive than from the human capacity to place supreme values upon transcendental ideas and to deduce an anthropology from them. The passions of revolutionary consciousness in the early years of this century revealed the new anthropology in the violence of the Cheka and its revolutionary justification of terror and torture. The torturers of Mussolini's OVRA contributed their own grim originality – the technique of pumping their victims' stomachs full of castor oil; the Nazis appear to have been the first to use electrical devices, although Argentine police officers proudly claimed to have invented the *picana electrica*, the thin metal rod attached to a source of electric current and then applied to different parts of the body. Subsequent testimony and research have revealed a much greater variety of torture techniques than these. Before considering them, however, it is necessary to trace another line of recent research. To understand the effects of the new technology of torture it is necessary to consider some aspects of human physiology and psychology and what its most able clinical students have termed 'the puzzle of pain'.

Among the many beauties and wonders of the human body is an

elaborate and highly articulate sensory system, part of which is assaulted in the process of torture with the deliberate intention of triggering pain mechanisms. The initial assault on the nervous part of the sensory system, by whatever means of torture, is designed to produce acute pain. The first stimulations excite complex sets of receptors, generate increased sweat and blood flow, and begin the process of synthesizing the major chemical components of pain: small amounts of histamine and serotonin, the larger peptides like bradykinin, and the prostaglandins. These chemicals start the coded pattern of nerve impulses, the message of pain, along a network of nerve fibres until it reaches the dorsal horn of the spinal cord, from which it contributes its information to the afferent (sensory) system travelling along the spine to the brain, first to the thalamus, which recognizes sensory experience, and finally to the cerebro-cortex, which recognizes pain intensity and localizes the pain. Since the discovery of chemicals known as endorphins in 1975, it has also been known that the body itself may provide its own analgesics, pain inhibitors, and the 'gate-control' theory of pain describes how a complex flow of pain and other stimulants may interact with the body's own natural pain inhibitors – the endorphins, enkephalins and neurotransmitters – to reduce direct pain stimulation internally.

Since most clinical research on the physiology of pain has been undertaken with the purpose of ameliorating pain, there is no public record of research on inflicting pain, although there is substantial evidence that a number of physicians and technicians have in fact performed such research, at least as early as the medical experimentation sponsored by the Third Reich. All such research would necessarily work within the physiology of pain outlined above. But in considering the deliberate infliction of pain, there are other elements that must be taken into consideration. Acute pain in itself causes other effects: it may interfere with breathing, cause nausea, place an undue strain on the heart and induce stroke. Since the methods of inflicting pain vary, many procedures of torture assault other parts of the sensory and other bodily systems as well, particularly the musculoskeletal, gastrointestinal and cardiovascular systems, the skin, and the mind itself.

Further, the experience of torture may also produce chronic pain in the victim, a distinct and separate syndrome marked by long-lasting distress which is characterized by depression, loss of appetite, profound fatigue and sleeplessness, as well as hypotension, vertigo, and syncope. Chronic pain may also produce long-term changes in the central nervous system itself, so that even after the original pain stimulus has ceased, the pain (or other related forms of pain) may continue or renew itself periodically. Finally, the deliberate infliction of pain in circumstances of the torture setting may actually overcome the body's natural capacity to produce its own analgesics (pain-killing substances) and the attendant fear, anxiety, stress (in both the clinical and common-language senses), powerlessness and hopelessness may actually increase the victim's perception of pain and therefore also lower the victim's natural mechanisms of enduring pain. In brief, the pain produced by torture is very likely to be stronger and perceived more intensely than a clinically comparable amount of pain might be if it occurred accidentally or in the course of disease etiology.

Pain is a complex structure, subjectively perceived and psychologically conditioned. As two pioneer pain clinicians, Melzack and Wall, have observed:

the psychological evidence strongly supports the view of pain as a perceptual experience whose quality and intensity are influenced by the unique past history of the individual, by the meaning he gives to the pain-producing situation and by his 'state of mind' at the moment. We believe that all these factors play a role in determining the actual patterns of nerve impulses that ascend from the body to brain and travel within the brain itself. In this way pain becomes a function of the whole individual, including his present thoughts and fears as well as his hopes for the future. (Melzack and Wall, *The Challenge of Pain*, 1983)

In spite of the long-recognized vagueness of the language of pain, the research of Melzack, Wall and others has indicated that pain may successfully be described, analysed and verbally communicated as a category of experience possessing both somato-sensory (physical) and negative affective (psychological) dimensions.

The techniques of torture used chiefly in early European history principally assaulted the musculoskeletal system, heat sensory receptors, and highly innervated tissue. The strappado – suspension by ropes – and the rack greatly distended and often dislocated muscles and joints. In the case of strappado by traumatically extending the muscles of the arms and the brachial plexus and by depriving the muscles of an adequate blood supply (muscle ischaemia) through constriction of the arteries, and by dislocating joints at hand and shoulder, intense pain was generated. In the case of the pressure-type legsplints and thumbscrews, the pain thresholds of innervating fibres were lowered by mechanical pressure. In that of the rack, tendons, tendon sheaths and joint capsules were assaulted. In addition to these pains, early European torture techniques may also have involved referred pain: pain in areas other than those directly stimulated, caused by the activity of 'trigger points', extremely sensitive areas of the upper chest and back which, when stimulated, produce oedema, which in turn releases free histamines into the nervous system. Histamines, vasodilators, are one of the strongest pain-producing agents known. It is said that modern techniques of torture sometimes include the direct injection of histamines in order to produce intense pain.

In the somewhat later techniques of the legsplint and thumbscrew, the skeletal and vascular systems and their surrounding highly innervated tissue are assaulted by mechanical pressure. Thus, the torture techniques of early Europe produced substantial amounts of pain, but a relatively limited number of types. The technique of filling the victim's stomach with water (or the Italian Fascist variant of castor oil) almost to the point of asphyxiation produced not only the pain of suffocation, but the unique pain to which the viscera are subject. The stomach and intestines respond to the stimulus of cutting or burning, but visceral pain is produced also by distension, dilation or spasm. The technique of forcibly filling the stomach with water or another liquid inflicts some of the most intense pain that visceral tissues can experience.

Until the mid-1970s there existed little verifiable data concerning either torture techniques or torture personnel. Much of the evidence was anamnestic – the subjective reports of individuals. There existed little clinical literature on the phenomenon of pain itself. Since the end of the Second World War, however, there had taken place in a number of countries, notably Denmark, extensive research on victims of concentration camps and the experiences of certain classes of military personnel. This research produced a substantial literature on 'concentation camp syndrome' and 'war sailor syndrome'. In 1973, at its annual conference in Paris, Amnesty International, which had just undertaken its campaign against torture, requested aid from physicians in order to provide clinical documentation for the existence of torture, information concerning its immediate somatic and psychological effects, its sequelae (long-lasting effects), and to consider the ethical professional implications for the participation of medical personnel in torture and in preventing its occurrence.

In 1974 at a meeting of the International Council of Amnesty International in Copenhagen, a group of Dutch and Danish physicians under the leadership of Dr Inge Kemp Genefke formed the first independent medical group assembled to study torture as a distinct phenomenon. The group began with small groups of Chilean refugees in Denmark, victims of torture in Greece after the overthrow of the Papadopoulos regime, and the clinical literature produced in the wake of the Second World War. In 1975 at its meeting in Tokyo, the World Medical Association adopted a declaration Concerning Torture and other Cruel, Inhuman and Degrading Treatment of Punishment in Relation to Detention and Imprisonment. In 1976, under the direction of A. Heijder and H. van Geuns, Amnesty International published a volume entitled *Professional Codes of Ethics*. In 1977 the first publication of the Danish Medical Group, *Evidence of Torture*, was published by Amnesty International. Subsequent professional medical congresses in Strasburg, Athens, Geneva, Copenhagen, Toronto, Lérida and Lyons have considered the results of recent research, provided extensive medical documentation of torture, and created a clinical literature on torture and its sequelae that is extensive and reliable. In 1978 Amnesty International and a number of specialized research groups separated organizationally in order more effectively to pursue their respective kinds of work. In that year an international biomedical society, Anti-Torture Research (ATR), was founded, and in 1980 the Danish Medical Group was given permission to admit, examine and treat torture victims at the Copenhagen University Hospital.

This group, the Internationalt Rehabiliterings- og Forsknings-center for Tortureofre – The International Rehabilitation and Research Centre for Torture Victims (RCT) – supported by the Danish government and private contributions, consists of teams of medical specialists, nurses, physical therapists and psychologists working together on the somatic and psychological rehabilitation of torture victims from all over the world. In the light of this history of the growing awareness, research and experience of significant parts of the world, medical professions and the ongoing research of ATR and Amnesty International, it is possible to analyse the manifestations of twentieth-century torture, its technology, and its sequelae more thoroughly than ever before.

The work of Amnesty International and other inter-governmental and non-governmental groups has documented a vast number of individual and regional case histories and assessments of governmental policies in more than a hundred different countries. This mass of testimony and investigation is readily available and need not be repeated here. The following list synthesizes the results of those investigations that have been documented and medically verified within the past decade. The techniques of Amnesty International and other investigatory groups and the medical research of ATR and RCT have now forged a tool that is accurate and convincing. Torture has its own pathology – and it leaves traces that are unmistakably its own.

METHODS OF TORTURE IN THE LATE TWENTIETH CENTURY

SOMATIC TORTURE

Beating: punching, kicking, striking with truncheons, rifle butts, jumping on the stomach

Falanga (falaka): beating the soles of the feet with rods

Finger torture: pencil placed between victim's fingers, which are then pressed together violently

Telephono: the torturer strikes with his flat hand at a victim's ear, imitating a telephone receiver, producing rupture of the tympanic membrane; *telephono* may also consist of blows delivered against a helmet worn by the victim

Electricity: probing with pointed electrodes (*picana electrica*); cattle prods (shock batons); metal grids, metal beds to which victims are tied; the 'dragon's chair' (Brazil), an electric chair

Burning: with lighted cigarettes, cigars, electrically heated rods, hot oil, acid, quicklime; roasting on a red-hot grill (e.g. the 'hot table' used by agents of SAVAK); by the rubbing of pepper or other chemical substances upon mucous membranes, or acids and spices directly on wounds

Submarino: the submersion of the victim's head in water (often filthy water) until on the brink of suffocation (called, in Argentina, 'the Asian torture'; elsewhere, the *banera*)

Dry *submarino*: the victim's head is covered by a plastic bag or blanket, or the mouth and nostrils gagged until the point of suffocation is reached

Suspension in mid-air: the Brazilian 'parrot's perch' – victim is suspended with knees bent over a metal rod and tied tightly to wrists

Prolonged assumption of forced and stressful positions of body

Prolonged standing

Traction alopecia: the pulling out of hair

The forcible extraction of nails

Rape and sexual assaults

Insertion of foreign bodies into vagina or rectum

'Operating table': table to which victim is strapped, either for being forcibly stretched, or secured only below the lower back, necessitating victim's supporting his or her own weight that is off the table; in Chile it is called *el quirófano*

Exposure to cold: submersion in cold air or water

Deprivation of water: providing only soiled, salty, or soapy water

Forced consumption of spoiled or deliberately heavily spiced food

Dental torture: forced extraction of teeth

PSYCHOLOGICAL TORTURE

Witnessing the torture sessions of others: relatives, children

Threats made to witness the torture of others

Sham executions

Sleep deprivation

Continuous exposure to light

Solitary confinement

Incommunicado (being held without any human communication)

Total sensory deprivation

Conditions of detention

Threats

Shame-infliction: stripping naked; forced participation in or witnessing of sexual activity

PHARMACOLOGICAL TORTURE

Enforced application of psychotropic drugs

Enforced application of nerve stimulants (histamines; aminazine; trifluoro perazine-stelazine)
Enforced injection of faecal matter
Enforced ingestion of sulphur or poison (thallium)

Several features of this list, particularly its divisions, ought to be noted. First, there are psychological sequelae to all of the examples of somatic torture cited, and there are physical aspects to a number of psychological tortures, particularly sensory deprivation, exhaustion and solitary confinement. Finally, the psychiatric-pharmacological tortures also act upon physical conditions. In addition, although most medical personnel who have worked with torture victims usually note that a combination of tortures is in general used upon each individual, not all of these tortures are used everywhere; there seem to be culturally-favoured forms of torture in different societies. In Latin America, for example, there is little use of the *falanga*-related tortures, and a great deal of use of electrical forms of torture; in Greece, however, *falanga* greatly predominated.

Another feature to be considered is the circumstances in which torture is applied. Most research on the nature of pain, as pointed out above, is directed towards acute or chronic pain caused by accident or disease, and such research recognizes the body's own capacity for producing pain inhibitors and focuses upon creating the optimal conditions for recovery from pain. In the torture process, however, the conditions under which torture is applied are specifically designed to enhance the experience of pain, to block the operation of natural pain inhibitors, to prevent optimal conditions for recovery from pain, and to increase the pain in as many ways as possible. To these ends, technical and medical personnel are often enlisted by torturers; their services are directed at increasing the pain while preventing the sensory and affective means of ameliorating it, on the one hand, and on the other maintaining the minimal physical status of the victim so that he or she will be able to experience yet more pain at the discretion of the torturers. Depending upon the society in which the torture takes place, such specialist personnel may also be there to advise about torture that leaves the fewest macroscopic traces, and so will leave less medical evidence for the certification that torture has in fact taken place.

The data in the above list has been extracted from more than a decade of investigation and testimony by Amnesty International,

ATR, and the Torture Rehabilitation Centre (RCT). It leads to some immediate conclusions. First, in spite of the increasing use of technical and medical personnel, most forms of torture now in use are capable of having been devised on fairly rudimentary principles, requiring only an enhanced knowledge of the paths of pain through the human body. Rather more psychological sophistication is evident than medical or technological, except in the use of pharmacological methods of torture. The mysterious machines of *Nineteen Eighty-Four* seem, for the most part, not yet to be in use. The key to the existence of torture, aside from official or unofficial state policy, seems to be the availability of torturers, a subject treated in the next section of this chapter; for the most part, torturers seem able to work with the rudimentary spectrum of instruments and techniques described above. In order to employ the full assistance of medical and scientific specialists, it may be necessary to recruit torturers from different social areas than those now used. Of the methods listed above, only the use of electrical instruments and dental torture require more than minimal skill, and in the cases so far reported, such skill is readily acquired with the minimum of military or police training. The willingness of the torturers to become torturers seems still to determine the sophistication of torture techniques, and insofar as information is available, as it was in the Greek trials of 1975, those who are recruited are given much more psychological conditioning than technical training.

Even though the degree of medical and scientific techniques of torture may have been exaggerated, the methods listed above still produce a range and intensity of pain that greatly exceeds that of earlier forms of torture. The varieties of twentieth-century torture techniques are far more capable than their predecessors of producing precise kinds and amounts of pain, intensifying it by using different techniques, adding a psychological dimension to the experience of torture that is far greater than that in early modern torture, and reducing the body's natural capacity to resist or endure pain. In addition, we now know a great deal more about what torture does to the human body, and we know infinitely more about its after-effects. The results of very recent medical research have revealed the *chronic* pain produced by torture, an equally important dimension to the nature of the *acute* pain produced at the time of torture and recorded in anamnestic testimony.

The following list sets out different kinds of torture sequelae, modified and expanded from the comparable table in M. Kosteljantez and O. Aalund, 'Torture: A Challenge to Medical Science', *Interdisciplinary Science Reviews*, 8, 1983.

TORTURE SEQUELAE

SOMATIC SEQUELAE
Gastro-intestinal disorders: gastritis, ulcer-like dyspeptic symptoms, regurgitation pains in the epigastrium, irritable spastic colon
Rectal lesions, sphincter abnormalities
Skin lesions, histological lesions
Dermatological disorders: dermatitis, urticaria
Difficulty in walking, tendon injury
Joint pains
Brain atrophy (parallel to post-concussion syndrome, determined by computer axial tomography of the brain) and organic brain damage
Cardio-pulmonary disorders, hypertension
Dental disorders
Residual trauma pain
Gynaecological symptoms: inflammation of the internal sexual organs, menstrual pains
Hearing impairment, lesions of the eardrum
Lowered pain threshold
Stress as an indirect sequela

PSYCHOLOGICAL SEQUELAE
Anxiety, depression, fear
Psychosis, borderline psychosis
Instability, irritability, introversion
Concentration difficulties
Lethargy, fatigue
Restlessness
Diminished control of expression of emotion
Communication disabilities
Memory and concentration loss
Loss of sense of locality
Insomnia, nightmares
Impaired memory
Headaches

Hallucinations
Visual disturbances
Alcohol intolerance
Paraesthesia
Vertigo
Sexual disturbances

SOCIAL CONSEQUENCES OF TORTURE SEQUELAE
Impairment of social personality
Inability to work
Inability to participate in recreation
Destruction of self-image
Stress placed upon family
Inability to socialize

Medical research has also revealed that few victims are without psychological sequelae, that few victims suffer from only one sequela, and that conventional methods of therapy are not always indicated in treating torture victims. Two characteristic methods of torture may suggest why this is so. The process of *falanga*, the relentless striking of the soles of the feet, has been clinically described by Nicholas Gage:

> Each blow of the rod is felt not just on the soles of the feet, painfully flexed upward as the club smashes the delicate nerves between the heel and the balls of the foot; the pain shoots up the stretched muscles of the leg and explodes in the back of the skull. The whole body is in agony and the victim writhes like a worm. (*Eleni*, p.521)

Pain and swelling are immediately felt by the victim, the latter extending well up past the ankle. There is reduced functioning of ankles, feet and toes. In half the cases later examined by experts, chronic sequelae of *falanga* were present from two to seven years after the application of the torture. In a clinical report on the somatic sequelae to torture, Ole Vedel Rasmussen and Henrik Marsussen ('The Somatic Sequelae to Torture', Danish Medical Group, Amnesty International, *Månedsskrift for praktisk laegegerning*, March, 1982) have suggested that *falanga* may produce a 'closed-compartment' syndrome: oedema and bleeding in compartments housing vessels and nerves passing from the sole to the feet, in this case indicated by tight soles of the feet, fixated tarsal bones, impaired walking, failure to use the entire foot, manifested as a syndrome of the crus (the portion of the leg between thigh and ankle). Similar syndromes in the upper extremities are known as Volkmann's contracture.

Among the particular interests of the ATR group has been the consequences of torture by electricity. The pain of burning, muscular contraction, convulsions and muscular paralysis are a consequence of all forms of such torture, and its use traditionally has left few marks. Recent research, however, has suggested that the application of electrical torture does leave specific histological changes in skin tissue, and that these may ultimately be used to prove the use of electrical tortures long after the experience has ceased, even when there is no other corroborating evidence. Thus, in the cases of two very different kinds of torture techniques, recent medical research has permitted a much more precise and clinical understanding of the acute and chronic pain effects and at the same time is shaping a pathology that can establish that torture did in fact take place through these methods in the cases of individual victims.

Short of the world of torture envisaged by Orwell, even the modest proliferation of medical and technological expertise and the extraordinarily broadened spectrum of torture techniques can be investigated and documented, legally and clinically. The victims of late twentieth-century torture have not all been de-personalized, nor have they all yet perished. Regimes, even torture regimes, still fall, and rival states or subsequent governments still investigate and denounce the techniques those regimes had employed in order to remain in power. And torture victims sometimes escape and face the need to rehabilitate themselves in a world that does not understand their ordeal and often provides no means of healing them.

Even standard therapeutic techniques often do not work well on victims of torture. In many cases later symptoms manifested by chronic conditions are not readily identifiable with specific forms of torture; in other cases, victims simply cannot (or are not permitted to) speak to medical personnel about what has happened to them. Even the Danish physicians and therapists who understand the sequelae of torture best have discovered that otherwise routinely indicated forms of therapy may not be ideal for victims of torture.

One of the most striking difficulties recorded by therapists who have treated victims of torture is the extraordinary degree of tact that must be used in therapeutic situations that bear even a slight surface resemblance to the original circumstances of torture. Questioning of victims must not be intensive; methods of physical therapy and medical examination must not be used if these (e.g., swimming or traction therapy, or EKG analysis) too strongly resemble the original methods of torture used. The temporary confinement in hospital quarters sometimes reminds patients involuntarily of their original confinement. Since torture victims' only previous contact with medical personnel may have been in the place of torture itself, the medical personnel involved in rehabilitation work under this further strain and a further irregular aspect of their normal professional treatment of patients.

Not only does the perversion of clinical behaviour by the original circumstances of torture affect subsequent rehabilitation procedures, but so too do the circumstances that often torture victims must find such rehabilitation outside their own country – in the case of Denmark, for example, in a country which may present language difficulties. For those who cannot leave their country, or where there has been no governmental change from the time of their torture, rehabilitation is virtually impossible.

This book began with a number of definitions of torture; those definitions dealt mainly with the forms and purpose of torture, and with its source in authority. The years since 1956 have revealed massive documentary evidence of the proliferation of instances and forms of torture, and the past decade has revealed a pathology of torture unavailable to previous historians and legislators. But for all of the new information, the general source of torture has not changed; it is still civil society that tortures or authorizes torture or is indifferent to those wielding it on civil society's behalf. The future of torture lies with civil society – and with the anthropologies that it devises or imagines.

Without end?

Historians possess no professional competence when they deal with the future, but the history of torture, as well as the presence of torture in the world today, has inspired more than one historian at least to think about the future. When the greatest of all historians of torture, Piero Fiorelli, brought his own monumental two-volume study, *La tortura giudiziaria nel diritto comune*, to a close, in 1954, he entitled his final section '*Senza una fine?*' – 'Without an end?' In 1953, the year before Fiorelli's work appeared, the Italian marxist political philosopher, Lelio Basso, had published a work entitled *La tortura oggi in Italia* (*Torture in Italy Today*). Fiorelli's concluding question proved to be more timely than he knew. Historians may indeed possess no professional competence in the matter of the future, but they possess curiosity. The case of torture necessarily sharpens that curiosity – and not only for historians.

In 1971, nearly two decades after the revelations of torture in Algeria and nearly a decade after the establishment of Algerian independence, General Jacques Massu published his memoirs of the Algerian war, under the title *La Vraie Bataille d'Alger*. In that book, and in subsequent interviews and public appearances, Massu defended his use of torture in Algeria on the grounds that the particular circumstances then obtaining demanded its use, and that military necessity dictated it. The book is a classic instance of one commonly used argument for the legitimacy of torture, an argument that Massu did not invent and was not alone in citing. Massu's defence of his policies coined a new word in French, *Massuisme*: the argument that torturers may be responsible servants of the state in times of extreme crisis. The response to this assertion was not long in coming. In 1972 Alec Mellor returned to the battle with his book *Je dénonce la torture*, which subjected Massu's arguments to a searing analysis. Jules Roy published *J'accuse le général Massu* in the same year, and Pierre Vidal-Naquet published the French translation of *Torture: Cancer of Democracy*.

The decade following 1972 witnessed the adoption of the UN Convention, the anti-torture campaign of Amnesty International, the formation of ATR and RCT, and yet another UN Convention, now under review, accompanied by a Draft Optional Protocol, submitted in 1980 by the government of the Republic of Costa Rica, originally created by the International Commission of Jurists and the Swiss Committee against Torture. But some ideas refuse to disappear, and *Massuisme* seems to be one of them. As late as 1982 an American academic philosopher, innocent of the literature and history of the subject, argued in the popular press a loud case for the selective value of torture, yet another version of *Massuisme*, of which the philosopher appeared to be ignorant. The scenario was the familiar idealized and sanitized version: interrogatory torture, in a case where information known only to the examinate could instrumentally prevent the deaths of hundreds of innocent people caused by the examinate's confederates, ought to be legally applied. Regardless of the fact that the legal philosopher Charles Black had raised (and dismissed) the same argument twenty years earlier – and Alec Mellor a decade earlier – the philosopher contributed to the sustaining of what has become the classic argument for retaining torture: the possibility of the heroic, unemotional torturer in the service of the state on behalf of innocent victims.

In *Je dénonce la torture* Mellor cites a document attributed to a French army officer in Algeria which purports to establish regulations for just such torture. Five points, the document states, must be meticulously observed:

1 It is necessary that torture be properly conducted.
2 It must not take place in front of children.
3 It must not be performed by sadists.
4 It must be done by an officer or another responsible person.
5 It must be *humane*, that is, it should cease immediately when the *type* [sic] confesses. And above all, it must leave no marks.

These are the ideal regulations for the dignified torturer, and conceivably they exist in the protocols or imaginations of governments that actually practise torture.

As Mellor observes, however, there are several flaws in such assumptions: 'It is not its qualifying phrases that make of this exercise of a code of Torture a criminal work, but its very admission of the principle of [legitimate] torture of any kind.' The most devastating criticism of *Massuisme* that Mellor cites, however, came from a former French career soldier, now a priest, Père Gibert, SJ:

The 'case' considered as the classic of its kind: if-the-arrested-terrorist-does-not-talk-then-hundreds-of-innocent-people-will-die, is, no matter what General Massu and the justifiers of torture claim, far from having constituted the only motivation for the use of torture in Algeria. People were tortured for far less reason than that, and by methods far worse than the superficial application of *gégène* [torture by the application of electrodes]. But let us admit for a moment that it might be possible to justify torture for the 'noble motives': have they thought for one moment of the individual who does it, that is, of the man whom, whether he wishes or not, one is going to turn into a torturer? I have received enough confidences in Algeria and in France to know into what injuries, perhaps irreparable, torture can lead the human conscience. Many young men have 'taken up the game' and have thereby passed from mental health and stability into terrifying states of decay, from which some will probably never recover.

General Massu exercises a 'high' responsibility: has he ever thought about those who do the dirty work? And in place of trying to satisfy us by arguments of a disquieting simplicity, and of justifying his own actions to himself by virtue of the 'theological memories' of some half-witted military chaplain, he might have done better to keep silent about all this. For the sake of his own peace and ours, if not for the truth.

So often have the effects of torture on the victims been the focus of discussion that its effects on the torturers have been neglected. Either torturers are written off as sadists, or, as in the case of *Massuisme*, they are blandly imagined to be loyal officers merely doing an unpleasant duty. The question of sadism among torturers is complex. Although many sadists are indeed drawn into the role of torturer when such a role is available, it is also arguable that the institution of torture creates as many sadists as it attracts. The creation or encouragement of sadism is not a proper – or safe – governmental function. The father of Alexander Lavranos, one of the defendants at the Greek torture trials of 1975, raised a poignant and relevant question: 'We are a poor but decent family . . . and now I see him in the dock as a torturer. I want to ask the court to examine how a boy whom everyone said was a "diamond" became a torturer. Who morally destroyed my home and my family?' Lavranos himself added: 'Now all my friends and relations look upon me with suspicion and pity. I can't find work. . . . I feel the need to tell this respected tribunal and the Greek people that I am a human being like you, like your neighbour's son, like a friend. When I struck it was not Lavranos' hand, but the hand of Spanos, of Hajizizis.'

We must postpone for a moment the question of whether or not Lavranos and other torturers are really 'a human being like you, like your neighbour's son, like a friend', to note that Lavranos' father was not the only person who asked the question. The prosecutor himself once asked: 'How could Greek officers sink to this moral degradation? Were they born with criminal instincts, or did external circumstances deform their characters?' In other discussions of the psychology of the Greek torturers, even many of their pronounced sexual perversities struck observers as the consequences, not the causes, of the practice of torture:

> It is important to see that these individual perversions are not the cause of a system of torture. Rather, once a system of torture has been created in order to support the political needs of those in power, the rulers' agents will exhibit patterns of behaviour that they would not otherwise be in a position to do.

In spite of the comforting aspects of writing torture off as the play of sadists, it seems wiser to apply psychological analysis to the torturers only *after* they have become torturers, and to assume as a working hypothesis that the institution of torture itself may act as an agent that transforms individual psyches. To apply such analysis retroactively is to face the dilemma that torturers may be made out of both people who have a psychological predisposition to cruelty with a sexual dimension, *and* young people who previously seem like 'diamonds'. The restriction of torture to the born sadist is thus too simple; it fails to account for the 'diamonds'.

But must the torturer be only either a born or a created sadist? Are the dignified torturers of *Massuisme* merely the figments of an old general's imagination? In 1974 the American psychologist Stanley Milgram published a controversial study called *Obedience to Authority*. The study used an experimental method upon human subjects that consisted of persuading average people (potential sadists were explicitly screened out) to inflict pain on others as an indication of their willingness to obey an authority they recognized as legitimate. The results of the Milgram experiment were complex, but one of their conclusions was that very ordinary people, out of neither psychological nor personal interests, could be induced with relative ease to become temporary torturers. A wise editor at *Harper's Magazine*, which published an article based on Milgram's research in December 1973, entitled it 'The Torturer in Everyman'.

Is there a torturer in Everyman? In 1963 Hannah Arendt published her study of the Eichmann case, *Eichmann in Jerusalem*, which carried the provocative subtitle, *A Report on the Banality of Evil*. A decade before Milgram, Arendt also claimed that, if there was not quite a potential torturer in Everyman, then there at least was, in the kind of society in which Eichmann worked, the possibility that a functionary might be so distanced from reality that in his detachment he failed to realize the consequences of what he was doing: 'That such remoteness from reality and such thoughtlessness can wreak more havoc than all the evil instincts taken together which, perhaps, are inherent in man – that was, in fact, the lesson one could learn in Jerusalem.' The brutal torturer – whether born or created – and the detached torturer are two late twentieth-century figures on the darker side of civil society.

Although the detached torturer seems closer to the ideal of *Massuisme*, there is a more detailed portrait of the ideal torturer in a recent series of fantasy novels written by Gene Wolf, entitled *The Book of the New Sun*. The hero, a professional torturer, raised as such from childhood in a dedicated, impersonal guild of torturers, possesses a highly skilled craft, which he wields with utter dispassion. He has been dismissed from the guild, however, and supports himself on his travels by serving in provincial capitals as a torturer and public executioner. Among his occasional justifications for his occupation are the observations that: torturers are not cruel, but efficient, and they work only under judges with legitimate authority; such formal public instruments are essential to prevent anarchy; only the judges have the power to decide who shall be tortured; forced labour as an alternative would be impractical, and prolonged imprisonment would be too expensive; the universal death sentence is too severely democratic and fails to distinguish between greater and lesser offences. Throughout this discourse the emphasis is upon the lack of emotion, the impersonality, utter lack of cruelty, strict legality and technical efficiency of the torturers themselves. Here, in Wolf's novel, is Massu's ideal and necessary torturer. Now, works of fiction obey their own rules, for their authors can safely adjust space and time – and anthropology – and too much must not be made of them, particularly when such a piece of rhetorical extravagance as this speech is under consideration. Except in novels, then, and the imaginations of men in high places, there are, so far, no such torturers.

Can they be created? Arendt and Milgram are not alone in seeing the possibility of a society which regards torture as routine and soberly solicits the assistance of physicians and scientists in its work. Lavranos and others were indeed created, but they were hardly the dispassionate torturers invoked by Massu and the American philosopher. Eichmann was created, and he may be the closest kind of human yet made to fit the idealized pattern of the modern torturer. In similar situations, some psychiatric physicians, police and military technicians, and psychologists may unwittingly be recruited as assistants to torturers, particularly if their work is solicited on the basis of clinical, therapeutic or professional reasons. In Mellor's discussion of the medical aspects of modern torture, for example, he focuses almost entirely upon the legality of truth-serum in police interrogations; in some countries forced sterilization of sexual offenders is accepted as legitimate; in Soviet psychiatry, in spite of worldwide objections to its forensic use, there is professed to be a clinical theory of neurosis that justifies the use of psychotropic drugs; the World Medical Association has forbidden the participation of member physicians in the forcible feeding of imprisoned hunger strikers. All of these instances may be considered as existing along the ambiguous edge between torture and legitimate state treatment of prisoners. Those who participate in them are not necessarily either Lavranos or Eichmann; indeed, the growth of what Mellor designates as *torture non douloureuse* – torture without suffering – is a large and as yet inadequately charted area. Except for such people, however, the training of modern torturers seems to have no such subtle and sanitized aim.

In spite of a large body of unverified testimony concerning the existence of specialized schools for torturers, the best evidence available comes either from official trial records, e.g., those of the Greek trials in 1975 and after, or from individual torturers who have left their countries and have spoken about their own experiences. This evidence suggests that potential torturers are recruited from conscript soldiers with family backgrounds politically sympathetic to the current regime, or from lower-level police personnel. These recruits receive intensive political indoctrination that emphasizes the danger to the country constituted by 'communists', 'fascists', 'terrorists', or 'imperialists', and after preliminary screenings a select group is invited to join an elite corps, whose exact function is not specified, but membership in which carries substantial privileges – higher rank, salary, access to cars and favours for one's family – that particularly appeal to rural or urban lower-class recruits, who are also promised civil-service positions when they leave the service.

The special training they undergo consists first of a violent programme of special training in which the recruits themselves are beaten and forced to beat others, perform self-abasing acts in front of their colleagues, and forced to accept both unquestioning obedience to superiors and excessive brutality among colleagues as a norm. After training, the recruits are assigned first to guarding prisoners, whom they routinely see being violently treated by others, then on arresting squads, and finally are assigned to torture details themselves. If they resist, they are threatened by loss of privileges and ignoble dismissal from the service, punishments for their families, or they themselves may be beaten and retrained until they comply. Once accustomed to the service, the torturers find their status enhanced by the names of their organizations, the privileges of a military or police elite, their independence from regular army or police structures, or from other governmental structures entirely, and the possibility of recruitment into private torture or terror organizations that exist under government patronage or with indirect governmental support. Their elite status and independence is enhanced by their high duties in protecting the state, by the rapid development of a specialized jargon to describe their work, by the psychological reinforcement of colleagues and superiors, and by the constant necessity of obtaining results from the torture.

As legal or other governmental safeguards of civilian rights are relaxed, the practice of torture generally spreads from victims charged with active terrorism or political mischief to other classes of victims, until the work of the torturer, himself conditioned to torture anyone at all, may be applied to any victim suspected of any sort of opposition to the government or indeed of any activities, such as labour union work or certain kinds of journalism or legal advocacy, that the government disapproves of. By this stage in his career, the torturer is hardly in a position to discriminate among his victims.

At this stage we may ask again the question raised above: is the torturer, as Alexander Lavranos claimed, 'a human being like you, like your neighbour's son, like a friend?' From the point of view of those best in a position to judge, the victims, there is a general consensus that, aside from a predictable number of constitutional sadists, the torturers were people who had been 'deprived of their personalities', 'dehumanized', by being forced to torture while among a group of torturers or in the presence of superiors. From all the evidence of torture training, then, we still do not find Massu's impersonal torturers. Torturers are deliberately trained in such a way as to alter their personalities, make them accept a fabricated political reality in which their victims have been set outside the pale of humanity, and sustain this illusion by both coercion and reward. The largest part of the future of torture depends upon the future of torturers. Although Massu's ideal torturer is not yet among us, thereby vitiating a substantial part of Massu's argument, it is not impossible that he may yet be created by the methods in use so far. And neither present torturers nor the ideal future torturer can be said to be exactly 'a human being like you, like your neighbour's son, like a friend'.

Another part of the future of torture lies with the possibility of action against torturers, either, as in the case of Greece, by public criminal trials conducted by a subsequent regime, or, as in many other cases, by criminal or civil suits brought by the victims or their families against accused torturers. In torture regimes, such action is unlikely to have more than a nuisance effect, although some legal doctrines, for example *habeas corpus*, still survive even in regimes that practice torture. A more useful example is provided by the relatively recent use, in the USA, of the Alien Tort Statute (*United States Code*, Title 28, Section 1350), which provides that: 'The [US Federal District] courts shall have original jurisdiction of any civil action by an alien for a tort [private or civil injury] only, committed in violation of the law of nations or a treaty of the United States.' Briefly, the statute permits one alien to initiate civil action against another in the US Federal courts, for an offence committed outside the United States, if that offence is a violation of the law of nations or a specific treaty to which the USA is a signatory. Between 1979 and 1983 such a suit was brought by the family of a Paraguayan torture victim against the Paraguayan torturer in the US District Court and later in the Federal Court of Appeals. The plaintiff won the case on appeal, thus creating a precedent for future use of the statute against other torturers, and possibly offering the Alien Tort Statute as a model for other countries with similar willingness to protect torture victims.

The Amnesty International Publication, *Torture in the Eighties*, lists a number of other kinds of action that may be and have been taken by national, international and other groups against torture and has assessed the relative success such movements have achieved – in some cases, notably those of Northern Ireland and Brazil – substantial success. On the other hand, there well may be, as the Swiss legal scholar Werner Kaegi has feared, 'an almost excessive activity in the field of human rights leading to a dangerous inflation of declarations, proclamations, and conventions. Many lawyers and politicians believe that the world will be changed by such documents with a tendency to universality.' Kaegi and other contributors to a small collection of statements on how to make the Draft Optional Protocol to the current Draft Convention Against Torture now being considered by the UN, all urge the adoption of the Draft Optional Protocol, which commits its signatories to permitting visits of an international commission to centres of detention. Kaegi and others argue that beginning with a small group of signatory states the number of participating states will increase because of the non-political and non-publicized character of the Commission and its agents. With the voluntary cooperation of an initially small group of states, it is argued, the experience of these states will encourage other states to sign the Protocol. Such a proposal has the virtue of beginning with the possible on a scale small enough to be realistic.

As to the larger Draft Convention itself, Amnesty International has raised some points that must be answered if the Convention is to be at all effective. First, no internal 'lawful sanctions' by individual governments may override the definition of torture or cruel, inhuman or degrading treatment or punishment contained in the Convention. Second, the Convention ought to recognize universal jurisdiction over alleged torturers no matter what country they may be in, a point similar to the use of the US Alien Tort Statute. Third, that victims have access to redress for their suffering and that no evidentiary use may be made of statements elicited by torture. Fourth, there must be effective implementation mechanisms for the Convention. The Draft Optional Protocol offers just such a set of implementation mechanisms.

The future of torture is thus partly determinable by the production of torturers and by the action of organizations from the family to the United Nations, including current material presently before the UN. But there is a final consideration upon which much of the success at eliminating torturers and torture itself must necessarily rest. Language that identifies torture with *inhuman* practices also presupposes an anthropology, one shaped in the late eighteenth century out of old and new principles of European thought. That anthropology has survived, barely, it sometimes seems, into the late twentieth century, but there is no guarantee that it will necessarily survive forever. It survived in part because it was embodied in jurisprudence, governmental policies and institutions, and international agreements, as well as in the literature of moral philosophy, in the arts, and in a high and low cultural consensus, indeed, in sentiment as well as law and morality. It may be possible to make torture disappear by making it effectively illegal and dangerous to those who practise it, but it seems necessary also to preserve the reason for making it illegal and dangerous – to preserve a notion of human dignity that, although not always meticulously observed, is generally assumed in the public language, if not the unpublic actions, of most modern societies, and assumed, moreover, in a generally universal and democratic sense. All human beings are assumed by this anthropology to possess a quality called human dignity. As Immanuel Kant once observed, punishments or other forms of treatment may be considered inhuman when they become inconsistent with human dignity. It is important to distinguish this operative idea of human dignity from what Malise Ruthven has acutely called the 'threshold of outrage' – a fluctuating notion of appropriate treatment of individuals depending upon social status, background or class. The idea of human dignity must not be distracted by momentary thresholds of outrage or momentary general designations of sentiment. It is sometimes easier to erode a large idea like that of human dignity slowly from its distant edges rather than to risk the abrupt introduction of torture outright into a society. It is easier to transform an anthropology slowly, for with such a transformation, torture may appear as a logical and predictable step.

From this assumption, the fallacies in several kinds of modern argument may become clearer. It is easy – and initially tempting – to correlate torture with a temper of brutality attributed to another race, culture, ideology, or particular regime. It is more reliable to observe the anthropology of particular cases than to make broad and unverifiable assumptions about the character of particular races or regimes. Historically, torture has proved to be adaptable to too many different cultures for it to be attributed exclusively to one or two especially feral ones. Second, meaning must be restored to the language of human dignity. Such observations as 'poverty is torture, frustration is torture', mean nothing except in the reversible mirror-language of ideology where meaning is deliberately detached from words and things. One of the most eloquent statements for the restoration of such meaning to human dignity is the argument of Francesco Campagnoni:

> Torture tends to the disintegration and consequent annihilation of the psychic and moral personality, to the non-physical destruction, practically speaking, of the human person, with lasting results . . . But from a theological point of view it seems to me that greater weight can be attributed to another consideration: that the human person cannot, literally speaking, be sacrificed, in that by which it is most properly constituted, namely its rational freedom, to the need of a social system, the ultimate purpose of which is the welfare of all individuals. . . . It seems to me that one of the central doctrines of theological anthropology is the absolute preeminence of man's dignity as a creature. . . This dignity, autonomous in the face of any juridical institution or community whatever, is the reason why, even after the worst (and verified) crimes, there is always the possibility of repentance.

The torturer too violates the same anthropological idea as does the torture of the victim; if the victim is conceived to be without human dignity and therefore vulnerable to torture, the torturer also divests himself of human dignity. And a new anthropology is substituted for the old.

Preserving an operative concept of human dignity may prove to be more difficult than it sounds. Such a concept may be attacked by different moralities, ideologies, thresholds of outrage, or sentimentality. It is probably wiser to preserve the concept in minimalist terms rather than attempting to enlarge it to its most ambitious dimensions.

Societies that do not recognize the dignity of the human person, or profess to recognize it and fail to do so in practice, or recognize it only in highly selective circumstances, become, not simply societies with torture, but societies in which the presence of torture transforms human dignity itself, and therefore all individual and social life. And a society which voluntarily or indifferently includes among its members both victims and torturers ultimately leaves no conceptual or practical room for anyone who insists upon being neither.

Bibliographical Essay

The following collections of documents and scholarly accounts have been of great assistance in my own research, and I have tried to list those accessible to diligent modern readers. On occasion, I have had to cite books not in English, particularly when these are the best – or, more often, the only – competent source for important points.

Throughout this book I have depended heavily upon the monumental work of Piero Fiorelli, *La tortura giudiziaria nel diritto comune* (2 vols., Milan, 1953–4), whose second volume takes brief account of torture up to the UN Declaration of 1948. There are many purported comprehensive histories of torture, few of them reliable and most of them at best picturesque. The most thorough attempt at a single history is that of Alec Mellor, *La Torture* (Paris, 1949; 2nd edn, Tours, 1961), a passionate and ambitious study that is seriously flawed but impossible to ignore, written by an outraged jurist who had lived through the 1930s and 1940s and wrote with a furious determination to prevent events like those of that period from happening again. After the publication of Henry Charles Lea, *Superstition and Force* (Philadelphia, 1866), the next extensive discussion of torture in English was the selective but generally astute study by Malise Ruthven, *Torture: The Grand Conspiracy* (London, 1978). A third work upon which I have drawn heavily is the volume *La Preuve*, Recueils de la Société Jean Bodin pour l'Histoire comparative des Institutions, vol. XIX, Parts 1–4 (Brussels, 1963), the various contributions to which are cited frequently in abbreviated form below. Among technical studies I have gratefully used John H. Langbein, *Torture and the Law of Proof* (Chicago, 1977), also cited and discussed below.

An interesting general historical survey of public rules for coercion, having no English equivalent, is Jean Imbert and Georges Levasseur, *Le Pouvoir, les juges et les bourreaux* (Paris, 1972). There is an important series of discussions in Franz Böckle and Jacques Pohier (eds), *The Death Penalty and Torture*, Concilium: Religion in the Seventies, vol.CXX (New York, 1979).

A number of specialized encyclopaedias contain excellent accounts of torture, although general encyclopaedias should be used with much caution. See, for example, L. Chevalier, 'Torture', in *Dictionnaire de droit canonique*, vol. VII (Paris, 1965), cols.1293–1314; A. Erhardt, 'Tormenta', in Pauly-Wissowa, *Real-Encyclopädie*, II.xii, cols.1775–94.

The rest of this bibliographical essay deals with the topics discussed in the text chapter by chapter and, in the more complicated fourth and fifth chapters, section by section.

A number of accounts of early European and modern torture provide illustrations (and in modern accounts, photographs). But the history of illustration of torture is not always reliable, nor can every picture (particularly those produced during the eighteenth and nineteenth centuries) be assumed to be graphically authentic. There are some reliable and important illustrations in the works of Fiorelli and Langbein and several more in the important work by Hans Fehr, *Das Recht im Bilde* (Munich and Leipzig, 1923), as well as in Fehr's companion work, *Das Recht in der Dichtung* (Bern, n.d.). A model study of the relation between art history and legal subject matter is that by Samuel Y. Edgerton, Jr., *Pictures and Punishment: Art and Criminal Prosecution during the Florentine Renaissance* (Ithaca, N.Y., 1984).

Films depicting torture are also usually unreliable. Two relatively recent exceptions are Herbert Radtke, *Im Jahr der Folter* (*In the Year of Torture*), and the Danish film *Your Neighbor's Son*, distributed by Amnesty International, Frederiksborggade 1, 1360 Copenhagen K, Denmark.

Chapter 1   *A Delicate and Dangerous Business*

It is hardly sufficient simply to recount what various sources and scholars have to say about torture alone; one must examine any legal phenomenon in its own historical and cultural context. Several general studies of Greek legal culture skilfully manage to do both. The handiest short introduction is George M. Calhoun, *Introduction to Greek Legal Science*, ed. F. de Zulueta (Oxford, 1944). Longer and more sophisticated are J. Walter Jones, *The Law and Legal Theory of the Greeks* (Oxford, 1956), esp. pp.141–3, and Eric A. Havelock, *The Greek Concept of Justice* (Cambridge, Mass., 1978). The most thorough recent study is A. R. W. Harrison, *The Law of Athens* (2 vols., Oxford, 1968), esp. vol. II, pp.147–50. The most detailed account of torture in Greek law is the learned study of Gerhard Thur, *Beweisführung vor den Schwurgerichtshofen Athens. Die Proklesis zur Basanos* (Vienna, 1977). In the first volume of *La Preuve*, see especially the essays by Gerard Sautel and Claire Preaux, which deal with heroic Greece and Greek Egypt respectively. Two technical works that deal specifically with the operation of Greek courts and the rules of evidence are Robert J. Bonner, *Evidence in Athenian Courts* (1905; rept. New York, 1979), and idem, with Gertrude Smith, *The Administration of Justice from Homer to Aristotle* (2 vols., 1930; rept. New York, 1970).

In Roman law, the best account of torture is in Fiorelli, *La Tortura Giudiziaria*, vol. I. There are a number of classic surveys, e.g., A. Esmein, *A History of Continental Criminal Procedure*, trans. J. Simpson (Boston, 1913), and Theodor Mommsen, *Römische Strafrecht* (rpt. Graz, 1955), pp.401–11. There is a good summary in Peter Garnsey, *Social Status and Legal Privilege in the Roman Empire* (Oxford, 1970). There is an important discussion in Alan Watson, 'Roman Slave Law and Romanist Ideology', *Phoenix* 37 (1983), pp.53–65.

Chapter 2   *The Queen of Proofs and the Queen of Torments*

For medieval and early modern Europe, the standard and exhaustive account is that of Fiorelli, *La tortura giudiziaria*. There are relevant articles in *La Preuve*, of which one of the most important, that of R. C. van Caenegem, has recently been translated into English by J. R. Sweeney and David A. Flanary, as 'Methods of Proof in Western Medieval Law', *Mededelingen van de Koninklijke Academie voor Wetenschappen, Letteren en Schone Kunsten van Belgie, Academiae Analecta*, 45 (1983), pp.85–127, with a bibliographical appendix. An extensive bibliography is printed as an appendix to my own study, *The Magician, the Witch and the Law* (Philadelphia, 1978), Appendix I, '*Res fragilis:* Torture in Early European Law'. There are important sections in Langbein, *Torture and the Law of Proof*, Mellor, *La Torture*, and Esmein, *A History of Continental Criminal Procedure*, as well. The most important primary source, the enormously influential *Tractatus de Maleficiis*, is printed in Herman Kantorowicz, *Albertus Gandinus und das Strafrecht der Scholastik*, vol. II (Berlin, 1926). A recent extensive discussion of the twelfth-century legal revolution is that of Harold J. Berman, *Law and Revolution* (Cambridge, Mass., 1983).

On the twelfth-century transformation of law, see the two important studies by Stephan Kuttner and Knut Nörr in Robert L. Benson and Giles Constable (eds), *Renaissance and Renewal in the Twelfth Century* (Cambridge, Mass., 1982). There is an extensive bibliography on the inquisition in my own *Heresy and Authority in Medieval Europe* (Philadelphia, 1980).

For the early modern period, the same general sources contain excellent references, as does John H. Langbein, *Prosecuting Crime in the Renaissance* (Cambridge, Mass., 1974), with English translations of key legislation. Although there are few English translations of the sixteenth and seventeenth century literature of criminal practice, many writers are extensively summarized in Henry C. Lea, *Materials for a History of Witchcraft*, ed. Arthur Howland (Philadelphia, 1939; rept. New York, 1957), particularly in vols. II and III. Some remarks of Sebastian Guazzini are translated in James C. Welling, *The Law of Torture: A Study in the Evolution of Law* (Washington, D.C., 1982).

In addition to the works on criminal procedure and punishment cited by Langbein and Lea, there has been much recent research dealing with crime as a social phenomenon in early modern Europe. See V. A. C. Gatrell, Bruce Lenman and Geoffrey Parker (eds), *Crime and the Law: The Social History of Crime in Western Europe since 1500* (London, 1980).

Chapter 3 *The Sleep of Reason*

Most Enlightenment histories comment extensively upon that aspect of Enlightenment penal theory that Langbein, *Torture and the Law of Proof*, dismisses as a 'fairy tale'. A convenient, persuasive and readable account of the conventional view is that of Marcello T. Maestro, *Voltaire and Beccaria as Reformers of Criminal Law* (New York, 1942). Langbein's criticisms of this view are laid out eloquently in *Torture and the Law of Proof*.

The fullest account of statutory abolition is that of Fiorelli, *La tortura giudiziaria*. In this instance, Mellor's *La Torture* is of little use, and most histories refer the reader back to Fiorelli's detailed account.

There is a good general account of Enlightenment moral thought on the subject in Ruthven, *Torture: The Grand Conspiracy*, pp.3–22, who also cites the important study of W. L. and P. E. Twining, 'Bentham on Torture', *Northern Ireland Legal Quarterly*, 24 (1973), pp.305–56.

For torture in the Ottoman Empire and traditional Islamic law, see Uriel Heyd, *Studies in Old Ottoman Criminal Law*, ed. V. L. Menage (Oxford, 1973), pp.252–4. On evidence in the *shari'a*, see Robert Brunschwig, 'La preuve en droit musulman', *La Preuve*, vol. III, pp.170–86, and Muhammad Hamidullah, 'La genèse du droit de la preuve en Islam', ibid., pp.187–200. In the same volume the study by Mario Grignaschi, 'La valeur du témoignage des sujets non-Musulmans (*dhimmi*) dan l'empire ottoman', pp.211–323, indicates that torture was not the only issue in which muftis found themselves at odds with imperial policy. In addition to the sources cited above, the essay by Mohammed Arkoun, 'The Death Penalty and Torture in Islamic Thought', in Böckle and Pohier (eds), *The Death Penalty and Torture*, pp.75–82, is a stimulating comparison between classical and modern Islamic law, with references to further literature. In 1982, the bar associations in Morocco called for an end to extraordinary criminal procedures, citing Islamic tradition as one of the juridical grounds for the appeal. This is described in the Amnesty International report, *Torture in the Eighties* (New York, 1984), pp.35–6.

For torture in Jewish law, see Clemens Thoma, 'The Death Penalty and Torture in the Jewish Tradition', in Böckle and Pohier (eds), *The Death Penalty and Torture*. For torture in Japanese law, see the essay by Ryosuke Ishii, 'The History of Evidence in Japan', *La Preuve*, vol. III, pp.521–34, and the sources cited here.

Although China is not considered in the text, there are some illuminating descriptions of torture in Chinese legal practice in an eighteenth-century Chinese novel, translated into English by Robert van Gulik as *Celebrated Cases of Judge Dee (Dee Goong An): An Authentic Eighteenth-Century Chinese Detective Novel* (rept. New York, 1976). Van Gulik's preface describes the reliability of the story for illuminating Chinese Judicial practice from ancient times to the establishment of the Chinese Republic in 1911.

For torture and the early development of law in Russia, see Daniel H. Kaiser, *The Growth of the Law in Medieval Russia* (Princeton, 1980), the definitive treatment of the subject, with an extensive bibliography. The period from the sixteenth to the nineteenth century is covered, with considerable hostility, in Ronald Hingley, *The Russian Secret Police: Muscovite, Imperial Russian and Soviet Political Security Operations, 1565–1970* (London, 1970). For the later Third Section, see the exemplary scholarly work of P. S. Squire, *The Third Department* (Cambridge, 1968), which also deals in a sophisticated manner with the early nineteenth century. Recent Soviet scholarship is noted in the review *Kritika* 19 (1983), pp.7–15. For later Russian police history, see below, references to chapter 4.

The classic account of torture in England is that of David Jardine, *A Reading on the Use of Torture in the Criminal Law of England Previously to the Commonwealth* (London, 1837). See also the recent extensive survey by James Heath, *Torture and English Law: An Administrative and Legal History from the Plantagenets to the Stuarts* (Westport, 1980), which should be read with Langbein, *Torture and the Law of Proof*, pp.73–179, John Bellamy, *The Tudor Law of Treason* (Toronto, 1979), and G. R. Elton, *Policy and Police* (Cambridge, 1972).

For France, see the generally uncritical work of Peter de Polnay, *Napoleon's Police* (London, 1970), which begins in 1667. Much more useful for the eighteenth century is Alan Williams, *The Police of Paris, 1718–1789* (Baton Rouge, 1979); John A. Carey, *Judicial Reform in France before the Revolution of 1789* (Cambridge, 1981);| Antoinette Wills, *Crime and Punishment in Revolutionary Paris* (Westport, 1981).

A classic work of enduring value on a specialized subject is that of Eugène Hubert, *La Torture au Pays-Bas autrichiens pendant le XVIIIe siècle* (Brussels, 1897). See also P. Parfouru, *La Torture en Bretagne* (Rennes, 1896).

For the problem of police and social order in France during and after the Revolution, see Richard Cobb, *The Police and the People: French Popular Protest, 1789–1820* (Oxford, 1970), and Howard C. Payne, *The Police State of Louis Napoleon Bonaparte, 1851–1860* (Seattle, 1966). For all of Payne's criticism of the police procedures of the Second Empire, he neither mentions nor indexes torture. Mellor, *La Torture*, deals extensively with nineteenth-century France, as does the fine recent study by Gordon Wright,

Between the Guillotine and Liberty: Two Centuries of the Crime Problem in France (New York, 1983), which does not, unfortunately, deal extensively with the police. Consideration of England, France and Germany should also be made in terms of Barton L. Ingraham's *Political Crime in Europe: A Comparative Study of France, Germany and England* (California, 1979). The thesis of Michel Foucault is laid out in his *Discipline and Punish: The Birth of the Prison* (New York, 1977), trans. Alan Sheridan. Sheridan in turn has devoted several illuminating pages to Foucault's study in his own *Michel Foucault: The Will to Truth* (London, 1980), pp.135–63. There is also a long discussion in Hubert L. Dreyfus and Paul Rabinow, *Michel Foucault: Beyond Structuralism and Hermeneutics* (Chicago, 1982), pp.143–67, and an active debate in Michelle Perrot (ed.), *L'Impossible Prison. Recherches sur le systeme pénitentiaire au XIXe siècle. Débat avec Michel Foucault* (Paris, 1980).

For those with an interest in the forms of punishment of the *ancien régime* there is a veritable encyclopedia on the subject in Hans von Hentig, *Die Strafe* (2 vols., Berlin, Göttingen and Heidelberg, 1954). On torture chambers and prisons, see vol. II, pp.178–83. Von Hentig also provides a description and extensive commentary and bibliography on medieval and early modern punishments in general in his essay, 'The Pillory: A Medieval Punishment', in von Hentig, *Studien zur Kriminalgeschichte* (Bern, 1962), pp.112–30.

Chapter 4   *'Engines of the State, not of Law'*

At the margins of the law. The subjects touched upon in this chapter each have considerable bibliographies. I cite only a few works in each category. I have relied upon the relevant chapters of Mellor, *La Torture*, virtually the only study of torture that attempts to deal, however topically, with the whole of the nineteenth and twentieth centuries. In general, I have found much guidance in Hannah Arendt, *The Origins of Totalitarianism* (1951, 2nd edn, New York, 1973) and the works of J. L. Talmon, *The Origins of Totalitarian Democracy* (rept. New York, 1970), *Political Messianism: The Romantic Phase* (New York, 1960), and *The Myth of the Nation and the Vision of Revolution* (Berkeley and Los Angeles, 1980). *La Preuve*, vol. IV, is also important, as well as the studies of Otto Kirchheimer cited below in this bibliography.

The police and the state. For the USA there is a large literature. Particularly useful are the works of Wilbur R. Miller, *Cops and Bobbies: Police Authority in New York and London, 1830–1870* (Chicago, 1970), Samuel Walker, *Popular Justice* (New York, 1980) and Eric H. Monkkonen, *Police in Urban America 1860–1920* (Cambridge, 1981), the last with much original material and an extensive bibliography. Ernest Jerome Hopkins, *Our Lawless Police*

(1931), and Emmanuel H. Lavine, *The Third Degree: American Police Methods* (1933), both remain the best popular expositions of the materials in the Wickersham Report, which is technically the *Report* of the National Commission on Law Observance and Enforcement (Washington, D.C.: U.S. Government Printing Office, 1930–1), Publications, No.1–14. For England and France, see the bibliographical discussion for chapter 3.

On the survival of torture in Naples and Austria during this period, see Ruthven, *Torture: The Grand Conspiracy*, 159–82.

Warfare, prisoners and military intelligence. The best general discussion of warfare, prisoners, and military intelligence in the light of the subject of this book is that of Mellor, *La Torture*.

Political crime. There is an immense bibliography on the problem of political crime and political justice, not all of it reliable. For the later Middle Ages, see S. H. Cutler, *The Law of Treason and Treason Trials in Later Medieval France* (Cambridge, 1982), and John Bellamy, *The Tudor Law of Treason* (Toronto, 1979), and in general, Pierre A. Papadatos, *Le Délit politique. Contribution a l'étude des crimes contre l'état* (Geneva, 1955). For the modern period, see Ingraham, *Political Crime in Europe*. For the purposes of this study, see especially Otto Kirchheimer, *Political Justice* (Princeton, 1961), idem, *Politics, Law and Social Change*, ed. Frederick S. Burin and Kurt L. Shell (New York, 1969), and idem, with Georg Rusche, *Punishment and Social Structure* (New York, 1939).

Of political crimes, the most important for this study have been treason and witchcraft, but in the nineteenth and twentieth centuries they have been ideological crime and terrorism. For the latter, see Walter Laqueur, *Terrorism* (Boston, 1977); and the studies edited by Yonah Alexander and Kenneth A. Myers, *Terrorism in Europe* (New York, 1982): cf. Hannah Arendt, *Crises of the Republic* (New York, 1972), esp. chapter 3, 'On Violence'.

Law and the state in revolutionary societies. The literature on fascist states is large, but the literature on fascist legal procedure is small. In addition to Mellor, *La Torture*, and Kirchheimer, *Political Justice*, the latter being the finest general study of modern jurisprudence of political crime, see for Italy, H. Arthur Steiner, *Government in Fascist Italy* (New York, 1938), pp.83–8; Gaetano Salvemini, *The Fascist Dictatorship in Italy* (New York, 1927), esp. chapters 3–4; Herman Finer, *Mussolini's Italy* (rept. Hamden, Ct. 1964), esp. parts III–IV. Some of the most important contributions to the study of Nazi legal ideas have been those of Peter Schneider: see, for example, 'Rechtssicherheit und richterliche Unabhängigkeit aus der Sicht des SD', *Vierteljahrshefte für Zeitgeschichte*, 4 (1956), 399–422. See also the large literature on the Nuremberg trials, as well as Arendt, *Crises of the Republic* and *The Origins of Totalitarianism*, and Ingraham, *Political Crime in Europe*.

A superb treatment of Germany is that of Otto Kirchheimer, *Von der Weimarer Republik zum Fascismus: Die Auflösung der demokratischen Rechtsordnungen* (Berlin, 1976). There is extensive critical discussion of the problem of Nazi torture in Ruthven, *Torture: The Grand Conspiracy*, pp.286–91.

The place of law in Soviet thought derives, through Lenin, from marxist legal thought. Three recent works contain good analyses of that thought: Maureen Cain and Alan Hunt, *Marx and Engels on the Law* (London, 1979); Paul Phillips, *Marx and Engels on Law and Laws* (Oxford, 1979); and Hugh Collins, *Marxism and the Law* (Oxford, 1982). Soviet legal thought must also be considered in terms of conventional crime and political crime, for the differences between procedures in each case are considerable. For the former, see Vladimir Gsovski and Kazimierz (eds), *Government, Law and Courts in the Soviet Union and Eastern Europe* (2 vols., New York, 1960), and more recently, Harold J. Berman and James W. Spindler (ed. and trans.), *Soviet Criminal Law and Procedure: The RSFSR Codes* (Cambridge, Mass., 1972). In *La Preuve*, vol. IV, see the studies by Jan Gwiazdomorski and Marian Cieslak, 'La Preuve judiciare dans les pays socialistes a l'époque contemporaine', and J. D. Kprevaar, 'La Preuve en droit| soviétique'. For criminology, see Peter H. Solomon, *Soviet Criminologists and Criminal Policy* (New York, 1978), and L. Fuller. 'Pashukanis and Vyshinsky', *Michigan Law Review* 47 (1949), pp.1159ff.

On political crime and the Cheka, see George Leggett, *The Cheka: Lenin's Political Police* (Oxford, 1981), the most thorough and best documented of all studies on the subject, and Lennard D. Gerson, *The Secret Police in Lenin's Russia* (Philadelphia, 1976), both with extensive bibliographies and documentation. Ruthven, *Torture: The Grand Conspiracy*, pp.218–78, offers an extensive and original treatment of these themes.

On relation between marxism and current Soviet practice, see R. W. Makepeace, *Marxist Ideology and Soviet Criminal Law* (London, 1980), Ivo Lapenna, *Soviet Penal Policy* (Toronto, 1968). The best recent study, O. S. Joffe, *Razvirie tsvilisncheskoi mysli v S.S.S.R.* (Leningrad, 1975), has not yet been translated into English.

The discovery of Algeria. For South Africa, see Hilda Bernstein, *South Africa: The Terrorism of Torture*, International Defense and Aid Fund, Christian Action Publications (London, 1972), and Albie Sachs, *Justice in South Africa* (London, 1973); William R. Frye, *In Whitest Africa: The Dynamics of Apartheid* (Englewood Cliffs, N.J., 1968). The classic work on the subject from the perspective of the colonized is that of Frantz Fanon, *The Wretched of the Earth* (rept. New York, 1968).

An example of early European concern for colonial practices like those discussed in this chapter is the *Report of the Commissioners for the Investigation of Alleged Cases of Torture in the Madras Presidency* (Madras, 1855); there is a thorough discussion of the circumstances and the context in Ruthven, *Torture: The Grand Conspiracy*, pp.183–217.

The best and most concise account of the problem of torture in Algeria is that of Alistair Horne, *A Savage War of Peace: Algeria, 1954–1962* (New York, 1977), a work to which I am much indebted. One of the most influential works to come out of Algeria during this period is that of Henri Alleg, *The Question*, trans. John Calder, with an introduction by Jean-Paul Sartre (New York, 1958). There is very little else in English. Among the indispensable works in French, see Pierre-Henri Simon, *Contre la torture* (Paris, 1957); Pierre Vidal-Naquet, *L'Affaire Audin* (Paris, 1958); idem, *La Raison d'état. Textes publiés par le Comité Maurice Audin* (Paris, 1962), the latter containing the text of the Willaume Report of 1955, pp.55–68, and other documents issued in the matter between 1954 and 1961. Vidal-Naquet's *Torture: Cancer of Democracy* first appeared in a French translation in 1972, as *La Torture dans la République*. In addition, see Fanon, *The Wretched of the Earth*.

The question of torture in France proper is considered in P. Péju, *Les Harkis à Paris* (Paris, 1961).

The most recent work of Alec Mellor, *Je dénonce la torture* (Tours, 1972), offers an analytical and topical history of torture in terms of confession, military and political information, and totalitarian politics, and in its fourth chapter deals with what the French now apparently term *Massuisme* – the justification of torture in extraordinary circumstances, a theme that is prominent in the memoirs of Gen. Jacques Massu, *La Vraie Bataille d'Alger* (Paris, 1971). The chapter is well-informed and substantial.

In one sense, at least, the American experience in Vietnam, particularly in its social and political consequences, served as an equivalent discovery made by one society about aspects of itself that parallels the French discoveries about Algeria a decade before. Although there is an immense literature on the subject, particularly representative without specifically mentioning torture is Nevitt Sanford, Craig Comstock, et al., *Sanctions for Evil* (San Francisco, 1971). There is a good general discussion of Vietnam in context in Telford Taylor, *Nuremberg and Vietnam: An American Tragedy* (New York, 1970), with extensive bibliographical references in the notes.

Chapter 5   *'To become, or to remain, human . . .'*

A new Enlightenment? Convenient texts of the United Nations documents, as well as the European Convention on Human Rights, may be found in Ian Brownlie, *Basic Documents on Human Rights* (2nd edn, Oxford, 1981), and in part VI of idem, *Basic Documents in International Law* (3rd edn, Oxford,

1983), both with useful annotation. Other collections include James Avery Joyce, *Human Rights: International Documents* (3 vols., Alphen, 1978). A good recent study of how international law operates in this context is Paul Sieghart, *The International Law of Human Rights* (Oxford, 1983).

See also B. G. Ramcharan (ed.), *Human Rights: Thirty Years after the Universal Declaration* (The Hague, 1979).

On current differing views of the nature and priority of human rights, see Fouad Ajami, *Human Rights and World Order Politics*, World Order Models Project, Working Paper No. 4, Institute for World Order (New York, 1978).

There is a complete edition of the preparatory materials for the European Convention on Human Rights: *Collected Edition of the 'Travaux Préparatoires'/Receuil des 'Travaux Préparatoires'* covering 1949–50 (7 vols., The Hague, 1957–79). For subsequent years, see *European Convention on Human Rights, Collected Texts/Convention européenne des droits de l'homme, Receuil de textes* (8th edn, Strasbourg, 1972). For the history of the application of the convention, see J. E. S. Fawcett, *The Application of the European Convention on Human Rights* (Oxford, 1969), and Frede Castberg, *The European Convention on Human Rights*, ed. Torkel Opsahl and Thomas Ouchterlony (Leiden and Dobbs Ferry, 1974). The Council of Europe also publishes an annual review, European Commission of Human Rights, *Annual Review/Compte Rendu Annuel* (Strasbourg, 1973–). There is a good introduction for the general reader in David P. Forsythe, *Human Rights and World Politics* (Lincoln and London, 1983), and a sophisticated exchange of very differing views on the part of experts in D. D. Raphael (ed.), *Political Theory and the Rights of Man* (Bloomington, 1967). See now also the Council of Europe, *Bibliography Relating to the European Convention on Human Rights* (Strasbourg, 1978) and Hurst Hannum (ed.), *Guide to International Human Rights Practice* (Philadelphia, 1984).

There is much documentation on torture and related offences against human rights in *Human Rights and the Phenomenon of Disappearance*, Hearings before the Subcommittee on International Organizations of the Committee on Foreign Affairs, House of Representatives, Ninety-Sixth Congress, First Session (Washington, D.C., 1980). Focusing chiefly on Latin America, the hearings offer a vivid context for the subject of this book. They are also eloquent testimony to the information elicited by the human rights policies of the Carter administration between 1976 and 1980.

The language of Eden. There is hardly a more accurate portrait of the mixture of intellectual confusion, anger and violence in the twentieth-century world than V. S. Naipaul, *The Return of Eva Perón* (New York, 1981).

On political language, aside from the works of Orwell themselves, I would suggest tracing the theme in the biography of Bernard Crick, *George Orwell: A Life* (Boston, 1980), a more reliable guide than the four volumes of *Essays and Letters*, which is not complete, and more accurate than other Orwell studies. See also Doris Lessing, *Documents Relating to the Sentimental Agents in the Volyen Empire* (New York, 1983). The debate over Arendt is responsibly described in Stephen J. Whitfield, *Into the Dark: Hannah Arendt and Totalitarianism* (Philadelphia, 1980).

After Algeria. Two studies of Amnesty International are: Egon Larson, *A Flame in Barbed Wire: The Story of Amnesty International* (New York, 1979), and Jonathan Power, *Amnesty International: The Human Rights Story* (New York, 1981). Both discuss the campaign against torture, although Larson's historical observations are not reliable, and Power's are based on Larson's. Amnesty International publications are available from various national headquarters, a list of which is appended to Power's book. Besides those cited in the text, there is a report on the *Republic of Korea: Violations of Human Rights* (1981), and in March 1984, Amnesty International published its extensive report *Torture in the Eighties* (London and New York).

For the Timerman case, see Jacopo Timerman, *Prisoner Without a Name, Cell Without a Number* (New York, 1981), trans. Toby Talbot, and the useful bibliography of the 'Timerman Case' in the review by Michael Walzer, 'Timerman and His Enemies', *New York Review of Books*, 24 Sept. 1981; Timerman's latest reflections are described in Jacopo Timerman, 'Return to Argentina', *New York Times Magazine*, 11 March 1984, 36f.

It is important to note that Amnesty International research has influenced scholarship as well. Peter Flynn's *Brazil: A Political Analysis* (London and Boulder, Colo., 1978) makes extensive use of the *Amnesty International Report on Allegations of Torture in Brazil* (London, 1977), and with its help, Flynn's account is a model of its kind. The kind of attention that such research and energy can bring to a subject often concealed by its perpetrators is illustrated by a comparison of Flynn's work to two independent works on torture in Argentina somewhat earlier: Roberto Estrella, *Tortura (Reportaje al Horror) 1943–1955* (Buenos Aires, 1956), and Raul Lamas, *Los Torturadores. Crimines y Tormentos en las Carceles Argentinas* (Buenos Aires, 1956).

Since 1970, torture has been the subject of a large number of publications, not all of which have been available to me. I cite here C. de Goustine, *La Torture* (Paris, 1976); A. Guindon, *La Pédagogie de la crainte* (Montreal and Paris, 1975); Gustav Keller, *Die Psychologie der Folter* (1978).

For Greece, besides Amnesty International's *Torture in Greece: The First Torturer's Trial 1975*, see especially the stunning and eloquent memoir by Nicholas Gage, *Eleni* (New York, 1983).

Testimony of torturers themselves is recorded in J. Victor, *Confessiones de un Torturador* (Barcelona, 1981), the author's name being a pseudonym for a group of torturers.

Room 101 – and other rooms. I have relied heavily upon Ronald Melzack and Patrick D. Wall, *The Challenge of Pain* (New York, 1983), a revision of Melzack's earlier pioneering work, *The Puzzle of Pain* (New York, 1973). On the physiology of torture, see J. Corominas and J.M. Farré, *Contra la Tortura* (Barcelona, 1978). I must again thank John T. Conroy, MD, for his advice about this section.

A brief history of recent professional awareness on the part of the medical profession is the article by Michael Kosteljanetz and Ole Aalund, 'Torture: A Challenge to Medical Science', *Interdisciplinary Science Reviews*, 8 (1983), with an extensive reference literature in the notes. I have very gratefully profited from a number of research papers provided me by the Internationalt Rehabiliterings- og Forskningscenter for Torturofre (RCT), the Torture Rehabilitation Centre, in Copenhagen, Denmark, whose director, Dr Inge Kemp Genefke, has played a prominent role in sensitizing the world medical profession to torture as a therapeutic and ethical problem. Much of my discussion of somatic and psychological sequelae to modern torture derives from the research papers of the RCT.

The Declaration of the World Medical Association at Tokyo in 1975 may be found in the *World Medical Journal*, 22, (1975), pp.87–8. Further texts are in *Professional Codes of Ethics*, Amnesty International Publications (1976); for the declaration of the Spanish Society of Psychosomatic Medicine and Psychotherapy at Lérida in 1977, see *Psiquiatrika* I/78, vol.I, no.1 (1978), pp.62–3. It is discussed by A. M. Ruiz-Mateos Jiminez de Tejada, 'Medical Care of Prisoners', in Böckle and Pohier (eds), *The Death Penalty and Torture*, pp.114–18.

Without end? The best recent survey of the present and the immediate future is the Amnesty International Publication, *Torture in the Eighties* (New York, 1984). The best survey of ideas for altering the future of torture is the pamphlet published by the International Commission of Jurists and the Swiss Committee Against Torture, *Torture: How to Make the International Convention Effective*, 2nd edn (Geneva, 1980). The debate – and the literature – will no doubt go on.

In August 1984, the Deutsche Presse-Agentur, a German news service, announced that the Swedish Red Cross plans to open a rehabilitation center in Stockholm for torture victims, along the lines of the RCT in Copenhagen. The news is not always bad. In November 1984, Amnesty International announced that half the member nations of the UN practise torture. Nor is the news invariably good.

Bibliographical Addendum: Torture— History and Practice, 1985–1995

Torture is a subject whose history continues to be studied and whose practice also continues. But its practice is also studied. We benefit from both kinds of study.

I

This account of recent historical research is discussed chronologically.

The best recent study specifically of torture in ancient Greece, but in a broad context of epistemology and intellectual history, is that of Page DuBois, *Torture and Truth* (New York-London, 1991). DuBois includes the most detailed discussion so far of the semantic history of the term *basanos* and its place in the mental world of fifth- and fourth-century Greece. As important has been the appearance of a number of recent studies in the larger area of criminal law and punishment in the ancient world. Most comprehensive among these is Mary Margaret Mackenzie, *Plato on Punishment* (Berkeley-Los Angeles, 1981); like DuBois's study, it is a wide-ranging address to questions as germane in the late twentieth century as in antiquity. Both these studies provide eloquent evidence of the value of what might otherwise seem to be recondite research to troubling aspects of the present human condition.

A number of studies have examined torture in the larger context of theories and practice of punishment and criminal law generally. The best of these are the volume *Du châtiment dans la cité: Supplices corporels et peine de mort dans le monde antique*, Collection de l'École Française de Rome 79 (Rome, 1984); Israel Drapkin, *Crime and Punishment in the Ancient World* (Lexington-Toronto, 1989); *La Peine/Punishment*, Receuils de la Société Jean Bodin pour l'Histoire Comparative des Institutions, Vol. 55, *Antiquité/Antiquity* (Brussels, 1991); Eva Cantarella, *I supplizi capitali in Grecia e in Roma* (Milan, 1991); Cinzia Vismara, *Il supplizio come spettacolo* (Rome, 1990). The use of terror in Roman law is analyzed in Alan Watson, "Law in a Reign of Terror," *Law and History Review* 3 (1985), 163–68. In much of the ancient world, both interrogative and punitive torture often shaded into aggravated sentences of death, the best known of which is crucifixion. On crucifixion, see Martin Hengel, *Crucifixion in the Ancient World and the Folly of the Message of the Cross* (Philadelphia, 1977)

The revival and reinterpretation of Roman law in the late eleventh and twelfth centuries and the emergence of a universally accepted and studied canon law led to the establishment of what the jurists called *Ius commune*, the "common law"—or the common learned law—of continental Europe. The best study of this process is that of Manlio Bellomo, *The Common Legal Past of Europe, 1000–1800*, trans. Lydia G. Cochrane (Washington, D.C., 1995). The broadest aspects of the process are surveyed by various scholars in the volume *La Peine/Punishment*, Receuils de la Société Jean Bodin pour l'Histoire Comparative des Institutions, Vol. 56, *L'Europe avant le XVIIIe siècle/Europe Before the Eighteenth Century* (Brussels, 1991). One element of the new learned law was the creation of the doctrine of notoriety of crimes and that of the infamy, the ill fame, of individuals who might be accused of crime. On infamy, see my essay, "Wounded Names: The Medieval Doctrine of Infamy," in *Law in Mediaeval Life and Thought*, ed. Edward B. King and Susan J. Ridyard, Sewanee Mediaeval Studies, 5 (Sewanee, Tenn., 1990), 43–89. The relationship of infamy to torture and to criminal legal procedure generally has now been traced in two important articles by Richard Fraher: "Preventing Crime in the High Middle Ages: The Medieval Lawyers' Search for Deterrence," in *Popes, Teachers, and Canon Law in the Middle Ages*, ed. James Ross Sweeney and Stanley Chodorow (Ithaca-London, 1989), 212–233, and "Conviction According to Conscience: The Medieval Jurists' Debate Concerning Judicial Discretion and the Law of Proof," *Law and History Review* 7 (1989), 23–88. Both studies have substantial remarks on the theory and practice of torture.

On the literature concerning procedure, see now Linda Fowler-Magerl, *Ordines iudiciarii and Libelli de ordine iudiciorum*, Typologie des Sources du Moyen Âge Occidental, Fasc. 63 (Turnhout, 1994).

Both the theory and the practice of torture are invoked in the excellent detailed study of Johannes Fried on the destruction of the Order of Knights Templar in early fourteenth-century France and elsewhere: "Wille, Freiwilligkeit und Geständnis um 1300: Zur Beurteilung des letzten Templergrossmeisters Jacques de Molay," *Historisches Jahrbuch* 105 (1985), 388–425. The results of Fried's scholarship as well as that of Fowler-Magerl and the present volume are assessed in Kenneth Pennington, *The Prince and the Law, 1200–1600: Sovereignty and Rights in the Western Legal Tradition* (Berkeley-Los Angeles, 1993), esp. 132–64. Dealing with some of the same materials, although from a strongly anthropological approach and using some dated sources, is Talal Asad, "Notes on Body Pain and Truth in Medieval Christian Ritual," *Economy and Society* 12 (1983), 287–327. Some of the ecclesiastical history is traced from a quite different perspective in F. Compagnoni, *La Peine de mort et la torture dans la tradition de l'Église catholique romaine* (Paris, 1979).

One particular aspect of torture in the Italian city-republics is considered in Mario Sbriccoli, "*Tormentum id est torquere mentem*: Processo inquisitorio e interrogatorio per tortura in Italia comunale," in *La Parola all'accusato*, ed. Jean-Claude Maire Vigueur and Agostino Paravicini (Palermo, 1991).

The theory and practice of criminal jurisprudence in one major Italian city-republic is considered in Laura Ikins Stern, *The Criminal Law System of Medieval and Renaissance Florence* (Baltimore, 1994), with considerable attention paid to torture. For the case of learned law in Germany during the same period, see Winfried Trusen, "Strafprozess und Rezeption: Zu den Entwicklung im Spätmittelalter und den Grundlagen der Carolina," in *Strafrecht, Strafprozess und Rezeption: Grunbdlagen, Entwicklung und Wirkung der Constitutio Criminalis Carolina*, ed. Peter Landau and Friedrich-Christian Schroeder (Frankfurt, 1984), 29–118, with detailed attention to the problem of torture. For France, see Robert Muchembled, *Le Temps des supplices: De l'obeissance sous les rois absolus, XVe–VIIIe siècle* (Paris, 1992), and Alfred Soman, *Sorcellerie et justice criminelle: Le Parlement de Paris, 16e–18e siècles* (London, 1992).

Two recent studies examine the criminal justice process broadly across early modern Europe, including torture: Pieter Spierenburg, *The Spectacle of Suffering: Executions and the Evolution of Repression from a preindustrial Metropolis to the European Experience* (Cambridge-New York, 1984), and Richard Van Dülmen, *Theatre of Horror: Crime and Punishment in Early Modern Germany*, trans. Elisabeth Neu (Cambridge, 1990). On the depiction of torments in art, see the classic study of Samuel Y. Edgerton, Jr., *Pictures and Punishment: Art and Criminal Prosecution During the Florentine Renaissance* (Ithaca-London, 1985), and Lionello Puppi, *Torment in Art: Pain, Violence and Martyrdom* (New York, 1991).

By far the most extensive and detailed study of the criminal jurisprudence of the later old regime is that of Richard Mowery Andrews, *Law, Magistracy, and Crime in Old Regime Paris, 1735–1789*, Vol. I, *The System of Criminal Justice* (Cambridge, 1994), 441–72. Andrews's exhaustive research does much to change our view of the routine severity of criminal justice at the end of the Old Regime. On the nineteenth century in France, see now Benjamin F. Martin, *Crime and Criminal Justice Under the Third Republic: The Shame of Marianne* (Baton Rouge, La., 1990), a study that considers the development of the French criminal justice system and its inability to prevent the growth of official brutality. It should be read with the important study by Douglas Porch, *The French Secret Services: From the Dreyfus Affair to the Gulf War* (New York, 1995).

The *Discurso sobre la tortura* of the eighteenth-century Spanish magistrate and writer Juan Pablo Forner (1756–1797) has been edited with an extensive critical introduction and bibliography by Santiago Mollfulleda: *Juan Pablo Forner, Discurso sobre la tortura* (Barcelona, 1990). There is a broad account of the history of Spanish torture and forms of public execution in Juan Esclava, *Verdugos y torturadores* (Madrid, 1991).

The most comprehensive and ambitious attempt to locate the use of torture in the process of modernization in a single extensive case study is that of Darius Rejali, *Torture and Modernity: Self, Society, and State in Modern Iran* (Boulder-San Francisco-Oxford, 1993). By considering Iran from the late nineteenth century to the present, Rejali has produced a work whose importance extends far beyond Iranian history.

The background to Algeria has been greatly illuminated by two studies. David Prochaska, *Making Algeria French* (Cambridge, 1990), reveals the profound differences between colonists and native Algerians that lay at the root of the disturbances leading to the French-Algerian war. Rita Maran, *Torture: The Role of Ideology in the French Algerian War* (New York, 1989) is the first of several volumes planned by Maran that locate torture in the ideology of French Algeria.

There is a recent and comprehensive study of Nazi justice by Ingo Muller, *Hitler's Justice: The Courts of the Third Reich* (Cambridge, Mass., 1991), and for the background, Hsi-Huey Liang, *The Rise of Modern Police and the European State System from Metternich to the Second World War* (New York-Cambridge, 1992).

On Greece, Professor Mika Haritos-Fatouros of the University of Thessaloniki has published a number of studies that deal with torture under the regime of the colonels: "The Official Torturer: A Learning Model for Obedience to the Authority of Violence," *Journal of Applied Psychology* 18 (1988), 1107–1120; with Janice T. Gibson, "The Education of a Torturer," *Psychology Today* (November 1986), 50–58; "Die Ausbilding des Folterers," in *Folter: Zur Analyse eines Herrschaftsmittels*, ed. Jan Philipp Reemtsma (Hamburg, 1991), 73–91. Her forthcoming book, *The Psychology of Torture* (New Haven, Conn.) will be the major work on the subject.

Nicholas Gage's memoir of his mother, Eleni Gatzoyannis, and his own search for her killer, *Eleni*, has been made into a film. It reflects accurately the occasions of torture both in postwar Greece and the world that succeeded it. Although the members of the film's cast traveled to the historical locations in Greece, the film had to be made in Spain, apparently because of the strong emotions that survive in Greece itself. With Gillo Pontecvorvo's *The Battle of Algiers* of 1966 it adds substantially to the small body of reliable filmography of torture.

It is appropriate to end this part of a bibliographical survey with the case of Greece and the aftermath of a torture regime. Christopher Hitchens has commented on that world:

A new garden is being created [in Athens] on a most unpromising site. Named *Parko Eleftheria*, or Freedom Park, it occupies the space that was tenanted until 1974 by the torture centre of ESA, the junta's military police. Those who remember those days have to check themselves from crossing the road at that point, and some of those who saw the inside of the building are incapable of speech. There was nothing to do but raze it after the restoration of democracy, turning the ancillary buildings into a hospital. As the grass grows over the scene, forming an extension to the Venizelos monument, and as cafés spring up to cater for the young couples who stroll by, it seems a pity that there is no plaque or inscription to immerse the casual visitor, however briefly, in acknowledgement. There would be an oblique tribute to continuity in that, too.

But there are other continuities in Greek life. In the thirteenth book of *The Odyssey*, Odysseus, finally washed up on the shore of his own Ithaka, but not knowing where he is, wonders:

> What am I in for now?
> Whose country have I come to this time? Rough
> Savages and outlaws are they, or
> godfearing people, friendly to castaways?
>
> (XIII, 200–203)

Hubristai or *philoxenoi*? It is a question that twentieth-century castaways must ask too, and never only, and now no longer in Greece. Of all the world's countries, Greece is still the only one to have asked that question of itself and publicly to have answered it.

There is another word that runs through much of Greek history, *philanthropia*. It is a concept severely tested by twentieth-century questions of human rights and human dignity. It may be expressed in ambitious declarations of principle on the international level, and in diplomacy, but it is invariably tested in individual households, churches, villages, and countries, full of human beings with passions and memories. And it is in a precarious balance of passions and memories that twentieth-century lives are lived in twentieth-century states. The early fifteenth-century Italian humanist and Chancellor of Florence, Leonardo Bruni, was one of the first to define what we may call the political dimensions of *philanthropia*, and his definition still holds good:

> Fellow citizens should hate one another in such a way that they do not forget that they are fellow citizens.

It is a minimalist *philanthropia*, indeed, but in many matters minimalism may be the only degree available, and it is vastly preferable to all lesser alternatives. The modern Greek experience, for all its shortcomings and bitter memories, now stands again alone, as a model for others.

II

The contemporary practice of torture is now better documented in many respects than ever before. The improved documentation appears to have done little to curtail the practice. Part of the problem stems from the disagreement over the priority of political or economic rights, usually represented respectively by western and by developing countries, intelligently considered in a *New York Times* editorial of June 13, 1993. This difference is reflected in the patterns adopted in countries in which torture regimes have been replaced by regimes that do not torture, but which nevertheless have to face the continuing consequences of past torture and the presence of former torturers in their midst. For a consideration of the atrocious past in a peaceful present, see Ian Buruma, *The Wages of Guilt: Memories of War in Germany and Japan* (New York, 1994). In Uruguay and El Salvador, amnesties have been given to torturers and other violators of human rights under previous regimes—in Uruguay by popular vote, in El Salvador by legislative act. The problem of reconciliation, however, is solved by neither process. A number of commentators have suggested that the very least a reformed state must do in this respect is to acknowledge publicly that torture had occurred, to pronounce governmental authorities responsible for it, and to pledge that it will not occur again. This minimalist approach also appears to satisfy the chief needs of torture victims—that their suffering will be testified to and that it will not be muffled in public silence. There is a serious discussion of the problem in the article by Ronald D. Crelinsten, "After the Fall: Prosecuting Perpetrators of Gross Human Rights Violations," *PIOOM Newsletter and Progress Report* 5 (1993), 4–7. On PIOOM, see below. See also Reemtsma, ed., *Folter: Zur Analyse eines Herrschaftsmittels*, and Lawrence Weschler, *A Miracle, a Universe: Settling Accounts with Torturers* (New York, 1990). But there are also many places where the torture has not stopped and still others in which, although it has stopped, accounts are still open.

Continuing reports of investigations conducted by Amnesty International, Middle East Watch, Helsinki Watch, and Human Rights Watch have provided descriptions of torture in particular states, most recently summed up in the *Human Rights Watch World Report 1994* (New Haven, Conn., 1995) and *Human Rights Watch 1995* (New York-Washington, 1995), a survey of sixty countries. In 1985, the year in which the present book was first published, Amnesty International accused South Korea of employing torture. The next year Helsinki Watch charged that torture was extensively used in

Turkish prisons, and a letter in *The Lancet* of June 10, 1989 issued by members of the London-based Medical Foundation for the Care of Victims of Torture repeated the charge, citing specifically its anti-Kurdish direction. Amnesty International reported on Israeli torture in 1993, charges which the Israeli government answered in a remarkable report to the Public Committee Against Torture in Israel. In turn, there appeared the study by Human Rights Watch, *Torture and Ill-Treatment: Israel's Interrogation of Palestinians from the Occupied Territories* (New York, 1994), and Neve Gordon and Ruchama Marcus have edited an important collection of essays with a strong medical component: *Torture: Human Rights, Medical Ethics and the Case of Israel* (London-Atlantic Highlands, N.J., 1995). These are simply isolated instances of a broad current of torture that still runs, but is now more frequently than ever reported upon—occasionally bringing changes in its wake, as has been the case in Israel. For individual countries it is advisable to follow the *Human Rights Watch World Reports* and the Amnesty International individual studies. The most recent international protocol is Protocol No. 2 to the European Convention for the Prevention of Torture and Inhuman or Degrading Treatment or Punishment (Strasbourg 4.XI.93), Council of Europe, European Treaty Series 152 (Strasbourg, 1994). The most recent comprehensive study is that of J. Herman Burgers and Hans Danelius, *The United Nations Convention Against Torture* (Dordrecht-Boston, 1988).

Among the most impressive of recent case studies that have used the historical dimension are those of Don Foster, *Detention and Torture in South Africa: Psychological, Legal and Historical Studies* (New York, 1987); Michael Dutton, *Policing and Punishment in China: From Patriarchy to the People* (Cambridge, 1992). A classic work of great importance for much of the Middle East is that of Uriel Heyd, *Studies in Old Ottoman Criminal Law* (Oxford, 1973).

Other recent regional case studies include Amnesty International, *Mexico: Torture with Impunity* (London, 1991); Gavan McCormick and Yoshio Sugimoto, eds., *Democracy in Contemporary Japan* (Armonk, N.Y., 1986), 186–214; Archdiocese of São Paolo, *Torture in Brazil: A Report*, trans. Jaime Wright, ed. Joan Dassin (New York, 1986); Shari Turitz, ed., *Confronting the Heart of Darkness: An International Symposium on Torture in Guatemala* (Washington, D.C., 1993).

The U.S. Alien Tort Statute has also been used successfully by a Paraguayan family against a Paraguayan torturer in the case of *Filártiga v. Peña-Irala* (630F.2d 876, second circuit, 1980), noted in Alexandra Stiglmayer, *Mass Rape* (see below), 218, and by three Ethiopian women in a U.S. court in 1993.

Medical science continues its double role: as inflictor of pain and as a body of healing. Besides the clinical work of Haritos-Fatouros and that of Gordon and Marton cited above, several studies have focused on the participation of members of the medical profession in the infliction of torture. In 1985 members of the American Committee for Human Rights charged Chilean physicians of aiding torturers under the Pinochet regime; Eric Stover and Elena O. Nightingale, eds., *The Breaking of Bodies and Minds: Torture, Psychiatric Abuse, and the Health Professions* (New York, 1985); Richard H. Goldstein and Patrick Breslin, "Technicians of Torture: How Physicians Became Agents of State Terror," *The Sciences* 26 (1986), 14–19. In June 1986 the Swiss section of the International Commission of Health Professionals held a seminar on the subject in Geneva, reported in *The Lancet* of June 28, 1986, and in 1989 the Danish Medical Group of Amnesty International organized the International Medical Congress on Detection and Examination of Human Rights Violations, co-sponsored by the Committee of Concerned Forensic Scientists and the Danish Center of Human Rights. See also Thomas Gordon, *Journey into Madness: Medical Torture and the Mind Controllers* (London, 1988), and *Médecins tortionnaires, médecins résistants*, edited by the Medical Commission of the French Section of Amnesty International and Valérie Marange (Paris, 1989). In 1986 the House of Delegates of the American Medical Association accepted Resolution 91, a condemnation of the participation in torture by physicians. The scholarship in this aspect of the field continues: Metin Basoglu, ed., *Torture and Its Consequences: Current Treatment Approaches* (Cambridge, 1992), and the British Medical Association, *Medicine Betrayed: The Participation of Doctors in Human Rights Abuses* (London-Atlantic Highlands, N.J., 1992). The Amnesty International *Selected Bibliography on the Health Professions and Human Rights* (1990) is comprehensive up to its date of publication.

On the reverse side, medical research on pain itself has developed beyond the stage represented by Melzack and Wall. See David B. Morris, *The Culture of Pain* (Berkeley-Los Angeles, 1992), and Peter Suedfeld, *Psychology and Torture* (New York-Washington, 1990). The most striking discussion is the monograph of Ole Vedel Rasmussen, *Medical Aspects of Torture* (Copenhagen, 1990). Rasmussen's text has been printed as a supplement to the *Danish Medical Bulletin* 37, 1 (1990), 1–88.

The most extensive recent research (aside from that dealing with the treatment of the victims, considered just below) has focused on the torturers. Here the work of Haritos-Fatouros has been path-breaking. At the University of Leiden, the Interdisciplinary Research Program on Root Causes of Human Rights Violations (PIOOM) has produced an important volume of studies on the subject, edited by Alex P. Schmid, research director of PIOOM, and the Canadian scholar Ronald Crelinsten, *The Politics of Pain: Torturers and Their Masters* (The Hague, 1993).

The study of torturers tells us why and how, but the most eloquent testimony—and the greatest urgency—is that of the victims. And for them, the most important center is still the Torture Rehabilitation Center (RCT) in Copenhagen, established in 1982. Its annual reports and its publication, *Torture: Quarterly Journal on Rehabilitation of Torture Victims and Prevention of Torture* (1991–) is still the most impressive record of the current practice, of diagnosis and a specific pathology and forensics of torture, and of steps to rehabilitate its victims. Although a number of other centers have opened since 1982—notably the Canadian Center for Investigation and Prevention of Torture and the Toronto Torture Treatment Center in 1983, the Center for Torture Victims in Minneapolis in 1985, the Marjorie Kovler Center for the Treatment of Torture Survivors in Chicago, and other centers in Europe and the United States—the RCT is still the most important in terms of research and publications. Much of its work has appeared in articles in the journal *Forensic Science International* over the past two decades.

Besides the quarterly journal *Torture*, the RCT has also published several supplementary numbers, particularly *Examining Torture Survivors* (Supplementum No. 1, 1992); Gregorio Martirena, *Uruguay: Torture and Doctors* (Supplementum No. 2, 1992); *Conceptualizing Anxiety in Torture Survivors* (Supplementum No. 1, 1993), and *Physiotherapy to Torture Survivors* (Supplementum No. 1, 1994).

The study of torture victims has also recently and properly expanded to consider the complex questions of the torture of children and women, especially, in the case of the latter in the quite recent recognition of the use of rape as torture.

On the torture of children, see Frederick Ahearn, Jr. and Jean L. Athey, eds., *Refugee Children: Theory, Research, and Services* (Baltimore, 1991); Jorgen Cohn et al., "The Torture of Children: An Investigation of Chilean Immigrant Children in Dennmark: Preliminary Report," *Child Abuse and Neglect* 5, 2 (1981), 201–3; Amnesty International, *Children: The Youngest Victims* (1990); Lois Whitman (for Helsinki Watch), *"Nothing Unusual": The Torture of Children in Turkey* (New York, 1991); Lawyers Committee for Human Rights, *The War Against Children: South Africa's Youngest Victims* (1986).

The emergence of a general recognition of at least some instances of rape as a form of torture, rather than a "sexually or privately motivated offense" distinct from torture, has been eloquently traced by Deborah Blatt, "Recognizing Rape as a Method of Torture," *Review of Law and Social Change* 19, 4 (1992), 821–65. The most recent and best-known instances are discussed in Ivan Lupis, *War Crimes in Bosnia Hercogovina* (New York, 1994), and in Alexandra Stiglmayer, *Mass Rape: The War Against Women in Bosnia-Herzegovina* (Lincoln, Neb., 1994). The best recent literature begins with Ximena Bunster-Burotto, "Surviving Beyond Fear: Women and Torture in Latin America," in *Women and Change in Latin America*, ed. June Nash and Helen Safa (South Hadley, Mass., 1985), 297–325, and continues with F. Allodi and S. Stiasny, "Women as Torture Victims," *Canadian Journal of*

Psychiatry 35 (1990), 144–48, and X. Fornazzari and M. Freire, "Women as Victims of Torture," *Acta Psychiatria Scandinavia* 82 (1990), 257–60. The most recent studies are those of Inge Lunde and Jorgen Ortmann, "Sexual Torture," in Basoglu, *Torture and Its Consequences*, 310–33; Barbara Chester, "Women and Political Torture: Work with Refugee Survivors in Exile," *Women and Therapy* 137, 3 (1992), 209–20, and S. K. Ghosh, *Torture and Rape in Police Custody: An Analysis* (New Delhi, 1993).

From the eighteenth century on, torture became a conspicuous component of various kinds of fiction. I have traced some of the process in my book *Inquisition* (New York, 1988; Berkeley-Los Angeles, 1989), and there is an interesting example of some of the imagery in the United States in Jenny Franchot, *Roads to Rome: The Antebellum Protestant Encounter with Catholicism* (Berkeley-Los Angeles, 1994), Index, s.v., Torture. The subject continues to inspire novelists as well as filmmakers. One of the most interesting of recent novels is Jonathan Dee, *The Liberty Campaign* (New York-London, 1993), a subtle examination of the encounter between an American suburbanite and a former Brazilian torturer in the ordinary setting of a late twentieth-century prosperous American town.

This addendum was completed in September 1995. The literature—and the practice—continue.

Appendix: Judicial Torture— Documents and Commentary

Some of the following documents were originally published as an appendix to my edition of Henry Charles Lea, *Torture*, published by the University of Pennsylvania Press in 1973. That book in turn was a separate reprint of Part IV of Lea's 1866 *Superstition and Force*, a pioneering work in legal history in the United States. Since the book is out of print, it seemed worthwhile to print these documents with others added for this edition in translation, with new commentary, again as an appendix, this time to a new edition of my own *Torture*.

One of the marked differences between the uses of torture in preindustrial and modern Europe (and the world) is that those who concerned themselves with torture in the Greek, Roman, medieval, and early modern European worlds wrote about it abundantly. Those who employ it today do not. The modern work, except when it is revealed by conquest, revolution, or the testimony of victims and occasional reformed torturers, must be found out by indirect means—by the inquiry of human rights groups, individuals, and the pathologists and other professional staff members of the various torture rehabilitation centers. Their work, too, is documentation, but it is more readily available than the materials included here, ranging from imperial Rome to the eighteenth century, with a few exemplary texts from the twentieth century.

I
The *Theodosian Code*, Book 9, Title 35

The *Theodosian Code*, issued by Theodosius II in 437, was the first official imperial collection of law in the Roman Empire. It was replaced a century later by the *Code* and *Digest* of Justinian, but the latter texts remained little known in western Europe, and the *Theodosian Code* was the form of Roman imperial law that most influenced later Germanic written law codes, including that of the Visigoths (below, No. V). On the work itself, see Jill Harries and Ian Wood, *The Theodosian Code* (Ithaca, N.Y., 1993).

TITLE 35:

Judicial Examination Under Torture (De Quaestionibus)

1. Emperors Valentinian, Valens, and Gratian Augustuses to Olybrius, Prefect of the City

No person whatever, without the consultation of knowledge of the Emperor, shall be stripped either of his position in the imperial service or of the defense of his birth and high rank, for the purpose of compelling him to submit to torture with cords, except in case of high treason, in which there is only one and the same status for all. Those persons also shall be subjected to judicial examinations under torture, without the restriction requiring a reference of the case to the Emperor, if by clear proofs they are shown to have forged Our imperial subscriptions. In this case, it is Our will that not even the assumption of the name of palatine shall exempt anyone from such judicial examination under torture.

Given on the eighth day before the ides of July in the year of the consulship of Emperor Designate Valentinian and of Victor.—July 8, 369.

2. The same Augustuses to Antonius, Praetorian Prefect of Gaul.

It is Our will that decurions shall be altogether exempt from punishments inflicted by cords and other instruments of torture, whether on account of another's debt or their own. Indeed, it shall be a capital offense on the part of a judge if he should attempt such punishment in contempt and nullification of this order. So bloody a condition awaits those of the order of the municipal senate only if they are guilty of high treason or if they are accomplices or principals in unspeakable practices. It is Our will that decurions who are debtors and those who are called tax gatherers or tax receivers, from the highest to the lowest rank, shall be exempt from such punishments. Severity has many means which it may take to confirm the discipline of public office, so that it may abstain from such bloody ones.

1. On the other hand, from beatings with leaden scourges, which We do not approve when inflicted upon the bodies of freeborn persons, We do not exempt all the aforesaid order, but We relieve only the decemprimi decurions of the order from the cruelty of such blows, and in the case of the rest, moderation in the use of this punishment shall be exercised by the judge.

Given on the fifteenth day before the kalends of October at Trier in the year of the fifth consulship of Valens Augustus and the consulship of Valentinian Augustus.—September 17, 376.

3. Emperors Valens, Gratian, and Valentinian Augustuses to Gracchus, Prefect of the City.

We exempt the Senatorial rank from harsh examination by torture.

Given on the day before the nones of January at Trier in the year of the fourth consulship of Gratian Augustus and the consulship of Merobaudes.— January 4, 377.

4. Emperors Gratian, Valentinian, and Theodosius Augustuses to Albucianus, Vicar of Macedonia.

During the forty days which anticipate the Paschal season by the auspicious beginning of ceremonies, all investigation of criminal cases through torture shall be prohibited.

Given on the sixth day before the kalends of April at Thessalonica in the year of the fifth consulship of Gratian Augustus and the first consulship of Theodosius Augustus.—March 27, 380.

INTERPRETATION: During the days of Quadragesima, in reverence for religion, all criminal actions shall be in abeyance.

5. Emperors Valentinian, Theodosius, and Arcadius Augustuses to Tatianus, Praetorian Prefect.

On the consecrated days of the Quadragesima, during which time the absolution of souls is awaited, there shall be no corporal punishment.

6. Emperors Arcadius and Honorius Augustuses to Messala, Praetorian Prefect.

Be it known that the indignation of trial judges, turning aside from the path of justice, and the venal terror caused by exactors of punishment shall not be permitted to inflict corporal injuries upon persons who are safe by the authority of innocence or protected by the rank of chief decurions. Their devotion, commended by the testimony of many public services, shall have this reward for its labor. (Etc.)

Given on the twelfth day before the kalends of September in the year of the consulship of the Most Noble Theodorus.—August 21, 399.

7. Emperors Honorius and Theodosius Augustuses to Anthemius, Praetorian Prefect.

The judges of the provinces shall be admonished that in the examination under torture of the Isaurian brigands, the betrayal of the wicked plans of the brigands shall not be deferred, although such betrayal must be sought through the torture of the brigands. They shall not suppose that any day of the Quadragesima or the holy day of Easter shall be excepted, since pardon of the Highest Divinity is very easily hoped for in regard to such action, by which the safety and welfare of many are obtained.

Given on the fifth day before the kalends of May at Constantinople in the year of the consulship of Bassus and Philippus.—April 27 (February 26), 408.

•   •   •

9. Emperors Valentinian, Theodosius, and Arcadius Augustuses to Cynegius, Praetorian Prefect.

If any person should unwittingly come upon a defamatory writing, either at home or in a public place or in any place whatsoever, he shall tear it to pieces before another finds it; he shall tell no person what he has found. Finally, if he is so curious as to read it, he shall report to no one what he learned in reading it. For if any person should report what he has found, he shall certainly himself be held guilty by law, unless he should betray the author, and he shall not escape the punishment that is established for such crimes, if he should be shown to have reported to anyone what he has read.

Given on the fourteenth day before the kalends of February at Constantinople in the year of the consulship of Emperor Designate Honorius and of Evodius.— January 19, 386.

INTERPRETATION: If any person should see and read a defamatory writing that is displayed in public for the injury or defamation of any person and should not immediately tear it to pieces, but perhaps should report to someone what he has read in it, he himself shall be held, just as the author of this crime.

10. Emperors Arcadius, Honorius, and Theodosius Augustuses to Anthemius, Praetorian Prefect and Patrician.

All those persons who by means of defamatory writings hurl against their enemies some poisonous weapon, so to speak, and those who do not tear in pieces immediately or burn in flames writings whose slanderous contents they learned by shameless reading, or those who do not betray the reader if they know him, shall dread the avenging sword upon their own necks.

Given on the fourth day before the kalends of May at Constantinople in the year of the sixth consulship of Arcadius Augustus and the consulship of Probus.— April 28, 406.

II
The *Digest* of Justinian, Book 48, Title 18

The torture of slaves and strangers in the Greek and Roman worlds may have had its origins in the denial of legal personality—and hence honor—to those from whom truth could only be extracted by force. The broad powers of the heads of Roman households, as well as the powers of enforcement of the commands (*coercitio*) of Roman lesser magistrates and the powers of military commanders and provincial governors, may also have contributed to the extensive ideas of the legitimacy of torture (and its control) found in the Roman jurists quoted by Justinian. The *Digest* is a vast anthology of excerpted texts that constitutes the sum of Roman jurisprudence.

The most explicit statement of the ideas behind the Roman laws governing torture is found in the *Digest*, Book 48, Title 18, the first several sections of which consist of extracts from the jurist Ulpian, whose murder in 226 A.D. is usually thought to signal the end of the classical period of Roman law. The *Digest* was issued in 534.

18

Torture

1. Ulpian, *Duties of Proconsul, book 8*:

It is customary for torture to be applied to unearth crimes; but let us see when and how far this should be done. The deified Augustus laid down that one should not begin with the application of pain, and that reliance should not be placed entirely on torture, as is contained also in the deified Hadrian's letter to Sennius Sabinus. 1. The words of the rescript are as follows: "Recourse should only be had to the infliction of pain on slaves when the criminal is [already] suspect, and is brought so close to being proved [guilty] by other evidence that the confession of his slaves appears to be the only thing lacking." 2. The deified Hadrian wrote the same in a rescript to Claudius Quartinus; in which rescript he stated that a start should be made with the most suspect person and the man from whom the judge believes that he can most easily learn the truth. 3. It is declared in a rescript issued by the deified brothers to Lucius Tiberianus that persons produced by the accuser from his own household should not be summoned to the torture, nor should it readily be believed that she whom both her parents are said to have treated

From *The Digest of Justinian*, Latin text ed. Theodor Mommsen with the aid of Paul Krueger, trans. Alan Watson (Philadelphia: University of Pennsylvania Press, 1985), vol. IV, pp. 840–45.

as their beloved daughter is a slave. 4. The same [emperors] sent a rescript to Cornelius Proculus that reliance should certainly not be placed on the torture of a single slave, but that the case should be examined by proofs. 5. The deified Antoninus and the deified Hadrian to Sennius Sabinus wrote in rescripts that when slaves were alleged along with their master to have sent gold and silver out of the country, they should not be questioned about the master in case they should of their own accord say something which would prejudice him. 6. The deified brothers wrote in a rescript to Lelianus Longinus that torture should not be applied to a slave belonging to an heir in matters concerning the inheritance, even though it had been suspected that the heir appeared to have sought the right of ownership over that [slave] by means of an imaginary sale. 7. It has very frequently been written in rescripts that a slave belonging to a municipality [may] be tortured in capital cases affecting the citizens because he is not their slave but the state's, and the same should be said of other slaves belonging to corporate bodies; for the slave appears to belong, not to a number of individuals, but to the body [itself]. 8. Should a slave serve me in good faith, even though I have not acquired actual ownership over him, it can be said that he should not be tortured in a capital case affecting me. The same applies to a freeman who serves in good faith. 9. It is also laid down that a freedman is not [to be] tortured in a capital case affecting his patron. 10. Nor indeed, as our emperor and his deified father wrote in the rescript, should a brother [be tortured] in [a capital case affecting] his brother, adding the reason that a person should not be tortured [to give evidence] against someone against whom he [can]not be compelled to give evidence against his wish. 11. The deified Trajan wrote in a rescript to Sernius Quartus that a husband's slave could be tortured in a capital case affecting his wife. 12. The same [emperor] wrote in a rescript to Mummius Lollianus that the slaves of a condemned man, because they have ceased to be his property, can be tortured [to give evidence] against him. 13. The deified Pius wrote in a rescript that if a slave is manumitted to avoid his being tortured, then, provided that he is not tortured in a capital case affecting his master, he can be tortured. 14. The deified brothers also wrote in a rescript that a [slave] who at the outset of a trial was the property of another, even if he subsequently becomes the property of the accused, can be tortured in a capital case against the latter. 15. If [a slave] should be said to have been bought invalidly, he cannot be tortured until it has been established that the slave was of no effect, according to a rescript of our emperor and his deified father. 16. Again, Severus wrote a rescript to Spicius Antigonus as follows: "Since information under torture ought neither to be obtained from slaves against their masters, nor, if this is done, should it guide the counsel of the person who is to pronounce sentence, much less should informations laid by slaves against their masters be admitted." 17. The deified Severus wrote in a rescript that the confessions of accused persons should not be taken as equivalent to crimes established by investigation, if there were no [objective] proof to guide the conscience of the judicial examiner. 18. Although a certain person had been prepared to put down the price of a slave, so that the slave might be tortured [to give evidence] against his master, our emperor and his deified father did not allow it. 19. Should slaves be tortured as participants in a crime in their own right and confess something concerning their master to the judge, the deified Trajan wrote in a rescript that [the judge] should pronounce as the case requires. In this rescript, it is demonstrated that masters may be injured by their slaves' confessions. But subsequent constitutions show a retreat from this rescript. 20. In a case involving tribute, in which no one doubts that the sinews of the state are concerned, the consideration of the risk, which threatens capital punishment to a slave who is privy to a fraud, corroborates his declaration. 21. The person who is going to conduct the torture should not ask specifically whether Lucius Titius committed a homicide, but in general terms who did it; for the former seems rather the action of someone suggesting [an answer] than seeking [the truth]. And so the deified Trajan wrote in a rescript. 22. The deified Hadrian wrote a rescript to Calpurnius Celerianus in these words: "Agricola, the slave of Pompeius Valens, can be interrogated concerning himself. If under torture he should say more than this, it is taken as evidence against the accused, not as a fault in the interrogation." 23. It is stated in constitutions that reliance should not always be placed on torture—but not never, either; for it is a chancy and risky business and one which may be deceptive. For there are a number of people who, by their endurance or their toughness under torture, are so contemptuous of it that the truth can in no way be squeezed out of them. Others have so little endurance that they would rather tell any kind of lie than suffer torture; so it happens that they confess in various ways, incriminating not only themselves but others also. 24. Moreover, you should not place confidence in torture applied to [a person's] enemies, because they readily tell lies. Not, however that [all] confidence in torture should be lost where enmity is alleged. 25. And it is [only] when the case has been investigated [that you will know] whether you can have confidence or not. 26. There is found in a number of rescripts [the principle] that when someone has betrayed brigands, reliance should not be placed on the latter's [accusations] against those who betrayed them; but in certain [rescripts] that deal with the subject more fully there is the proviso that you should neither make it a rigid rule not [to rely on them], nor rely on them as you would in the case of other witnesses; but when the case has been examined, it should be considered whether to trust them or not. For most people, when they fear that [others], on being arrested, may perhaps name them, are accustomed to betray those [others first] as it were clutching at immunity for themselves; for it is not easy to believe those who inform on their own betrayers. But immunity should not indiscriminately be allowed to those making betrayals of this kind, nor should the [counter] allegations of those who say that they were accused solely because they themselves had handed over men [who have now denounced them] be disregarded; nor should any argument that they put forward of falsehood or calumny deployed against them [necessarily] be treated as invalid. 27. If a person should confess to wrongdoing of his own accord, he should not always be believed; for sometimes people confess out of fear or for some other reason. There is extant a letter of the deified brothers to Voconius Saxa, in which is contained the principle that a man should be freed who had made a confession against himself but who, after condemnation, had been found to be innocent. Its words are as follows: "My dear Saxa, you have acted prudently and with the excellent motive of humanity in condemning the slave Primitivus, who had been suspected of fabricating [a confession of] homicide against himself for fear of going back to his master and was persisting in his false evidence, with the aim of interrogating him about the accomplices whom he had equally mendaciously declared himself to have, so that you could get a more reliable confession than his about himself. Nor was your prudent scheme in vain, since under torture it was established that they had not been his accomplices and that he had rashly told lies about himself. You can, therefore, set aside the verdict and by virtue of your office order him to be sold off with the proviso added that at no time is he to return to the power of his master, who, we are advised, now that he has received compensation will gladly be rid of such a slave." By this letter it is indicated that a seemingly condemned slave, if he be reinstated, will be the property of him who owned him before he was condemned. A provincial governor, however, does not have the power to reinstate a person whom he has condemned, since he does not [even] have the power to revoke his own imposition of a fine. What then [must he do]? He should write to the emperor if at any time proof of innocence is subsequently established for a person who had appeared to be guilty.

2. Ulpian, *Edict, book 39*:

As long as there is doubt about the ownership of the property the slaves of an inheritance cannot be tortured in a capital case affecting their master.

3. Ulpian, *Edict, book 50*:

By a constitution of our emperor and the deified Severus, it was settled that a slave who belongs to a number of persons cannot be tortured in a capital case affecting any one of them.

4. Ulpian, *Disputations, book 3*:

As Papinian stated in an opinion, and as is laid down by rescript, in a cast of incest the torturing of slaves is not applicable, since the *lex Julia* on adultery also does not apply.

5. Marcian, *Institutes, book 2*:

If anyone has sexual relations with a female relative, whether a widow or married to another, with whom he cannot contract a marriage, he is to be deported to an island, since his crime is twofold: both incest, because he has violated a kinswoman contrary to what is lawful, and adultery, or *stuprum*. Finally, in this case, slaves are liable to torture [to give evidence] against their master's person.

6. Papinian, *Adulteries, book 2*:

When a father or husband is bringing action for adultery and they request the torturing of the slaves of the accused, then, if an acquittal should follow after the case has been wound up and the witnesses produced, an assessment is made of the value of the slaves who have died; however, if a condemnation follows, the surviving [slaves] are forfeit to the state. 1. When there is an investigation into a forged will, the slaves of the inheritance can be tortured.

7. Ulpian, *Adulteries, book 3*:

The prevailing view is that it is the duty of the judges to weigh the degree of torture; for the torture should be so conducted that a slave survives, whether for acquittal or punishment.

8. Paul, *Adulterers, book 2*:

An edict of the deified Augustus, which he issued to the consuls Vibius Habitus and Lucius Apronianus, is extant as follows: "I do not think that interrogations under torture ought to be requested in every case and person; but when capital or more serious crimes cannot be explored and investigated in any other way than by the torturing of slaves, then I think that those [interrogations] are the most effective means of seeking out the truth and I hold that they should be conducted." 1. A *statuliber* can be cited in a case of adultery for examination under torture, because he is the slave of the heir; but he will retain his hope [of freedom].

9. Marcian, *Criminal Proceedings, book 2*:

The deified Pius wrote in a rescript that interrogation under torture may be applied to slaves in a case involving money, if the truth cannot be found in any other way. The same provision is found in other rescripts. But it is the case that torture may not readily be applied in a matter involving money; but if the truth cannot be found otherwise than by physical pains, then it is permissible to use torture, as the deified Severus also wrote in a rescript. Therefore, it is lawful to torture the slaves of other persons also, if the case so suggests. 1. In those cases, where the torture of slave against their masters should not be employed, it has been stated that not even interrogation [without torture] is valid; much less admissible are [voluntary] informations laid by slaves against their masters. 2. The deified Pius wrote in a rescript that a person who has been deported to an island should not be interrogated under torture. 3. Neither is a *statuliber* to be tortured in cases involving money, unless the condition [on which he is to be freed] is not satisfied.

10. Arcadius Charisius, *Witnesses, sole book*:

A person below the age of fourteen is not to be interrogated under torture, as the deified Pius wrote in a rescript to Caecilius Juventianus. 1. But all persons without exception are subject to torture if they are called to give evidence, when the case requires it, in a charge of *majestas*, because it touches on the persons of the emperors. 2. It is possible to ask whether interrogation under torture cannot be applied to the slaves of a son's *peculium castrense* in a capital case affecting his father; for it is laid down that the father['s slaves] ought not to be tortured [to give evidence] against the son. I think it is correctly stated that neither ought the son's slaves to be interrogated in a capital case affecting his father. 3. Tortures, however, are not to be applied to whatever extent the accuser demands, but as the due measure of well-regulated reason requires. 4. Nor should the accuser make a beginning of his proofs from the household of the accused, calling the freedmen or slaves of him whom he is accusing to give evidence. 5. Again, in sifting out the truth, the actual voice [of the witness] and the subtle persistence of the judicial examination yield the greatest [result]; for from his speech and from the firmness or hesitancy with which a person says something, or from that reputation which everyone has in his own *civitas*, there come to light revelations of the truth. 6. Also, in actions concerned with establishing free status, the truth should not be sought to torturing those whose status is at issue.

11. Paul, *Duties of Proconsul, book 2*:

Even if a slave has been returned to the seller, he is not to be tortured in a capital case affecting the buyer.

12. Ulpian, *Edict, book 54*:

If someone, to avoid interrogation under torture, alleges himself to be free, the deified Hadrian has written in a rescript that he is not to be tortured before an action to determine his status has been heard.

13. Modestinus, *Rules, book 5*:

It is accepted that a slave who has been valued at a particular price is to be put to the torture [only] when there has been a stipulation.

14. Modestinus, *Rules, book 8*:

A *statuliber* found out in a delict is, in token of his expected freedom, to be punished not as a slave because of his doubtful condition that as a freeman.

15. Callistratus, *Judicial Examinations, book 5*:

Interrogation under torture ought not to be applied to a freeman whose evidence is not inconsistent. 1. Again, the deified Pius wrote in a rescript to Maecilius that a person under fourteen should not be tortured in a capital case affecting another, especially when the accusation might be completed without outside evidence. It does not, however, follow from this that such [young persons] are to be believed even without torture; for, said [Pius], their age, which is regarded as safeguarding them for the time being against the harshness of torture, makes them also the more suspect of a readiness to tell lies. 2. A person who has given a slave as security to someone who claims ownership [in the slave] is to be regarded as in the position of master, and accordingly [such] slaves can not be tortured in a capital case affecting him, as the deified Pius wrote in a rescript in these words: "You must furnish your case with other proofs; for interrogation under torture must not be applied to slaves when the possessor of the inheritance, who has given security to the plaintiff, is regarded for the meantime as in the position of master."

16. Modestinus, *Punishments, book 3*:

The deified brothers wrote in a rescript that interrogation under torture may be renewed. 1. A person who has made a confession on his own account shall not be tortured in a capital case affecting others, as the deified Pius wrote in a rescript.

17. Papinian, *Replies, book 16*:

It has been argued that even when a person outside the family is bringing the accusation, slaves may be interrogated [to give evidence] against their master in a question of adultery. The deified Marcus and subsequently our own great emperor have followed this principle in their judgments. 1. However, in a case of *stuprum*, slaves are not tortured [to give evidence] against their master. 2. Where the question is one of substituted birth, or if [someone] is claiming an inheritance whom the other sons allege not to be their brother, interrogation under torture will be applied to the slaves of the inheritance, because the interrogation is not [to provide evidence] against their masters, the other brothers, but concerns the succession to their [former] master who is dead. This agrees with what the deified Hadrian wrote in a rescript; for when one partner was being prosecuted for murdering another, he wrote in a rescript that a slave who was their joint property should be examined under torture, since it seemed that this would be for the benefit of his [dead] master. 3. I gave the opinion that a slave condemned to the mines should not be tortured [to give evidence] against the person who was previously his owner; and that it does not affect the case even if he confesses that he assisted in the crime.

18. Paul, *Views, book 5*:

Where a number of persons are charged with the one crime, they are to be heard in such a way that a beginning is made with the one who is the more afraid or appears to be of tender years. 1. An accused who has been overwhelmed with clearer proofs can be recalled to interrogation under torture, especially if he steels his body and spirit against the pains. 2. In a case where the accused is not hard-pressed by any proofs, tortures should not readily be applied, but the accuser should be urged [himself] to make good and prove true his charges. 3. Witnesses are not to be tortured for the sake of demonstrating falsehood or discovering the truth unless they are alleged to have had a hand in the act. 4. A judge, when he cannot put reliance on the family, will be able to put to the torture slaves of the inheritance. 5. Credence is not given to a slave who confesses something relating to his master of his own accord; for it is not right in matters of doubt for the master's well-being to be entrusted to the whim of his slaves. 6. A slave cannot be interrogated [to give evidence] in a capital case against a master by whom he was sold off and whom he formerly served, in memory of the former ownership. 7. A slave, even if he is offered for torture by his master, is not to be interrogated [in a capital case affecting the master]. 8. Indeed, whenever the question arises of whether slaves are to be interrogated in capital cases affecting their master, [the nature of] his ownership over them must first be investigated. 9. A governor who is about to conduct a hearing into charges should, before the day [of the trial], make it public that he is going to hear the persons in custody, so that persons who need a defense may not be assailed by charges brought suddenly by their accusers; although an accused who requests a defense at any time should not be denied it, so much so that for that reason persons in custody may [have their appearance] deferred and postponed. 10. Persons in custody can be heard and condemned not only before the tribunal but also outside the court.

19. Tryphoninus, *Disputations, book 4*:

A person to whom freedom is due under a *fideicommissum* may not be subjected to interrogation as a slave unless and only unless he is accused as a result of the interrogation of others.

20. Paul, *Decrees, book 3*:

A certain husband as his wife's heir was claiming from Surus money which he said the dead woman had lodged with Surus, while he himself was absent, and he had produced a single witness to this, the son of his freedman, before the procurator; he had also sought the interrogation under torture of Surus's handmaid. Surus continued to deny that he had received [the money], and [said] that the testimony of a single person should not be admitted, and that it was not customary to begin with interrogations under torture, even if the handmaid had belonged to a third party. The procurator put the maid to the torture. When the case came to the cognizance of the emperor on appeal, he pronounced that the torture had been conducted unlawfully, that reliance should not be placed on the evidence of one witness, and that therefore the appeal had been rightly lodged.

21. Paul, *Punishments of Civilians, sole book*:

The deified Hadrian wrote in a rescript that no one should be condemned for the purpose of putting him to the torture.

22. Paul, *Views, book 1*:

Persons taken into custody without accusers are not to be subject to torture unless there are any suspicions strongly attaching to them.

III
The *Code* of Justinian, Book 9, Title 41

Justinian's *Code* supplanted the *Theodosian Code* and differed from it in many respects. It consists of imperial laws that formed the basis of Ulpian's and other jurists' legal analysis in the *Digest*, as well as the laws that Augustine held up for the dilemma of the conscientious judge (see next selection).

TITLE XLI

Concerning Torture

1. The Emperors Severus and Antoninus to Antiana

Slaves should not be subjected to torture against their masters except in cases of adultery, accusations of fraud having reference to taxation, and the crime of high treason, which involves the safety of the Emperor. So far as other offences are concerned, although judges should not formulate hurriedly a decision based on testimony given by a slave against his master, still, if the truth is established by other testimony, an exception cannot be pleaded. It is, however, clear that, in pecuniary cases, slaves should be interrogated against their masters, where other evidence is lacking.

Published on the *Kalends* of January, during the Consulate of Fuscus, Consul for the second time, and Dexter, 197.

2. The Same Emperors and Cæsars to Catullus

It is unusual, and furnishes a bad precedent, for slaves to be heard against their guardians, or the mother of their master, unless the administration of the guardianship is involved.

Published on the third of the *Ides* of September, during the Consulate of Chilo and Libo, 205.

3. The Emperor Antoninus When Deciding a Case, Said:

Slaves belonging to another should first be interrogated under torture, when there is sufficient evidence that a crime of such atrocity has been perpetrated; and the woman herself may afterwards be put to the question, for it is not inhuman for her to be tortured who destroyed her husband by poison.

Published on the seventh day of the *Kalends* of April, during the Consulate of Sabinus and Anulinus, 217.

From *The Civil Law, Including the Twelve Tables, the Institutes of Gaius, the Rules of Ulpian, the Opinions of Paulus, the Enactments of Justinian, and the Constitutions of Leo*, trans. S. P. Scott (Cincinnati, 1932; reprint New York: AMS Press, 1973), vol. XV, pp. 66–70.

4. Extract from a Rescript of the Emperor Antoninus

As too much reliance should not be placed on the statements of criminals who, having been convicted, allege that those by whom they were arrested and kept in custody are their accomplices, so, if it is clearly proved that they only divulged the crime committed in common for the purpose of avoiding the penalty, they shall not escape public punishment.

Published on the fifth of the *Kalends* of April, during the Consulate of Sabinus and Anulinus, 217.

5. The Emperor Alexander to Respectus

Slaves who have obtained their freedom by the last will of a testator should not be indiscriminately subjected to torture, even where his death should be avenged.

Published on the sixth of the *Ides* of March, during the Consulate of Sabinus and Venustus, 241.

6. The Emperor Gordian to Herodian

It was long since decided that slaves or freedmen ought not to be tortured in cases having reference to the domestic affairs of their owners, or patrons, as what might be obtained by their confessions would not have the force of truth either for or against them, in capital or pecuniary cases.

Published on the seventh of the *Ides* of May, during the Consulate of Sabinus and Venustus, 241.

7. The Emperors Diocletian and Maximian to Urbana

If the slaves have been proved without doubt to belong to you, We do not permit them to be put to torture, even though you suggest that this be done; and, so far from doing so, We are unwilling that they should be compelled to violate their fidelity to their mistress, even against your consent.

Published on the *Kalends* of November, during the Consulate of Maximus, Consul for the second time, and Aquilinus, 286.

8. The Same Emperors and Cæsars to Sallust, Governor

We do not permit soldiers to be subjected to torture, or to the penalties imposed upon plebeians in criminal cases, even when it appears that they have been dismissed from the service without the privileges of veterans, with the exception of those who have been dishonorably discharged. This rule shall also be observed with reference to the sons of soldiers and veterans.

In the prosecution of public crimes, judges should not begin the investigation by resorting to torture, but should first avail themselves of all accessible and probable evidence. If, after having obtained information relative to the crime, they think that torture should be applied for the purpose of ascertaining the truth, they only ought to resort to it where the rank of the persons involved justifies such a course; for, by the terms of this law, all the inhabitants of the provinces have a right to the benefit of the natural benevolence which We entertain for them.

Without date or designation of Consulate.

9. The Same Emperors and Cæsars to Our Beloved Governor of Syria

In the investigation of the question of free birth, every form of interrogation and torture should be resorted to in order that persons of low and debased origin may not venture to claim for themselves a position among those who are distinguished and freeborn, and that the succession to which the latter are entitled may not through a fraudulent assumption be denied to them.

Given on the sixth of the *Ides* of May, during the Consulate of Diocletian, Consul for the fourth time, and Maximian, Consul for the third time, 290.

10. The Same Emperors and Cæsars to Ptolmæus

As you allege that the will is forced, the slaves forming part of the estate may, under the Constitutions of the Emperors, be put to torture, even though they were granted freedom by the person who asserts that he is the heir.

Published on the sixth of the *Kalends* of September, during the Consulate of Diocletian, Consul for the fourth time, and Maximian, Consul for the third time, 290.

11. The Same Emperors and Cæsars to Boëthus

It was decided by the Divine Marcus that the descendants of men who are designated "Most Eminent and most Perfect," to the degree of great-grandchildren, shall not be subject either to the penalties or the tortures inflicted upon plebeians, if no stigma of violated honor attached to those of a nearer degree, through whom this privilege was transmitted to their descendants.

The learned jurist Domitius Ulpianus, in his works treating of public law, states for the knowledge and information of future ages that this rule shall also be observed with reference to decurions and their children.

Published on the fifth of the *Kalends* of December, during the Consulate of Diocletian, Consul for the fourth time, and Maximian, Consul for the third time, 291.

12. The Same Emperors and Cæsars to Asper

Whenever the ownership of slaves is involved, and the truth cannot be ascertained by other evidence, eminent legal authorities hold that the slaves themselves can be interrogated under torture.

Published at Sirmium, on the third of the *Ides* of May, during the Consulate of Tiberianus and Dio.

13. The Same Emperors and Cæsars to Philippa

It can be of no advantage to you for the slaves forming part of the estate to be tortured in the case in question, as the ownership of the same is not in dispute; for where it is uncertain who is entitled to it, it is but reasonable that, in order to ascertain the truth, the slaves belonging to the estate should be subjected to torture; but, as you assert that the slave is common property, you should entertain no doubt that half of him belongs to the person against whom you desire the said slave to be interrogated. This fact presents an obstacle to the application of torture, as slaves of two joint-owners cannot be put to the question and interrogated against either of them, except where one is said to have killed the other.

Ordered at Heraclia, on the third of the *Kalends* of May, during the Consulate of the above-mentioned Emperors.

14. The Same Emperors and Cæsars to Constantius

It is settled that slaves cannot be tortured any more in favor of their masters, to whom they now belong, than in favor of those who formerly owned them.

Ordered on the eight of the *Ides* of April, during the Consulate of the Cæsars.

15. The Same Emperors and Cæsars to Maximus

There is no doubt that slaves can be put to torture on account of acts committed by them, not only in criminal cases, but also in those involving the payment of money, where property is entrusted to them for deposit or loan, or for other purposes authorized by law.

Ordered on the fifth of the *Ides* of April, during the Consulate of the Cæsars.

16. The Emperors Valentinian, Valens, and Gratian to Antonius, Prætorian Prefect of the Gauls

We desire decurions to be absolutely exempt from the suffering inflicted by instruments of torture, not only with reference to the debts of others, but also on account of their own. If any magistrate should attempt to insult the Order of Decurions in this manner, he shall be put to death. This severe proceeding shall only be permitted in the case of persons belonging to this municipal order, who are accused of high treason, and who are either accomplices or principals in this infamous crime.

Given on the fifteenth of the *Kalends* of October, during the Consulate of Valens, Consul for the fifth time, and Valentinian, 376.

17. The Emperors Arcadius and Honorius to Messala, Prætorian Prefect

Let every magistrate understand that he cannot, when inflamed with resentment, deviate from the course of justice; nor, if influenced by bribery, inflict corporeal injury by torturing persons who are innocent, or of exalted rank; as the devotion manifested by such persons through long service and arduous labors entitles them to this privilege.

The same rule applies where anyone has retired from the office of decurion, for, on account of his former position, he must not be subjected to torture.

Given on the twelfth of the *Kalends* of September, during the Consulate of Theodore, 299.

18. The Emperor Justinian to Demosthenes, Prætorian Prefect

So far as the torture of slaves belonging to an estate is concerned, We order that, in accordance with former laws and constitutions, no distinction shall be made, whether a question has arisen among the heirs as to the title to the entire estate, or only to a portion of the same, or to both; for the slaves can only be interrogated concerning certain property of the estate, and those alone shall be liable to torture who had charge of its administration, whether they were left in servitude, or were directed to obtain their freedom by the last will of the testator, so that any property belonging to the estate which may have been concealed can be discovered. Before this is done, however, he who demands the torture of the slaves must take the oath prescribed by Us in such cases.

Given on the fifteenth of the *Kalends* of October, at Chalcedon, during the Consulate of Decius, 529.

IV
Augustine: *The City of God,* XIX.6

The Christianization of the Roman Empire by the end of the fourth century did not initially change Roman institutions, including the use of torture in criminal cases. Although a number of early Christian thinkers, including Tertullian, bitterly opposed torture, others, often reluctantly, permitted it, particularly those who, like Augustine, regarded all human efforts in this world from a bleak perspective that saw little hope for either justice or righteousness in the city of the world. As Robert Markus has said of this passage, "No political thinker, not even excepting Hobbes, has ever given a more powerful or more disturbing description of the contradictions in human society than Augustine gives in this image of the conscientious judge." See the discussion in Markus, "Saint Augustine's Views on the Just War," *Studies in Church History* 20 (1983), 1–13, some topics in which are expanded in Markus, *The End of Ancient Christianity* (Cambridge, 1990), 45–62.

On the parallel subject of religious coercion, see Peter Brown, "Religious Coercion in the Later Roman Empire: The Case of North Africa," in Brown, *Religion and Society in the Age of St. Augustine* (New York-Evanston, 1972), 301–31.

What shall I say of these judgments which men pronounce on men, and which are necessary in communities, whatever outward peace they enjoy? Melancholy and lamentable judgments they are, since the judges are men who cannot discern the consciences of those at their bar, and are therefore frequently compelled to put innocent witnesses to the torture to ascertain the truth regarding the crimes of other men. What shall I say of torture applied to the accused himself? He is tortured to discover whether he is guilty, so that, though innocent, he suffers most undoubted punishment for crime that is still doubtful, not because it is proved that he committed it, but because it is not ascertained that he did not commit it. Thus the ignorance of the judge frequently involves an innocent person in suffering. And what is still more unendurable—a thing, indeed, to be bewailed, and, if that were possible, watered with fountains of tears—is this, that when the judge puts the accused to the question, that he may not unwittingly put an innocent man to death, the result of this lamentable ignorance is that this very person, whom he tortured that he might not condemn him if innocent, is condemned to

From St. Augustine, *The City of God,* trans. Marcus Dods, XIX.6.

death both tortured and innocent. For if he has chosen, in obedience to the philosophical instructions to the wise man, to quit this life rather than endure any longer such tortures, he declares that he has committed the crime which in fact he has not committed. And when he has been condemned and put to death, the judge is still in ignorance whether he has put to death an innocent or a guilty person, though he put the accused to the torture for the very purpose of saving himself from condemning the innocent; and consequently he has both tortured an innocent man to discover his innocence, and has put him to death without discovering it. If such darkness shrouds social life, will a wise judge take his seat on the bench or no? Beyond question he will. For human society, which he thinks it a wickedness to abandon, constrains him and compels him to this duty. And he thinks it no wickedness that innocent witnesses are tortured regarding the crimes of which other men are accused; or that the accused are put to the torture, so that they are often overcome with anguish, and though innocent, make false confessions regarding themselves, and are punished; or that, though they be no condemned to die, they often die during, or in consequence of, the torture; or that sometimes the accusers, who perhaps have been prompted by a desire to benefit society by bringing criminals to justice, are themselves condemned through the ignorance of the judge, because they are unable to prove the truth of their accusations though they are true, and because the witnesses lie, and the accused endures the torture without being moved to confession. These numerous and important evils he does not consider sins; for the wise judge does these things, not with any intention of doing harm, but because his ignorance compels him, and because human society claims him as a judge. But though we therefore acquit the judge of malice, we must none the less condemn human life as miserable. And if he is compelled to torture and punish the innocent because his office and his ignorance constrain him, is he a happy as well as a guiltless man? Surely it were proof of more profound considerateness and finer feeling were he to recognise the misery of the necessities, and shrink from his own implication in that misery; and had he any piety about him, he would cry to God, "From my necessities deliver Thou me."

V
The *Visigothic Code*: On Torture

The Visigothic kingdom in the Iberian peninsula borrowed heavily from Roman criminal and other law, including the use of torture. These texts offer an example of how some Roman criminal procedures were adapted to societies consisting of both Roman and non-Roman peoples and ruled by kings who were shaping kingship and law into entirely new institutions. On Visigothic law, see P. D. King, *Law and Society in the Visigothic Kingdom* (Cambridge, 1972).

A

Flavius Chintasvintus, King

IV. Torture shall, in no Case, be inflicted upon Persons of Noble Birth who are acting as Representatives of Others; and, In what way a Freeman of the Lower Class, or a Slave, may be subjected to Torture

No person of noble rank shall, under any circumstances, be put to the torture by authority of a commission given to another. It is, however, hereby permitted that any freeborn person of low rank who is poor, and has already been convicted of crime, may be tortured under such a commission; but only when the principal gives authority in writing to do this, signed by him, and attested by three witnesses, which shall be entrusted for delivery, to a freeman, and not to a slave. And if he should cause the torture to be inflicted upon an innocent person, the aforesaid principal is hereby admonished, that he has incurred the penalty of the law which is found in the sixth book, first title, second chapter; wherein it is stated for what things freeborn persons are to be put to the question. It is lawful for other criminal causes to be prosecuted under commission; and, as has been said above, tortures may be applied to a freeman by the representative of another who is also free. And it is granted by the law to a freeman or a slave, to subject a slave to torture, with this provision, to wit: that if either torture or injury should be inflicted upon an innocent person, the principal shall be compelled to give complete satisfaction, under the instructions of the judge. Nor is he to be discharged who received the commission, until either the principal may be produced in court, or shall make amends according to law. And whoever desires to inflict the torture, having received authority to do so under a commission, shall be compelled by the judge to give bond.

From *The Visigothic Code (Forum Judicum)*, trans. S. P. Scott (Boston: Fred B. Rothman, 1910; reprinted 1982), (A) Book II, Title III, IV, p. 49; (B) Book VI, Title I, I–IV, pp. 194–99.

B

The Glorious Flavius Chintasvintus, King

II. For what Offences, and in what Manner, Freeborn Persons shall be put to the Torture

If moderation is displayed in the treatment of crimes, the wickedness of criminals can never be restrained. Therefore, if anyone should, in behalf of the king or the people, bring an accusation of homicide or adultery against a person equal to him in rank, or in palatine dignity, he who thus seeks the blood of another shall first have an opportunity to prove what he alleges. And if he cannot prove it in the presence of the king, or those appointed by the royal authority, an accusation shall be drawn up in writing, and signed by three witnesses; and the accused person may then be put to the question.

If the latter, after undergoing the torture, should prove to be innocent, the accuser shall at once be delivered up to him as a slave, to be disposed of at his will, except that he shall not be deprived of life. But if he should be willing to make a compromise with his accuser, he may accept from the latter as large a sum as may compensate him for the sufferings he has endured. The judge shall take the precaution to compel the accuser to specifically describe the alleged offence, in writing; and after he has done so, and presented it privately to the judge, the torture shall proceed; and if the confession of him who is subjected to the torture should correspond with the terms of the accusation, his guilt shall be considered to be established. But if the accusation should allege one thing, and the confession of the person tortured the opposite, the accuser must undergo the penalty hereinbefore provided; because persons often accuse themselves of crime while being tortured. But if the accuser, before he has secretly given the written accusation to the judge as aforesaid, should, either in his own proper person, or by anyone else, inform the party of what he is accused, then it shall not be lawful for the judge to subject the latter to torture, because the alleged offence has become publicly known. This rule shall also apply to all other freeborn persons. But if the accusation should not be that of a capital crime, but merely of theft, or of some minor breach of the law, nobles, or persons of superior rank, such as the officials of our palace, shall, upon such an accusation, under no circumstances, be put to the question; and if proof of the alleged offence is wanting, he who is accused must declare his innocence under oath.

All persons of inferior rank, and freeborn persons, when accused of theft, homicide, or any other crime, shall not be tortured upon such an accusation, unless the property involved is worth more than fifty *solidi*. But if the property is of less value than fifty *solidi*, and the accused is convicted upon legal testimony, he shall be compelled to make restitution, as prescribed by other laws; of if he should not be convicted, after purging himself by oath he shall receive the satisfaction granted by the law for those who have suffered from an improper demand for torture.

We hereby especially provide that a lowborn person shall not presume to accuse a noble or one of higher rank than himself; but if such a a person should accuse another of crime, and proof of the same should be wanting, the person accused shall at once purge himself of all guilt by oath, and swear that he never took, nor has in his possession, the property on account of which he was prosecuted; and oath having been made, as aforesaid, he who brought the false accusation shall undergo the penalty for the same, as prescribed by a former law. But, whether the person subjected to the torture is a noble, one of inferior rank, or a freeman, he must be tortured in the presence of the judge, or of certain respectable men appointed by him; and in such a way as not to lose his life, or the use of any of his limbs; and because the torture must be applied for the space of three days, if, as the result of accident, or through the malice of the judge, or the treachery of anyone else, he who is subjected to it should die; or if the judge, having been corrupted by the bribes of the adversary of the accused, should not prohibit the infliction of such torments as are liable to produce death; the judge himself shall be delivered up to the nearest relatives of the accused person, that, on account of his injustice, he may undergo at their hands the same sufferings which he unlawfully inflicted upon the accused.

If, however, he should declare himself under oath to be innocent, and witnesses who were present should swear that death did not result from any malice, treachery, or corruption of which he was guilty, but only as a result of the torture itself; for the reason that the said judge did not use his discretion to prevent excessive cruelty, he shall be compelled to pay fifty *solidi* to the heirs of the deceased; and if he should not have sufficient property to pay said sum, he shall be delivered up as a slave to the nearest heirs of the former. The accuser shall be surrendered to the nearest relatives of the deceased, and shall suffer the penalty of death, which he suffered who perished through his accusation.

Ancient Law

III. For what Offences, and in what manner, Slaves, of Either Sex, shall be put to the Torture, on account of the Crimes of their Masters

No slave, of either sex, shall be tortured in order to obtain evidence of crime against either his or her master or mistress, unless for adultery; or for some offence against the Crown, or against their country; or for counterfeiting, homicide, or witchcraft. And if slaves tortured for such reasons should be proved to be cognizant of the crimes of their masters, and to have concealed them, they shall be punished along with their masters in such a way as the king may direct. But if they should voluntarily confess the truth before being put to the question, it will be sufficient if they undergo the torture in order to confirm their testimony, and they shall not suffer the penalty of death. But any slave of either sex, who, after being put to the torture for a capital crime, should also implicate his or her master, and the commission of said crime can be proved by competent evidence, they shall be subject to the same punishment as their master.

Flavius Chintasvintus, King

IV. For what Offences, and in what manner, a Slave, or a Freedman, shall be Tortured

Where a slave is accused of any crime, the accuser must, before the torture is inflicted, bind himself to give to the master in his stead, another slave of equal value, if the innocence of the slave should be established. But if the accused slave should be found innocent, and should die, or be disabled from the effects of the torture, the accuser must at once give to the master two other slaves, each equal in value to the one killed or disabled. The one who was injured shall be free, and remain under the protection of his master; and the judge who neglected to use moderation in the infliction of torture, and thus violated the law, shall give to the master another slave equal in value to the one who perished by torture.

In order that all doubt may be removed concerning the value of slaves in dispute, no statement of artificial or fraudulent value of the same shall be accepted; but information of their age and usefulness shall be obtained by personal examination of the slaves themselves; and if he who was disabled was skilled in any trade, and he who injured him when he was innocent possesses no slave proficient in the same trade, he shall be forced to give to the master a slave skilled in some other trade; but if he should not have such a skilled artisan, and he whose slave was injured by the torture should not be willing to accept another in his stead, then the accuser shall pay to the master the value of the slave that was injured, according to a reasonable estimate made by the judge, or by men of respectability and established character. It must, however, be observed, that no one shall presume to subject any free-born person or slave to torture, unless he shall make oath in the presence of a judge, or his representative, the master of the slave or his agent being also present, that through no artifice, fraud, or malice, he is inflicting torture upon an innocent person. And if, after having been put to the question he should die, and his accuser should not have the means to make the reparation required by law, he himself shall be reduced to slavery, for the reason that he was the cause of the death of an innocent man. And if anyone, through treachery, should attempt to subject the slave of another to torture, and the master of said slave should prove that he was innocent of crime, the accuser shall be compelled to give to the master of the accused slave another of equal value, and to reimburse said master for any reasonable expense that he has incurred in defence of his slave, until, in the opinion of the judge, full satisfaction has been rendered by the unjust accuser to the master of the innocent slave.

In case a slave is found guilty of a minor offence, the master, if he chooses to do so, shall have a right to compound the same; but every thief shall be scourged according to the degree of his guilt. Where a master is not willing to give satisfaction for graver offences, he must immediately surrender the slave to justice. Any freeborn person who desires to subject a respectable freedman to the torture, in the case of a capital crime, or of offences of less gravity, shall not be permitted to do so, unless the value of the property involved in the accusation amounts to at least two hundred and fifty *solidi*. But if said freeborn person should be of inferior rank, and a boar, he may be tortured, if the value of the property amounts to a hundred *solidi*.

Where he who is put to the question should, through want of proper care, be disabled, then the judge who did not exercise moderation in the infliction of torture, shall pay two hundred *solidi* to him who suffered his negligence; and he who caused him to be tortured unjustly, shall be compelled to pay him three hundred *solidi*; and if he should die, while undergoing torture, the judge, as well as the accuser, shall each pay to the nearest relatives of the deceased the sums of money aforesaid. And, in like manner, in the case of freedmen of still lower rank, should anyone of them undergo mutilation or death, through want of caution on the part of those employing the torture, half of the sum hereinbefore mentioned as applying to respectable freedmen shall be paid to him who was tortured, should he be still living, or, if he is dead, to his heirs.

VI
Torture by Inquisitors: Innocent IV and Alexander IV

The introduction of torture into the procedure of the inquisitorial office was first authorized by Pope Innocent IV in the decretal *Ad extirpanda* of 1252. Even this remarkable document, however, did not permit the Inquisitors themselves to apply torture, because the twelfth-century attack upon early procedures, particularly the ordeal, had laid down that the clergy could not shed blood, a doctrine that was enunciated with great force and widespread influence at the Fourth Lateran Council of 1215. Inquisitors, even after *Ad extirpanda*, could not apply torture themselves without becoming canonically irregular. Not until the next pontificate, that of Alexander IV, did Inquisitors obtain the authority to absolve one another from canonical irregularities incurred by their work. The following are extracts from the decretals *Ad extirpanda* of Innocent IV (1252) and *Ut negotium* of Alexander IV (1256), the two most important documents in the history of judicial torture in ecclesiastical courts. The first text begins with the introduction of Francesco Peña, a sixteenth-century commentator.

A

Originally, when the inquisitorial office was first constituted, it seems that it was not permitted to the inquisitors to torture offenders under the danger (as I believe) of incurring irregularity, and so torture was used against heretics or those suspected of heresy by lay judges; however, in the constitution of Innocent IV beginning *Ad extirpanda*, it is written:

In addition, the official or Rector should obtain from all heretics he has captured a confession by torture without injuring the body or causing the danger of death, for they are indeed thieves and murderers of souls and apostates from the sacraments of God and of the Christian faith. They should confess to their own errors and accuse other heretics whom they know, as well as their accomplices, fellow-believers, receivers and defenders, just as rogues and thieves of worldly goods are made to accuse their accomplices and confess the evils which they have committed.

(A) From *Directorium Inquisitorum F. Nicolai Eymerici . . . Cum Comentariis Francisci Pegnai* (Rome, 1587), pp. 592–593; (B) from Henry Charles Lea, *A History of the Inquisition of the Middle Ages* (New York: Harper, 1888; reprint New York: AMS Press, 1966), Appendix Doc. XII, p. 575.

B

In order to expedite the work of faith that you carry out, we authorize you by this permission that if you incur in any cases the sentence of excommunication or irregularity, whether it should occur from human weakness or if you should incur it later on because you are not able to have recourse to your superiors at the moment, you may absolve each other of these things according to the proper form of the Church and by this authority you are enabled to dispense each other, just as this power has been conceded to your superiors by apostolic authority.

VII
The *Constitutio Criminalis Carolina*

John Langbein's comparative study of criminal prosecutions in sixteenth-century England, Germany, and France contains several useful translations of official legislation. The selection here is from criminal procedural sections the *Carolina*, issued by the emperor Charles V in 1532. One purpose of the *Carolina* was to establish the inquisitorial judicial procedure in criminal cases, and with it, torture, but in a highly regulated way, one that led to the qualifications by such jurists as Guazzini, considered in the next section. Langbein's discussion of torture in this process and in the text itself is on pp. 179–86.

Concerning the cases in which a legally sufficient indication of a crime shall be made out

18. In this our and the holy Empire's criminal courts ordinance, conforming to the common law (*gemeynem rechten*), the arrest and confinement, and also the examination by torture of one who is accused and suspected as the criminal and has not confessed, is based upon legally sufficient indication, sign, and suspicion of the wrongdoing (as dealt with above and below); yet it is not possible to set forth all of these matters or signs which suffice for legally sufficient indication or suspicion. Nonetheless, however, in order that the officials, judges, and judgment-givers, who are otherwise uninstructed in these matters, may be the better informed as to what establishes a legally sufficient indication or suspicion, the following examples of legally sufficient indication or suspicion are hereafter set forth in a manner that everyone, to the extent of his German, can identify or distinguish.

Concerning the meaning of the word "indication" (*anzeygung*)

19. Where hereafter we discuss "legally sufficient indication" (*redlich anzeygen*), we intend thereby also to have consistently meant legally sufficient signs, suspicion, and presumption, and therefore we drop the residual words.

That no one shall be examined under torture without legally sufficient indication

20. When legally sufficient indication of the crime which it is desired to investigate has not been produced and proven beforehand, then no one shall

Translation based on the edition of the *Carolina* in *Die Peinliche Gerichtsordnung Kaiser Karls nebst der Bamberger und der Brandenburger Halsgerichtsordnung*, ed. H. Zoepfl, 2nd ed. (Leipzig and Heidelberg, 1876). From John H. Langbein, *Prosecuting Crime in the Renaissance: England, Germany, France* (Cambridge, Mass.: Harvard University Press, 1974), pp. 272–84.

be examined; and should, however, the crime be confessed under torture, it shall not be believed nor shall anyone be condemned upon that basis. When, notwithstanding, some of the authorities or the judge proceed in this way, then they shall be bound to make appropriate compensation to the person who was tortured in this illegal way without the proven indication for his injury, pain, costs, and damage.

Furthermore, no authority or judge in this situation shall support, protect, or uphold any recognizance (*urphede*) such that the tortured person cannot legally recover for his injury, pain, costs, and damage—quite excluding his own wrongful acts.

Concerning indication produced by those who dare to soothsay with sorcery

21. No one shall be gaoled or examined under torture upon indication of those who purport to be able to soothsay through sorcery or other artifice. Rather these pretended soothsayers and complainants shall in consequence be punished. If, however, the judge should nonetheless continue to proceed upon such soothsayers' denunciation, then he shall be obliged to compensate the tortured person for costs, pain, injuria (*injurien*), and damage, as set out in the previous article.

That upon indication of a crime only examination under torture, and not further penal sanction, shall be ordered

22. It is further to be noticed that no one shall be definitely sentenced to penal sanction on the basis of any indication of a suspicious sign or upon suspicion, rather on that basis there may only be examination under torture; when the indications are sufficient (as will be found below), then the person shall be finally condemned to penal sanction; however, that must take place upon the basis of his own confession or a witness proof procedure (*beweisung*) (as will be found plainly elsewhere in this ordinance), and not on the basis of presumption or indication.

Concerning how the sufficient indication of a crime shall be proven

23. Every sufficient indication upon which it is sought to examine under torture shall be proven with two good witnesses, as described below in several articles concerning sufficient proof. When, however, the essential element of the crime is proven with one good witness, then this, as a half proof, serves as sufficient indication, as set out below in Article 30 ("a half proof, as when someone is caught in [*sic*] the essential element, etc.").

That an analogy may be inferred from the indications following below for unnamed and herein unexpounded suspicions of crime

24. From these articles below following treating, suspicion and indication of crime, an analogy shall be drawn in cases not named in these articles. For it is not possible to set forth all cases and circumstances which raise suspicion.

Concerning general suspicion and indications which relate to all crimes

25. To begin with[:] concerning matters which raise suspicion, with explanation following, how and when these suffice as legally sufficient indication.

[And as a second purpose of this article:] When the indication does not appear among those described in numerous following articles and regulating sufficiency for examination under torture, investigation shall correspond to the following and to similar circumstances of suspicion, because not all can be set forth.

First: When the accused is an insolent and wanton person of bad repute and regard, so that the crime could be credibly ascribed to him, or when the same person shall have dared to perform a similar crime previously or shall have been accused of having done so. However, this bad repute shall not be adduced from enemies or wanton people, rather from impartial and upright people.

Second: When the suspected person has been caught or found at a place suspicious in the context of the deed.

Third: When a culprit has been seen in the deed or while on the way to or from it; in the case when he has not been recognized, attention shall be paid to whether the suspect has such a figure, such clothes, weapon, horse, or whatnot corresponding to what the above-mentioned culprit was seen to have.

Fourth: When the suspected person lives with or associates with such people who commit similar crimes.

Fifth: In cases of damage to property or person, attention shall be paid to whether the suspected person could have been motivated to the present crime out of envy, enmity, former threat, or in the expectation of some advantage.

Sixth: When a victim injured in person or property himself accuses someone of the crime on various grounds, and thereafter dies or affirms it with his oath.

Seventh: When someone flees on account of a crime.

Eighth:

26. When someone is in litigation with another concerning substantial property, which thereby constitutes the larger part of his support, goods, and possessions; he will be regarded as a grudge-holder and great enemy of his opponent; should the opponent be secretly murdered, a presumption arises against the other party that he committed this murder; and when this person is otherwise inherently suspect of having done the murder, he may be gaoled and examined under torture, when he has in the matter no legally sufficient excuse.

A rule concerning when the above-mentioned matters of suspicion together or singly suffice as adequate indications for examination under torture

27. In the last article[s] above are found eight matters of suspicion concerning indication for examination under torture; none of these matters of suspicion alone suffices as legally sufficient indication upon which basis tor-

ture may be employed. When, however, more than one of these matters of suspicion concerning someone are found together, then those persons who are responsible for ordering and conducting examination under torture shall decide whether the aforementioned or corresponding matters of suspicion established really provide as much legally sufficient indication of the suspected crime as in the following articles (concerning that which singly constitutes legally sufficient indication for examination under torture).

Another rule in the above-mentioned matters

28. In addition, it is to be borne in mind when someone is suspected of a crime on the basis of more than one matter of suspicion (as above), that two things must always and invariably be observed[:] First, the suspicions uncovered; second, what favors the suspected person—that which could exculpate him of the crime. And when in consequence it is decided that the weight of suspicion is greater than the weight of exculpation, then torture may be employed. When, however, the grounds of exculpation have higher regard and attention than some lesser suspicions which have been made out, then examination under torture shall not be employed. And when something is doubtful in these matters, those responsible for ordering and conducting examination under torture shall seek advice from the legally knowledgeable and at those places and locations set out at the end of this our ordinance.

General indications each of which singly suffices for examination under torture

29. When someone in the committing of the crime loses something or lets it fall or be left behind, so that it can afterwards be found and determined to have belonged to the criminal, examination under torture is appropriate in order to discover who had the thing immediately before it was lost—unless he interposes something to the contrary, and were it to turn out or be established, the said suspicion would thereby be resolved, in which case this excuse shall first be investigated, before any examination under torture.

30. A half proof, as when someone thoroughly proves the essential element of the crime with a lone good and upright witness (as discussed below concerning good witnesses and witness proof proceedings)—that is and is called a half proof, and such a half proof also constitutes a legally sufficient indication of suspicion of the crime. When, however, someone wants to prove sundry circumstances, signs, indication, or suspicion, he shall do it with at least two good upright and unimpeachable witnesses.

31. When a proven criminal who has had accomplices in his crime informs while gaoled against someone who helped him with the crime he committed and was detected at, that is a ground of suspicion against the person so denounced, insofar as there are found and observed in connection with such denunciation the following matters and circumstances.

First: That the informer has not been asked after the denounced person by name under torture, hence has not been particularly examined or tortured with reference to just this person; rather that he have named and himself revealed the denounced person in the course of general examination regarding who helped him with his crime.

Second: It is pertinent that the said informer be particularly questioned as to how, where, and when the denounced person helped him and what relationship he had to him; and in such situations the informer shall be questioned about all possible and necessary details which can, according to the circumstances and character of each individual instance, best serve the subsequent discovery of the truth; and which can not all be described here, but which, however, every diligent and knowledgeable person can himself upon reflection work out.

Third: It is pertinent to inquire whether there is particular enmity, conflict, or ill will between the informer and the person he accuses. Because, were such enmity, conflict, or ill will obvious or revealed, then such accusation against the denounced person would not be believed from the informer, unless he otherwise credibly indicated adequate basis and signs, which would then hold up when investigated and constitute legally sufficient indication.

Fourth: That the person denounced be so suspicious that the accused crime can be believed of him.

Fifth: Where the informer has held to his denunciation, some priest-confessors nonetheless practice the abuse of instructing the miserable fellows in confession eventually to recant upon their truthful statement[s]; to the extent possible the priest-confessors shall be prevented from that, for no one is authorized to help criminals conceal their evil, which can disadvantage innocent people and the common weal. When, however, the informer in the end repudiates his denunciation or statement, which he himself has earlier made with great detail; and when it is thought that he wishes thereby to abet his accomplices, or that he was perhaps instructed to it by his father-confessor as above discussed; then the informer's statement and the other investigated circumstances must be considered and it must be thereupon decided whether or not the denunciation is adequate as legally sufficient indication. And in such a case it must be noticed and inquired, what sort of good or evil standing or reputation the denounced person has, and what sort of association or relationship he has had with the informer.

32. When someone is sufficiently convicted, as has been previously mentioned concerning a complete witness proof proceeding, through things he himself has needlessly said out of conceit or otherwise—that he committed the alleged or suspected crime or that he threatened to do such a crime before this one happened and the crime actually thereupon followed within a short time—and he is also the sort of person of whom such a deed could be believed, that can also be taken as legally sufficient indication of the crime upon which to examine under torture.

Concerning indications relative to particular crimes; and each article is enough for legally sufficient indication of that crime and therefore for examination under torture

Concerning sufficient indication of a murder committed clandestinely

33. When the person suspected and accused of the murder was seen in a suspicious manner at the time the murder occurred with bloody clothes or weapon; or when he has taken, sold, given away, or still retained property of the murder victim; that may be deemed legally sufficient indication upon which examination under torture may be employed, unless he can contradict such suspicion with credible indication or proof (which shall be heard before any examination under torture).

Concerning sufficient indication of publicly committed homicides happening in brawls or riots among many people, and which no one admits to having done

34. A homicide which occurred in a public brawl or riot, which no one will admit[:] When the suspected person who was at the brawl has also been an enemy of the deceased, and when he has taken his knife and slashed, hacked, or otherwise maliciously struck at the deceased, that is, as regards the crime committed, a legally sufficient indication for examination under torture; and it is yet more suspicious of such a suspect should his weapon be seen bloody. When, however, such or similar is not present, and particularly when he was present at the event in a harmless manner, then he shall not be examined under torture.

Concerning sufficient indication of the clandestine having of children and their killing by their mothers

35. When a girl, purportedly a maiden, comes under suspicion of having secretly had and killed a child, it shall be especially inquired, whether she was seen with a large and unusual body, and further, whether the body then became smaller and she was then pale and weak. When such and similar is discovered, and where this girl is a person of whom such a suspected crime could be believed, then she shall be inspected by knowledgeable women in an enclosed place, so far as that facilitates further inquiry; and if the suspicion is there confirmed, and nonetheless she will not confess the deed, she may be examined under torture.

36. When, however, the baby was killed only such a short time before that the milk in the breasts of the mother has not yet gone away, then she may be milked in her breasts; and when mother's milk is found in the breasts, there is in consequence a strong presumption for the use of examination under torture. Since, however, some physicians say that for several natural reasons a woman who has not borne a child may have milk in the breasts, when, therefore, a girl exculpates herself in this way, she shall be further investigated by the midwife or other.

Concerning sufficient indication of secret poisoning

37. When it is found that the suspect brought or otherwise dealt with poison, and the suspect had quarreled with the poisoned person or could have anticipated gain or advantage from his death or was otherwise a wanton person of whom the crime could be believed, that then suffices for legally sufficient indication of the crime unless he can produce credible indication that he used or wanted to use the said poison for other noncriminal ends.

Further: when someone buys poison and denies it to the authorities, and then the purchase is nonetheless proven, then this constitutes a sufficient ground for examining him as to why he used or wanted to use this poison.

Further: all authorities shall everywhere put the apothecaries and others who sell or deal in poison under vow and oath that they shall not sell any poison to anyone, nor allow him to get it, without indication, prior knowledge, and permission of these authorities.

Concerning sufficient indication of the suspicion of being a robber

38. When it is discovered that someone has with him goods that have been robbed; has sold, passed on, or otherwise dealt with them in a suspicious way; and he refuses to identify the person who sold or supplied him; he has raised against himself a legally sufficient indication, unless he demonstrates that he did not know that these goods were robbed and that he took them upon himself in good faith.

39. When horse soldiers or foot soldiers regularly tarry and eat and drink in inns and cannot demonstrate the sort of honest service relation, trade, or income on hand from which they could suitably defray their expenses, they are suspected of many evil deeds, and in particular of robbery, as especially to be understood from our and the Empire's common *Landfrieden,* wherein it is provided that such villains shall not be tolerated, rather proceeded against and rigorously examined and severely punished for their crimes; likewise shall every authority pay diligent regard to suspicious beggars and vagrants.

Concerning sufficient suspicion of those who aid robbers or thieves

40. When someone knowingly and maliciously takes robbed or stolen goods or loot, or shares therein; or when someone knowingly and maliciously gives the culprits food or drink, or knowingly takes in, conceals, or harbors the culprits or takes in, conceals, harbors, sells, or disperses the said illegal goods in whole or in part; or when someone otherwise in some similar way maliciously furnishes the culprits with help, advice, or assistance or had improper association with them in their crime, that is also an indication upon which to examine under torture.

Further: when someone has concealed prisoners, who leave him and then reveal where they were; further, when a suspect who is rather distrusted in the matter, but who feels good reason to be partial and on the side of the culprit, makes a contract of composition without telling the gaoling authorities, and does compose it or go surety therein—all these things in both the above articles are collectively and singly signs which constitute legally sufficient indication of criminal complicity and may be examined under torture.

Concerning sufficient indication of clandestine arson

41. When someone is suspected or accused of a covertly committed act of arson, and when this person is otherwise a fellow to be suspicious of, and it can be discovered that shortly before the fire he was in a stealthy and suspicious manner concerned with unusual and suspicious incendiary materials of the sort typically used to set fires clandestinely, that provides legally sufficient indication of the crime unless he can show with good, credible basis that he used or wanted to use them to noncriminal ends.

Concerning sufficient indication of treason

42. When the suspect has been seen behaving stealthily, unusually, and insidiously with those he is suspected of having betrayed, and when he pretends that he is afraid of them, and when he is a sort of person of whom such a crime can be believed, this is an indication for examination under torture.

Concerning sufficient suspicion of theft

43. When the stolen property is found with the suspect, or when it is discovered that it was, in whole or in part, possessed, sold, dispersed, or squandered by him, and he refuses to name his seller or supplier, he has raised a legally sufficient indication of the crime against himself, so long as he does not establish that he brought the said property upon himself in an undeceitful, noncriminal manner in good faith.

Further: when the theft was accomplished with special lock opening or breaking tools, then when the suspect has been at the very place dealing with such insidious lock opening or breaking tools with which the theft was committed, and the suspect is a sort of person of whom the crime can be believed, examination under torture is to be employed.

Further: when a particularly large theft occurs and there is suspected of it someone who, after the crime, is found to be more effusive with his spending than could be within his means apart from the crime; and when the suspect cannot show other good ground, where he got the indicated suspect wealth, and he is a sort of person of whom the crime could be believed, then there is present against him legally sufficient indication of the crime.

Concerning sufficient indication of sorcery

44. When someone offers to impart sorcery to other people, or threatens to bewitch someone and such befalls the threatened person, and the aforesaid person otherwise has associated with men or women sorcerers, or has employed suspicious things, gestures, words, and signs such as characterize

sorcery, and when, further, the said person has a bad reputation of similar sort, then that constitutes a legally sufficient indication of sorcery and is adequate basis upon which to examine under torture.

Concerning examination under torture

45. When the suspicion of a crime complained of and denied is established as above provided, and taken or recognized as proved, then a day for examination by torture shall be notified to the complainant upon his demand.

46. When it is desired to examine the prisoner under torture, either ex officio or upon demand of the complainant, then the said prisoner shall first, in the presence of the judge and of two of the court and of the court scribe, be diligently exhorted to speak up, with words (appropriate to the circumstances of the person and case) best serving to further understanding of the crime or the suspicion; and he shall be interrogated under threat of torture, whether or not he confesses to the alleged crime and what he knows about the said crime; and what he then confesses or denies shall be transcribed.

Regarding demonstration of innocence before threatened torture, and further proceeding thereupon

47. When, in the case now being discussed, the accused denies the crime under consideration, then it shall be assiduously inquired of him whether he can show that he is innocent of the alleged crime, and the prisoner shall in particular be asked to remember whether he can prove and establish that at the time the crime under consideration was committed he was with people or at a place or location whereby it can be recognized that he cannot have done the crime of which he is suspected. And such exhortation is thus needed because many a person out of simpleness or fright, even when he is quite innocent, does not know how he should proceed to exculpate himself of the thing. And when the prisoner in this manner or in like-serving way indicates his innocence, then the judge shall as quickly as possible investigate the exculpation proffered at the cost of the accused or his friends; moreover, when, with the approval of the judge, the witnesses which the prisoner or his friends wish in proper manner to proffer—as hereafter set forth concerning witness proof proceeding in Article 62 ("Where the accused will not confess, etc.") and in several subsequent articles—want on their own request to be examined, then the aforementioned hearing of the witnesses, also of the prisoner and of his friends on their demand, shall not be denied or disallowed without good and lawful ground. When, however, on account of poverty, the accused or his friends cannot bear or suffer such aforementioned costs, then nevertheless, in order that evil be punished while the innocent be not unlawfully taken advantage of, the authorities or the court shall put up the costs and the judge shall proceed with the case.

Further: when in the investigation now under discussion the innocence of the accused is not established, then he shall be examined under torture concerning the aforementioned, established legally sufficient suspicion in the presence of the judge and of at least two of the court and of the court scribe; and that which is revealed in the confession or in his admission and in all [subsequent verifying] investigation shall be particularly transcribed, and insofar as it concerns the accuser, disclosed to him, and at his request a copy shall be given to him without any intentional procrastination or delay.

How those who confess a crime when examined under torture shall be questioned subsequently without torture for further information

First, concerning murder

48. When the person examined confesses the crime under consideration through torture (as above) and his confession is transcribed, those persons who examine him on account of his confession shall diligently question him with great care to the extent that it serves the discovery of truth (as will be further treated to some extent hereafter); and indeed, when he has confessed to a murder, he shall be asked the reason he did the crime, on which day, at what hour, and at what place, whether anyone helped him to it and who; also where he buried or put the dead man, with what weapons the said murder was committed, how and what sort of blows or wounds he gave or inflicted upon the dead man, or how otherwise he killed him, what the murdered person had upon him by way of money or other things, and what he took from him, where he put this, or sold, dispersed, parted with, or hid it; and such questions as in many respects apply just as well to a robber or thief.

When the examined person confesses treason

49. When the prisoner confesses treason, he shall be asked who put him up to it and what he got for it, also where, how, and when this happened, and what motivated him to it.

Upon confession of poisoning

50. When the person examined confesses that he poisoned or wanted to poison someone, he shall also be asked about all the reasons the circumstances (as above), and moreover, what motivated him to it, also wherewith and how he employed or meant to employ the poison, and where he got the said poison, and who helped him or advised him to it.

When the person examined confesses arson

51. When the person examined confesses a fire, he shall be particularly questioned as to the reason, time, and company (as above), and furthermore, with what incendiary materials he set the fire and from whom, how, or where he procured the said incendiary materials or the corresponding tools.

When the person examined confesses sorcery

52. When someone confesses sorcery, he shall also be questioned about the causes and circumstances (as above), and moreover, with what, how, and when the sorcery occurred—with what words or deeds. Further, when the person examined states that he hid or held on to something which allegedly facilitated the said sorcery, then afterwards there shall be an attempt to find it; when, however, the said sorcery was committed with other things through word or deed, then they too shall be investigated to see whether they are infected with sorcery. The person shall also be asked from whom he learned such sorcery, and how it came about; whether he also employed such sorcery against more people, and against whom, and what damage thus occurred.

Concerning general, unparticularized questions regarding a confession secured under torture

53. From the brief instructions above any knowledgeable person can well gather what should be further and additionally inquired about concerning the confessed crime of the person examined, according to the circumstances of each case—what serves to the discovery of the truth, although it is all too long to be described. Any knowledgeable person can surely deduce from the above exposition how he should handle such additional questioning in other cases in order that one who has confessed a crime can be questioned about those signs and circumstances which no innocent person can know or discuss, and it shall be carefully transcribed how the person questioned explains the details.

Concerning the checking out and investigating of the incriminating circumstances confessed

54. When there is employed the aforementioned questioning of a confession secured with or without torture, the judge shall send to the places and shall (with all diligence, appropriate to the circumstances which the person examined told of in confessing the crime to the extent useful to precise knowledge of the truth) have it inquired whether the confession of the aforementioned circumstances is or is not true; because when someone declares the extent and mode of a crime as explicated in part above, and when just these circumstances are discovered, then it can be firmly established that the person committed the crime confessed, particularly then when he discloses such circumstances as occurred in the event and which no innocent person can know.

Where investigation reveals the circumstances confessed to be untrue

55. When it is determined in the aforementioned investigation that the circumstances confessed were untrue, this falsehood shall be put to the prisoner, who shall in consequence be verbally severely chastised, and he may then be brought to examination under torture a second time, in order that

he declare the above-mentioned circumstances truly and properly, because sometimes the guilty falsely declare the circumstances of a crime and believe that they can thereby make themselves appear innocent when the investigation discloses the untruth.

That the circumstances of the crime not be told to any prisoner beforehand, rather that they be told entirely by him alone

56. In the previous articles it is plainly set forth how someone who confesses under torture or threat of torture to an unsolved crime shall be questioned about all the circumstances of the said crime and how on that basis subsequent investigation shall take place, in order thus to get at the truth thoroughly, etc.; that would, however, probably be frustrated when the said circumstances of the crime were previously told to the prisoner upon arrest or examination and he thereupon examined. For that reason we want judges to take precautions against such happening; instead we want nothing to be put to the accused before or during examination other than according to the manner plainly written out in the articles just concluded.

Further: the prisoner shall also, at minimum two or more days after the torture and his confession (as set by the judge), be brought before the competent judge and two Schöffen in the guard room or in another room and his confession read to him by the court scribe, after which he shall be asked a second time whether his confession is true, and what he says to that shall also be transcribed.

When the prisoner retracts the confession

57. When the prisoner denies the previously confessed crime, and the suspicion is nonetheless manifest (as above), then he shall be returned to the gaol and again examined under torture, in addition to there being a thoroughly diligent investigation of the circumstances (as above) to the extent the examination under torture turns upon them—unless the prisoner adduces such reason for his denial that the judge is persuaded that the prisoner made the confession in error, in which case the judge may allow the said prisoner to detail and prove such error.

Concerning the extent of torture

58. Torturing shall be conducted according to the circumstances of the suspicion regarding the person—much, often or seldom, hard or lenient—according to the discretion of a good, sensible judge; and what the tortured person says shall not be taken down or transcribed while he is being tortured, rather he shall make his statement when he is released from the torture.

When the miserable fellow to be examined has serious wounds

59. When the accused has serious wounds or other injury to his body, examination under torture against him shall be conducted so that he is as little as possible hurt in these wounds or injury.

Establishing when the confession arising from examination under torture is ultimately to be believed

60. When, upon the making out of legally sufficient indication of a crime, examination under torture is conducted (as all that is plainly set out in the articles just concluded) and all possible subsequent investigation and interrogation has taken place and the sort of truth is revealed respecting the said confessed crime that no innocent person can tell or know, then this confession is soundly and undoubtedly credible; and upon it, according to the nature of the case, penal sanction is to be pronounced, as hereafter set forth in Article 104 ("When, according to our common written law, someone, etc.") and to be found in several articles following concerning penal sanctions.

When the prisoner has been put to examination under torture upon legally sufficient suspicion and not found guilty or the guilt not proven

61. When the accused on the basis of such a suspicion as is deemed sufficient for examination under torture (as above) has been gaoled and examined under torture and nonetheless is not convicted through his own confession or through proof of the alleged crime, then the judge and complainant have notwithstanding incurred no penalty on account of the aforementioned legal and proper examination under torture, because the incriminating indications made out gave reason and excuse for the examination which took place; for the law says that one should keep oneself not only from the committing of crime, but also from all appearance of evil, of the sort that can cause ill repute or indication of crime, and he who does not do that has himself in this way caused his own complaint. And in this case the complainant shall bear his own costs; and the accused shall bear his own support [while in gaol], since he supplied ground for his being suspected; and the authorities shall themselves bear the remaining court costs, for example, for the executioner and other court and gaol attendants. When, however, such examination under torture was employed in violation of this and the holy Empire's lawful ordinance, then, the said judges, as causes of such unjust examination under torture, are subject to punishment, and they shall in consequence suffer punishment and make recompense according to the law corresponding to the nature and circumstances of the violation, and further, shall be brought to account before their next appropriate authorities.

VIII
The Jurisprudence of Torture: Sebastian Guazzini

Torture entered most of the criminal courts of Europe, clerical and lay, during the thirteenth century, in the Romano-canonical system now commonly called *Ius commune*. Along with the incidence of torture in criminal procedure, there also grew up a jurisprudence of torture that imposed at least a theoretical control over it. Guazzini's "defense" echoes both the jurisprudence of Justinian's *Digest* and the experience of the jurists of the *Ius commune*. On the system itself, see now Manlio Bellomo, *The Common Legal Past of Europe, 1000–1800*, trans. Lydia G. Cochrane (Washington, D.C.: 1995).

What is called Torture is distress of body devised for extracting truth. The mode of administering torture by the use of the rope was invented by the Civil Law, and this torment of the rope, sometimes called the queen of torment, was justly invented by the Civil Law, as a mode of discovering truth, for the sake of the public welfare, to the end that crimes might not remain unpunished. It is called a species of evidence substituted to supply the lack of witnesses.

But let judges be on their guard against resorting to torture with facility, as it is an expedient which may prove fragile and perilous, and may play false to truth; because some persons have such an incapacity for the endurance of pain that they are more willing to lie than to suffer torments. Others again are so obstinate that they are more willing to suffer any torments whatsoever than to confess the truth.

Having been invented only as a subsidiary form of evidence where truth cannot be otherwise discovered in the ordinary way, *i.e.*, by witnesses, the authorities say that this rule holds good in every case whatsoever, in which resort is had, either by law or usage, to the institute of torture. It is always a subsidiary remedy, to be invoked only when truth cannot be discovered in any other way."

Torture cannot be repeated more than three times on the same subject, and then only for justifying reasons and with respect had to the persons and the crimes involved.

Confession of guilt made under torture works no damage to the party confessing until the confession has been reaffirmed without torture. Under this head the lawyer has the firmest rule for his guidance, and the rule has been established, as the text-writers say, because the remedy of torture "is falla-

From Sebastian Guazzini, *Tractatus ad Defansam Inquisitorum, Carceratorum, Reorum, et Condemnatorum super Quocumque Crimine*, 1612 (Geneva, 1664), pp. 71–130, *Defensio XXX, Circa Torturam pro habenda veritatem*; abbreviated translation from James C. Welling, *The Law of Torture: A Study in the Evolution of Law* (Washington, D.C., 1892), pp. 6–15.

cious, fragile, and perilous" for reasons already given; and this ratification should be made outside of the place of torment, at the bar of public justice, and in presence of the witnesses required by law. It should also be made at a sufficient interval after the torture to protect it from the suspicion of being made under the surviving stress of the torture which has extorted the confession. But in practice this rule is very elastic, and the interval, according to the discretion of courts or judges, may vary from three days to four or five hours.

Torture legally administered in a legal case and sustained with constancy has for its effect to work the legal absolution of the party accused.

More than this, if after a person has confessed his guilt, has been convicted, and has been condemned, the judge shall proceed to torture him for ulterior information concerning his accomplices, suborners, or abettors without first premising and protesting that the torture *does not relate to the matters confessed and of which the culprit has been convicted*, or without first premising and protesting that the torture is inflicted *without prejudice to his condemnation*, in such cases the torture, if sustained, will work not only his expurgation from the presumptions, but also from the proofs on which he has been convicted. But where such a precautionary reservation has been made the judge may proceed to torture a confessed or convicted culprit for the discovery of accessories before or after the fact.

Torture, in cases where it is applicable, works the rehabilitation of competent witnesses who are affected with a single defect, but will not deliver from a multiplicity of defects. It cannot be used to purge the defect of perjury, of personal enmity, etc.

A judge who unduly tortures an accused party from malice, hatred, enmity, or for reward, is guilty of a capital offence if the patient dies under torture. Some writers hold that the victim of unjust torture may slay the judge who ordered it, and may do so without being subject to the ordinary penalty of homicide, especially when this vengeance is taken by the victim immediately on being dismissed from torture.

The text-writers hold that prisoners who make or take remedies to harden the body against torture should be punished, since such remedies are altogether prohibited; and, as such, the text-writers are likely to characterize all incantations and malefic arts, if they induce taciturnity or insensibility to bodily torture. If anybody desires to know how accused parties make use of such-like incantations and remedies, let him consult Paul. Grill., *De quæst. et tort., quæst.* 4, *numer.* 11. If anybody desires to know the remedies which the judge should use against the remedies of the accused, let him consult Grill., *ibid., numer.* 16. The authorities lay down many other antidotes against these diabolic incantations, but Cavalcanus thinks, for his part, that there is no remedy more appropriate than the upright mind of the judge himself, when he directs it solely to the end of attaining the way of truth and justice, and not to the end of clutching after vainglory or striving for the sake of gain.

Hence the judge should pray God to be propitious to him in the way of truth and justice.

If a prisoner about to be tortured shall use the words of the Holy Evangely or Prophets, even though the words should induce taciturnity or silence, he may not deserve for this reason to be punished in this world or in the secular forum. Such, at least, is the opinion of certain commentators.

Even when these legitimate presumptions exist, the judge, before he proceeds to torture, must file a decree or an interlocutory plea stating his purpose to resort to torture, and alleging the grounds on which this plea is based. After a decree of torture shall have been allowed, an appeal may be taken from it by the counsel of the accused, and, pending this appeal, at least in most jurisdictions (that of the French Parliament and of other courts in Dauphiny being exceptions), the judge cannot renew any proceedings in the way of torture. If, in spite of the appeal, a judge shall have proceeded to torture and extorted a confession, such a confession shall be wholly null. It is not competent for the government prosecutor or for the plaintiff to take an appeal from a decree disallowing torture. Wary judges, it is true, when they wish to torture and do not want to have their hands tied, are accustomed to pass the decree of torture secretly, and do not interpose it until it is too late for the accused to take an appeal. But this surprise action on the part of judges may be counterminded by wary attorneys, who are wont to obtain in advance an inhibition [from the superior court] against the menace of torture; and, the instant that the judge shows a disposition to proceed to torture, they present the inhibition to him, and thus compel him to stay his hand and to consign the case to the court above. A frivolous and false appeal can be rejected at once, and it resides in the discretion of the judge to decide when an appeal is manifestly frivolous and false. In such case he can administer torture without usurpation; but if any doubt remain, whether of fact or law, he must wholly desist from torture, or he will expose himself to punishment and peril.

If the decree of torture shall be overruled [by the court of appeals], there are regulations which prescribe who shall hear the principal matter involved in the case—*an judex a quo vel judex ad quem.*

Torture can be administered only in cases which involve a heavy penalty such as banishment, death, or severe bodily punishment of some kind. In nowise should a resort to torture be allowed in actions at law sounding in money damages alone. In an action, for instance, arising from contract, express or implied, torture is not to be thought of, even though the truth cannot otherwise be attained, because in civil suits the laws afford other remedies, for if the plaintiff makes complete proof of his declaration judgment is given; if a half-complete proof is made, the supplementary oath is administered to him; if a proof less than half complete is made, then the oath of purgation is granted to the defendant; if the plaintiff makes no proof at all, the defendant is acquitted.

Sometimes, however, or at least in the judgment of some authorities, it may be competent to torture vile persons in actions where only a money penalty is involved, it being presumed that such persons will make more account of money, "the second blood of men," than of their physical comfort; but in all such cases the torture inflicted must be moderate or even light."

1. The first principal requisite is that the truth of the facts cannot be otherwise elicited, and that the torture, as declared in the decree allowing it, is employed only as a subsidiary remedy and for the reasons already assigned by the judge in his interlocutory plea.

2. The second principal requisite is that the *corpus delicti* be manifest before resort is had to torture.

3. The third principal requisite is that legitimate presumptions of fact held sufficient to justify torture shall precede its administration, it being abhorrent both to the canon and the civil laws that the judge should begin his inquest with torture. These presumptions should be so accusatory, according to some authorities, as to leave nothing wanting except the confession alone of the culprit—that is, in their character as accusatory indications they should be, so to say, clearer than light; and let judges beware lest, in virtue of any discretion conceded to them, either by law or by man, they push on to torture without the legitimate presumptions precedent, because this discretion of theirs should be regulated by the rules of the common law. Some authorities hold that a judge who has the faculty of proceeding with the Royal Arm [that is, by Prerogative Right] can resort to torture, in cases of difficult proof, because of the bad character of the accused; because of the atrocity of the crime alleged; because of a widespread public rumor, or such like probable indication; yet even in such cases there should be certain concurrent and precedent indications.

The Prince [that is, in the Italian diction of the time, the Government] cannot order that anybody should be tortured without legitimate indications, nor can a judge be held to obey him, as, by so obeying, the judge is subject to public impeachment [*tenetur in syndicatu*].

Just as little can a judge lawfully terrorize an accused party without legitimate presumptions precedent. Yea, many hold that, in default of legitimate indications precedent, an accused party cannot be tortured even with his own consent.

If the prosecutor shall say, "I have no presumptions of fact and no proofs against the accused, but I wish to stand with him in torture, and in this way prove the crime imputed to him," such a prosecutor shall not be heard, and the accused shall not be tortured on this plea.

And let the judge make sure that the indications are not only sufficient for torture, but that they are such as can be lawfully received; and this rule holds good even where the judge has the faculty of proceeding summarily in the administration of torture.

Nor let the [ordinary] judge suppose that without the legitimate indications precedent he can proceed to torture because of the gravity of the crime, for the rule that in atrocious crimes 'it may be lawful to exceed the laws' is a rule which holds good only after the accused has been found guilty, and cannot be pleaded in regard to the mode of procedure. The logic of the rule would seem to be that the greater the crime is, so much the more vehement should be the presumptions of fact which ought to precede torture; and, without these legitimate presumptions of fact, the judge must be on his guard against resorting to torture under the pretext that the crime is hard to prove. Just as little can a judge use torture to extract truth, under pretext that on account of torture inflicted for certain crimes even without legitimate presumptions of fact, a great public scandal may be allayed.

All the indications which may suffice for inflicting torture cannot be enumerated, nor can any certain or determinate doctrine on the subject be propounded; but the whole matter is committed to the discretion of the prudent judge, having regard to the nature of the facts, of the crime, of the person involved, and of other circumstances and characteristics deduced from the process. This discretion, however, must not be based on any indication at the pleasure of the judge, but only on certain concurrent circumstances and characteristics implicit in each case. The judge's discretion is a regulated discretion, because regulated by rules of common law, and does not spring out of the judge's mere brain. The faculty of torturing accused parties is so far restricted and limited to terms of law that, in my opinion, not even the Royal Bailiffs [*Trunculatores*] sent to try highway robbers should presume that God has created human bodies to be agonized and lacerated at the torturer's free will. Yet true it is that if the judge has the Royal Arm he may torture on the strength of indications which hold good under natural, divine, or canon laws.

Thus far the whole question has moved in presumptions of *fact* resulting from the inquest. It is otherwise where presumptions of *law* are concerned, and where any indication shall have been *proved*, whether by confession made out of court or by the testimony of a single witness, because in such cases it will not reside in the discretion of the judge to decide whether the indication is sufficient for torture or not. He will be bound to torture the accused without demur. If anybody is curious to see certain particular indications which are sufficient for torture, let him consult Campeg. *de testib. reg.*, 395; Menoch. *de præsumpt.*, lib. 9, *quæst.* 89, where the latter heaps up forty-three indications for torture, while Cavalcanus discusses indications that may be used before an ordinary judge and indications that may be used before a judge of the Royal Arm.

Question has been raised whether one indication will suffice for torture or whether several indications should be required. The distinction to be observed is that one may suffice provided it is proximate to the crime [that is, very close to the crime in its accusatory significance]. Where the indications are remote in their bearing, several are required. The common rule is, in both the canon and the civil laws, that at least two indications should be required for torture, and that one remote indication is not enough to justify torture. If, however, there shall be several remote indications, which are proved by single witnesses, the accused can be tortured on the strength of them. If there should be at least three indications, proved by single witnesses, they will suffice for torture, though the indications may not be very cogent, especially where the witnesses are men of known probity and of high authority.

4. The fourth requisite for torture is that the issue at law with the accused shall be fully and legally joined, except where the judge has the power of proceeding summarily.

5. The fifth requisite is that the interlocutory plea for torture shall have been filed and duly allowed after the suit has been made public, and after the matter has been discussed with the counsel of the accused; though, as before implied, such a decree of torture is not required where the judge has the faculty of proceeding summarily. Maur. Burg. lays down in such cases a form for the summary procedures to torture, and enumerates eight special prerogatives which a judge has in virtue of such faculty of summary procedure. In passing a decree of torture the judge should collect and, as it were, condense into a brief compass all the several indications scattered through the process in its several parts, by way of exhorting the accused to make a clean breast of it, inasmuch as, in the fact of so many indications, he cannot persist in a denial. In this way accused parties may place themselves in the clemency of the Prince, and will do a service to their lawyers, who will clearly discern wherein the difficulty of a case may lie.

6. The sixth requisite is that a copy of the indications and of the whole process must be furnished to the accused, and that the process itself must be published. Where the accused is found *in flagranti delicto*, no copy, either of the indications or of the process, need be furnished, as, for instance, in the celebrated case of the noblemen who were caught with their ladders at the windows of a certain noble lady [in the act of abduction]. In a crime like that, the rule is not to observe rule.

7. The seventh requisite is that inspection be made of the person of the accused, to ascertain whether he is privileged or not, because a privileged person cannot be tortured even with legitimate presumptions precedent.

8. The eighth requisite is that if the accused shall ask that the accuser make oath to the good faith of the charge, no torture shall be inflicted until such oath shall have been made.

9. The ninth requisite is that the accuser, in the presence of the judge, shall demand the torture of the accused, and shall swear that he has no further proofs; but this rule had fallen into desuetude in the whole of Italy.

10. The tenth requisite is that the accused shall not have eaten for nine or ten hours before torture, that the process of digestion may have been com-

pleted before the torture begins. If accident happen and suffering ensue to the accused from a failure to observe this rule, the judge will be liable to public impeachment.

11. The eleventh requirement is that if the accused be under the age of twenty-five years the judge shall appoint a curator to watch for his safety under torture. In such cases, a confession made without a curator is null and void. Of late years, however, an exception of nullity, when based on this ground, has been so reduced as to extend only to minors under the age of fourteen years; but it will always be competent for counsel to insist, in such cases, that special usage shall not prevail against common law.

12. The twelfth requisite is that the judge must have plenary power for the administration of torture. A *Locumtenens Potestatis* [an acting judge] or a simple assessor on the bench has not the power of torture.

13. The thirteenth requisite is that indications of the government prosecutor, if sufficient for torture, shall not have been quashed by the counter-indications of the accused.

14. The fourteenth requisite is that when several persons are to be tortured they shall not all be tortured alike, but some more severely and others more mildly, according to the quality of the persons and the presumptions lying against them, having regard to their age, their physical constitution, their mental habits, and their social status.

15. The fifteenth requisite is that the accused must not be disabled in any of his members, for in that case, as for instance, if he has an issue of blood, has a wound in the breast, is troubled with shortness of breath, has hernia, or is suffering from venereal disease, he cannot be tortured.

16. The sixteenth requisite is, as before stated, that torture cannot be employed to make manifest the *corpus delicti* (since this must appear *aliunde*), but only for the purpose of discovering the authors and accomplices of the crime. It also ought to be inflicted [as before implied] only in cases in which a confession can and ought to sound in felony (*possit et debeat sonare in delictum*), since torture should not be inflicted uselessly.

17. The seventeenth requisite is that before accused parties can be tortured their counsel should be inquired of and duly heard on the question whether the accused can be tortured or not. The rule that counsel should be inquired of holds good especially in the Kingdom of Naples, though little observed in practice; but counsel ought to be heard if they wish to be heard.

After counsel have been duly heard for a client they are not permitted, by usage, to be present at the act of torture, though, of right, it should be said otherwise; and, of right, the government prosecutor should not be present at the infliction of torture, though, by custom, it is sometimes allowed. Baiardus says that for the sake of suppressing the vain exclamations of the government, he always wished the presence of the government prosecutor or of some substitute for the said prosecutor—a rule which I have always observed for the sake of avoiding the vain acclamations of the aforesaid attorney for the government.

18. The eighteenth requisite is that in inflicting torture on a clergyman degradation from office shall precede the infliction, though this rule is poorly observed in practice.

19. The nineteenth requisite is that an accused party shall not be tortured on a Feast Day celebrated in honor of God, except in grave cases. Judges who fear god observe this rule, says Julius Clarus, but judges otherwise minded do not pay much respect to it.

A culprit pardoned by the Prince can be tortured as to any contingent remainder of suspected guilt not covered by the pardon. For instance, a pardoned culprit may be tortured in order to remove the stain of his guilt, so that his testimony under torture may be held valid against his accomplices. But a full pardon works exemption from torture.

Where a party confesses the act, but denies criminal intent, as in case of homicide alleged to have been committed in self-defence, it is a moot point whether such a mixed confession should be received at all, or whether it should be received by the government as a confession of guilt unless the accused can establish the absence of criminal intent. In case of such mixed confession it would be safer not to torture, for torture sustained in such a case would work the acquittal of the accused.

A culprit, confessing a crime, cannot be tortured to procure the confession of other crimes, in the absence of competent presumptions to that effect. The contrary usage prevails, however, in the whole of Italy. But such torture is subject to the following qualifications: It must be moderate; it cannot be applied to clergymen; it is applicable only to notorious criminals, and it is abolished in the States of the Church.

Whether benefit of clergy works immunity from torture or not, is a disputed question among the authorities. Some hold that a clergyman can be tortured, but not so severely as a layman, and not by a lay judge, nor by a lay minister even at the mandate of a bishop. A clergyman should not be admitted to canonical purgation when he is weighed down with presumptions that justify torture.

A deaf-mute from birth cannot be tortured, though opinion and practice are at variance on this point. A pregnant woman and a woman giving suck to her children cannot be tortured.

Torture must be suspended so soon as the victim falls into a faint under its effects, and unless the judge, in the act of such suspension, is careful to reserve a right of renewing torture, the right lapses. The notary is bound to make a minute of all proceedings in torture, with its effect on the subject, and the measures taken to recover him from a faint. The prisoner's counsel, in such moments, must watch for his rights and protect him from the renewal of the torture, if the judge, in his alarm at the fainting spell, forgets to reserve the right of renewing the torture. [Guazzini confesses that he had several times fallen into negligence under this head when he first began to practice the duties of his office.]

Bishops and others in which civil dignity are exempt from torture even under strong presumptions of guilt. Noblemen, town councillors, doctors, lawyers, have a general immunity from torture, though the practice varies under these heads. Privilege from torture works a perfectly valid defence against all confessions extorted under its illegal infliction, except in cases of high treason. When several persons are to be tortured at the same time the general rule is that the judge should begin with the more timid, with the weaker, with the meaner [in social rank], with the younger, with the one who stands more nearly related to the charge, and with men before women, though some authorities hold that it is better to begin with women, because women are less afraid of torture than men, and will longer persist in a negative. In such cases the judge may proceed at his discretion.

In administering torture it is competent for the judge, according to some authorities, to begin with the culprit who, from the name he bears, is known to belong to a family of criminals, and, as examples of such bad names, may be cited the names of Forabosco, Sgaramella, Saltalamachia, Mardolino, Spazzacroce, Pizzaguerra, Falameschia, Mazzasette, etc. Some hold that it is proper to begin with the man who has a bad hold that it is proper to begin with the man who has a bad physiognomy, provided he labors under other presumptions.

Where father and son rest under the same charge and the same presumptions, it may be proper to begin with the son rather than the father, that the father, being more tortured in the person of his son than in his own proper person, may be the sooner urged to confession. [But Guazzini says he had never seen this rule observed, and had not observed it himself when once, in Perugia, he had a father and a son before him *in pari delicto*.] The preponderant weight of opinion would seem to be that the judge should begin with the person to whom the strongest suspicions of guilt attach.

Let judges beware of aspiring after a vainglory in the infliction of torture, and let them strive only to attain truth through legitimate channels, conducting themselves with moderation and considering the physical condition, temperament, age, social status, etc., etc., of the accused. Torture must be administered only with the usual and established instruments. The accused is to be so tortured that his life may be safe, whether with a view to his innocence [in case his innocence shall be demonstrated by his constancy] or with a view to his punishment [in case he shall confess his guilt].

The judge must not administer torture by his own hands, but by the intervention of satellites and bailiffs.

IX
John Locke: *Letter on Toleration*

Locke's *Letter on Toleration,* one of the landmarks in the history of religious toleration, was printed anonymously in Latin in the town of Gouda in the Netherlands in 1689 while Locke himself was in exile. Locke had long thought about the problems raised by religious coercion and looked back upon a century of both religious and political wars and persecutions. The generally tolerant atmosphere of the Netherlands and the friendship of such figures as Philip van Limborch seem to have contributed to the letter, whose opening pages are printed here. The Preface by Klibansky and the Introduction and notes by Gough in the volume from which this selection is taken provide ample background. For the long tradition of which the letter is a part, see my book, *Inquisition* (New York, 1988; Berkeley-Los Angeles, 1989), 155–88.

A LETTER ON TOLERATION

Honoured Sir,

Since you ask my opinion about mutual toleration among Christians, I reply briefly that I regard it as the chief distinguishing mark of a true church. For however much some people boast of the antiquity of places and names, or of the splendour of their ritual; others of the reformation of their teaching, and all of the orthodoxy of their faith (for everyone is orthodox to himself): these claims, and others of this kind, are more likely to be signs of men striving for power and empire than the signs of the church of Christ. If a man possesses all these things, but lacks charity, meekness, and good will in general towards all mankind, even towards those who do not profess the Christian faith, he falls short of being a Christian himself. *The kings of the Gentiles exercise lordship over them,* said our Saviour to his disciples, *but ye shall not be so* (Luke xxii. 25). The business of true religion is something quite different. It is not made for outward pomp, nor for ecclesiastical dominion, let alone for force; but for regulating men's lives in accordance with virtue and piety. He who wishes to enlist under the banner of Christ must first of all declare war upon his own vices, his own pride and lusts; otherwise, without holiness of life, purity of manners, benignity and meekness of spirit, it is in vain for him to seek the name of Christian. *Thou, when thou are converted, strengthen*

From John Locke, *Epistola de Tolerantia: A Letter on Toleration,* ed. Raymond Klibansky, trans. J. W. Gough (Oxford: Clarendon Press, 1968), pp. 59–68 (notes deleted). Reprinted by permission of Oxford University Press.

thy brethren, said our Lord to Peter (Luke xxii. 32). For one who is careless about his own salvation will hardly persuade people that he is extremely concerned about someone else's. No man can sincerely strive with all his might to make other people Christians, if he has not really embraced the Christian religion in his own heart. For if the Gospel and the Apostles are to be believed, no man can be a Christian without charity, and without the faith which worketh, not by force, but by love. Now, I appeal to the consciences of those who persecute, mutilate, despoil, and kill other men on the plea of religion, whether they do it out of friendship and kindness. And then indeed, and only then, will I believe that they do so, when I see those fanatics in the same manner correct their friends and familiar acquaintance, who manifestly sin against the precepts of the Gospel; when I see them persecute with fire and sword their own brethren, who are corrupted with vices and unless they mend their ways will assuredly perish; and when I see them remonstrate their love and desire for the salvation of their souls by the infliction of all kinds of cruelties and torments. For if it is out of charity, as they pretend, and care for men's souls, that they deprive them of their property, mutilate their bodies, torment them in noisome prisons, and in the end even take away their lives, all to make them believers and procure their salvation, why do they allow fornication, deceit, malice, and other vices, which according to the Apostle (Rom. i) so plainly smell of paganism, to run riot among their own people? These, and such-like practices are more contrary to the glory of God, the purity of the church, and the salvation of souls, than any conscientious dissent, however erroneous, from ecclesiastical decisions, or separation from public worship, if it is accompanied by innocence of life. Why then does this burning zeal for God, for the church, and for the salvation of souls—actually burning at the stake—pass by, without any chastisement or censure, those wickednesses and moral vices which all men admit to be diametrically opposite to the profession of Christianity, and devote itself entirely and bend all its energies to the introduction of ceremonies, or the correction of opinions, which for the most part are about subtle matters that exceed the ordinary man's grasp? Which of the parties contending about these questions is more in the right, which of them is guilty of schism or heresy—those that domineer or those that submit—will then at last be manifest, when the cause of their separation comes to judgement. For he is not a heretic who follows Christ and embraces his doctrine, and takes up his yoke, though he forsake father and mother, the public ceremonies and assemblies of his country, and indeed all other men.

Now, however much the divisions among sects obstruct the salvation of souls, yet *adultery, fornication, uncleanness, lasciviousness, idolatry, and the like* are none the less works of the flesh, concerning which the Apostle expressly declares that *they who do such things shall not inherit the kingdom of God* (Gal. v). Whoever, therefore, is sincerely solicitous about the kingdom of

God, and thinks it his duty to strive for its enlargement, ought to apply himself with no less care and industry to the rooting out of these vices than to the extirpation of sects. But if anyone does otherwise, and while he is cruel and implacable to sins and moral vices that are unbecoming the name of a Christian, however much he may prate of the church, he plainly demonstrates that he aims at another kingdom, and not the kingdom of God.

If anyone wishes to make a soul, whose salvation he heartily desires, expire in torments, and that even in an unconverted state, I shall be greatly surprised, and so, I think, will others also. But nobody, surely, will ever believe that such an attitude can proceed from love, good will, and charity. If men are to be driven by fire and sword to profess certain doctrines, and forced to adopt a form of outward worship, but without any regard for their morals; if anyone endeavours to convert those that are in error to the faith, by forcing them to profess things they do not believe, and allowing them to practice things which the gospel does not permit to Christians, and which no believer permits to himself, I do not doubt that such a one desires to have a numerous assembly joined in the same profession with himself; but who can believe that what he desires is a Christian church? No wonder therefore if men who, whatever they pretend, do not fight for the advancement of true religion and the Christian church, make use of arms that do not belong to Christian warfare. If, like the Captain of our salvation, they sincerely desired the salvation of souls, they would tread in his steps and follow the perfect example of the Prince of peace, who sent out his disciples to subdue nations and gather them into his church, not armed with sword, or with force, but furnished with the Gospel, the message of peace, and the exemplary holiness of their conduct. Though if infidels were to be converted by force of arms, if the blind or the obstinate were to be recalled from their errors by armed soldiers, it would be easier for him to do it with the army of the heavenly legions, than for any protector of the church, however powerful, with his dragoons.

The toleration of those who hold different opinions on matters of religion is so agreeable to the Gospel and to reason, that it seems monstrous for men to be blind in so clear a light. I will not here blame the pride and ambition of some, the passion and the harsh, uncharitable zeal of others. These are faults which perhaps cannot be eradicated from human affairs, yet they are such that no one is willing to have them openly imputed to him; there is hardly anyone who when led astray by them does not seek to win praise by disguising them with some specious colour. But that some may not mask their persecution and unchristian cruelty with a pretence of care for the commonwealth and observance of the laws; and that others, in the name of religion, may not seek licence for their immorality and impunity for their misdeeds; in a word, that none may impose upon himself or others, either as a faithful subject of his prince, or as a sincere worshipper of God, I regard it as necessary above all to distinguish between the business of civil government and that of religion, and to mark the true bounds between the church and the commonwealth. If this is not done, no end can be put to the controversies between those who truly have or pretend to have at heart a concern on the one hand for the salvation of souls, and on the other for the safety of the commonwealth.

X
The Moral Protest: Cesare Beccaria

As a number of scholars have observed, the meticulous subtleties of jurists like Guazzini, with their interminable restrictions, shadings of the weight of different kinds of evidence, technical considerations, and meticulous insistence on legal minutiae may well reflect the process within jurisprudence by which judicial torture was finally abolished in the late eighteenth century. Guazzini was certainly not the only jurist who produced detailed accounts. Far better known are those eighteenth-century denunciations that reflect an outraged humanity rather than judicial thought. The most famous indictment of torture came from the pen of Cesare Beccaria, the eighteenth-century Italian publicist whose essay *On Crimes and Punishments* became the foremost treatise on penal reform produced by the Enlightenment. The work circulated widely in both the original Italian and in many translations. Beccaria was not himself a jurist, and he drew what he knew of jurisprudence from his friends, the Verri brothers.

Beccaria's inaccuracies derived partly from his lack of legal training and partly from his dependence on the work of Pietro Verri, whose *Osservazioni sulla tortura* appeared in 1804. Some of these are reviewed in Alessandro Manzoni, *The Column of Infamy, Prefaced by Cesare Beccaria's "Of Crimes and Punishments,"* trans. Kenelm Foster, O.P. and Jane Grigson, with an Introduction by A. P. d'Entrèves (Oxford, 1964); see now Marcello Maestro, *Cesare Beccaria and the Origins of Penal Reform* (Philadelphia, 1973). Three recent studies shed considerable light on Beccaria's moral and rhetorical arguments: Richard Mowery Andrews, "The Cunning of Imagery: Rhetoric and Ideology in Cesare Beccaria's Treatise *On Crimes and Punishments*," in *Begetting Images: Studies in the Art and Science of Symbol Production*, ed. Mary B. Campbell and Mark Rollins (New York-Bern, 1989), 113–32; J. S. Cockburn, "Punishment and Brutalization in the English Enlightenment," *Law and History Review* 12 (1994), 155–79; and especially the magisterial study by Richard Mowery An-

From Cesare Beccaria, *On Crimes and Punishments, and Other Writings*, ed. Richard Bellamy, trans. Richard Davies with Virginia Cox and Richard Bellamy (Cambridge and New York: Cambridge University Press, 1995), Chapter 16, pp. 39–44. Reprinted by permission of Cambridge University Press.

drews, *Law, Magistracy, and Crime in Old Regime Paris, 1735–1789*, vol. I, *The System of Criminal Justice* (Cambridge, 1994), 441–72.

OF TORTURE

The torture of a criminal while his trial is being put together is a cruelty accepted by most nations, whether to compel him to confess a crime, to exploit the contradictions he runs into, to uncover his accomplices, to carry out some mysterious and incomprehensible metaphysical purging of his infamy, (or, lastly, to expose other crimes of which he is guilty but with which he has not been charged).

No man may be called guilty before the judge has reached his verdict; nor may society withdraw its protection from him until it has been determined that he has broken the terms of the compact by which that protection was extended to him. By what right, then, except that of force, does the judge have the authority to inflict punishment on a citizen while there is doubt about whether he is guilty or innocent? This dilemma is not a novelty: either the crime is certain or it is not; if it is certain, then no other punishment is called for than what is established by law and other torments are superfluous because the criminal's confession is superfluous; if it is not certain, then an innocent man should not be made to suffer, because, in law, such a man's crimes have not been proven. Furthermore, I believe it is a wilful confusion of the proper procedure to require a man to be at once accuser and accused, in such a way that physical suffering comes to be the crucible in which truth is assayed, as if such a test could be carried out in the sufferer's muscles and sinews. This is a sure route for the acquittal of robust ruffians and the conviction of weak innocents. Such are the evil consequences of adopting this spurious test of truth, but a test worthy of a cannibal, that the ancient Romans, for all their barbarity on many counts, reserved only for their slaves, the victims of a fierce and overrated virtue.

What is the political purpose of punishment? The instilling of terror in other men. But how shall we judge the secret and secluded torture which the tyranny of custom visits on guilty and innocent alike? It is important that no established crime go unpunished; but it is superfluous to discover who committed a crime which is buried in shadows. A misdeed already committed, and for which there can be no redress, need be punished by a political society only when it influences other people by holding out the lure of impunity. If it is true that, from fear or from virtue, more men observe the laws than break them, the risk of torturing an innocent ought to be accounted all the greater, since it is more likely that any given man has observed the laws than that he has flouted them.

Another absurd ground for torture is the purging of infamy, that is, when a man who has been attained by the law has to confirm his own testimony by the dislocation of his bones. This abuse should not be tolerated in the eighteenth century. It presupposes that pain, which is a sensation, can purge infamy, which is a mere moral relation. Is torture perhaps a crucible and the infamy some impurity? It is not hard to reach back in time to the source of this absurd law, because even the illogicalities which a whole nation adopts always have some connection with its other respected commonplaces. It seems that this practice derives from religious and spiritual ideas, which have had so much influence on the ideas of men in all nations and at all times. An infallible dogma tells us that the stains springing from human weakness, but which have not earned the eternal anger of the great Being, have to be purged by an incomprehensible fire. Now, infamy is a civil stain and, since pain and fire cleanse spiritual and incorporeal stains, why should the spasms of torture not cleanse the civil stain of infamy? I believe that the confession of guilt, which in some courts is a prerequisite for conviction, has a similar origin, for, before the mysterious court of penitence, the confession of sin is an essential part of the sacrament. It is thus that men abuse the clearest illuminations of revealed truth; and, since these are the only enlightenment to be found in times of ignorance, it is to them that credulous mankind will always turn and of them that it will make the most absurd and far-fetched use. But infamy is a sentiment which is subject neither to the law nor to reason, but to common opinion. Torture itself causes real infamy to its victims. Therefore, by this means, infamy is purged by the infliction of infamy.

The third ground for torture concerns that inflicted on suspected criminals who fall into inconsistency while being investigated, as if both the innocent man who goes in fear and the criminal who wishes to cover himself would not be made to fall into contradiction by fear of punishment, the uncertainty of the verdict, the apparel and magnificence of the judge, and by their own ignorance, which is the common lot of both of most knaves and of the innocent; as if the inconsistencies into which men normally fall even when they are calm would not burgeon in the agitation of a mind wholly concentrated on saving itself from a pressing danger.

This shameful crucible of the truth is a standing monument to the law of ancient and savage times, when ordeal by fire, by boiling water and the lottery of armed combat were called the *judgements* of God, as if the links in the eternal chain which originates from the breast of the First Mover could be continually disrupted and uncoupled at the behest of frivolous human institutions. The only difference which there might seem to be between torture and ordeal by fire or boiling water is that the result of the former seems to depend on the will of the criminal, and that of the latter on purely physical and external factors; but this difference is only apparent and not real. Telling the truth in the midst of spasms and beatings is as little subject to our will as is preventing without fraud the effects of fire and boiling water. Every act of our will is always proportional to the force of the sensory impression which gives rise to it; and the sensibility of every man is limited. Therefore, the impression made by pain may grow to such an extent that having filled the whole of the sensory field, it leaves the torture victim no freedom to do anything but choose the quickest route to relieving himself of the immediate pain. Thus the criminal's replies are as necessitated as are the effects of fire and boiling water. And thus the sensitive but guiltless man will admit guilt if he believes that, in that way, he can make the pain stop. All distinctions between the guilty and the innocent disappear as a consequence of the use of the very means which was meant to discover them.

(It would be redundant to make this point twice as clear by citing the numerous cases of innocent men who have confessed their guilt as a result of the convulsions of torture. There is no nation nor age which cannot cite its own cases, but men do not change nor do they think out the consequences of their practices. No man who has pushed his ideas beyond what is necessary for life, has not sometimes headed towards nature, obeying her hidden and indistinct calls; but custom, that tyrant of the mind, repulses and frightens him.)

The result, therefore, of torture depends on a man's predisposition and on calculation, which vary from man to man according to their hardihood and sensibility, so that, with this method, a mathematician would settle problems better than a judge. Given the strength of an innocent man's muscles and the sensitivity of his sinews, one need only find the right level of pain to make him admit his guilt of a given crime.

A guilty man is interrogated in order to know the truth, but if this truth is hard to discover from the bearing, the gestures and the expression of a man at rest, it will be much the harder to discover it from a man in whom every feature, by which men's faces sometimes betray the truth against their will, has been altered by spasms of pain. Every violent action confuses and clouds the tiny differences in things which sometimes serve to distinguish truth from falsehood.

These truths were known to the ancient Roman legislators, who only allowed the torture of slaves, who were denied the status of persons. They are also evident in England, a nation the glory of whose letters, the superiority of whose trade and wealth, and hence power, and whose examples of virtue and courage leave us in no doubt about the goodness of her laws. Torture has been abolished in Sweden and by one of the wisest monarchs of Europe who, bringing philosophy to the throne and legislating as the friend of his subjects, has set them equal and free under the law, which is the only equality and freedom which reasonable men could demand in the present state of things. Martial law does not believe torture necessary for armies, which are made up for the most part of the scum of society whom you might have thought more in need of it than any other class of person. How strange it must seem to anyone who does not take account of how great the tyranny of habit is, that peaceful laws should have to learn a more human system of justice from souls inured to massacre and blood.

This truth is also felt, albeit indistinctly, by those very people who apparently deny it. No confession made under torture can be valid if it is not given sworn confirmation when it is over; but if the criminal does not confirm his crime, he is tortured afresh. Some learned men and some nations do not allow this vicious circle to be gone round more than three times; other nations and other learned men leave it to the choice of the judge, in such a way that, of two men equally innocent or equally guilty, the hardy and enduring will be acquitted and the feeble and timid will be convicted by virtue of the following strict line of reasoning: *I, the judge, had to find you guilty of such and such a crime; you, hardy fellow, could put up with the pain, so I acquit you; you, feeble fellow, gave in, so I convict you. I know that the confession extorted from you in the midst of your agonies would carry no weight, but I shall torture you afresh if you do not confirm what you have confessed.*

A strange consequence which necessarily follows from the use of torture is that the innocent are put in a worse position than the guilty. For, if both are tortured, the former has everything against him. Either he confesses to the crime and is convicted, or he is acquitted and has suffered an unwarranted punishment. The criminal, in contrast, finds himself in a favorable position, because if he staunchly withstands the torture he must be acquitted and so has commuted a heavier sentence into a lighter one. Therefore, the innocent man cannot but lose and the guilty man may gain.

The law which calls for torture is a law which says: *Men, withstand pain, and if nature has placed in you an inextinguishable self-love, if she has given you an inalienable right to self-defence, I create in you an entirely opposite propensity, which is a heroic self-hatred, and I order you to denounce yourselves, telling the truth even when your muscles are being torn and your bones dislocated.*

(Torture is given to discover if a guilty man has also committed other crimes to those with which he is charged. The underlying reasoning here is as follows: *You are guilty of one crime, therefore you may be of a hundred others; this doubt weighs on me and I want to decide the matter with my test of the truth; the laws torture you because you are guilty, because you may be guilty, or because I want you to be guilty.*)

Finally, torture is applied to a suspect in order to discover his accomplices in crime. But if it has been proven that torture is not a fit means of discovering the truth, how can it be of any use in unmasking the accomplices, which is one of the truths to be discovered? As if a man who accuses himself would not more readily accuse others. And can it be right to torture a man for the crimes of others? Will the accomplices not be discovered by the examination of witnesses, the interrogation of the criminal, the evidence and the *corpus delicti,* in short, by the very means which ought to be used to establish the suspect's guilt? Generally, the accomplices flee as soon as their partner is captured; the uncertainty of their fate condemns them to exile and frees the nation of the danger of further offences, while the punishment of the criminal in custody serves its sole purpose, which is that of discouraging with fear other men from perpetrating a similar crime.

XI
A Twentieth-Century Interrogator's Manual on Torture

The Interrogator's Manual is a handwritten, 42-page notebook covering a wide variety of subjects pertaining to the Tuol Sleng extermination center, including the need for secrecy and the centrality of the revolution in Cambodia. The passage printed here is from the third section and sets much of modern torture in a common context, including the diverse purposes in using torture.

VIEWS AND STANCES CONCERNING METHODOLOGY OF INTERROGATION

The measures for each of us during our interrogation of prisoners are of two types:

a. Political pressure, i.e., we propagandise and pressure them constantly, consistently and continuously at all times.

b. The use of torture is a supplementary measure.

Our experience in the past has been that our interrogators for the most part tended to fall on the torture side. They emphasised torture over propaganda. This is the wrong way of doing it. We must teach interrogators how to do it.

The enemy will not confess to us easily. When we use political pressure, prisoners confess only very little. Thus, they cannot escape from torture. The only difference is whether there will be a lot of it or a little. Torture is a necessary measure, we must also nevertheless try our best with political pressure, to make them confess fully. Only when we put maximum political pressure on them, when we put them in a corner politically and get them to confess, will torture become productive. Our political efforts also make the prisoners clear in their answers. And, whether or not we use torture later, make them quicker to confess.

It's better than if we were to just think of only beating them and not to think of propaganda at all. The doing of politics demands a stance of utmost perseverance. Don't be hasty. The forms of propaganda that we have made use of in the past are:

a. Reassure them by giving them something, some food for instance. Reassure them that the Party will give them back their posts.

b. Terrify them, confuse them in clever ways. Arrange little ploys to make them give up any hope that they will ever live again or ever be able to survive.

From David Hawk, "S21, Tuol Sleng Extermination Center, Cambodia," *Index on Censorship* (1986). Reprinted by permission of Writers and Scholars International, Ltd.

c. Draw them into some ordinary conversation, but formulated so that it is of some use.

d. Bring them over to thinking about their families, their wives, their children and their life. Make it clear to them that their guilt is a minor one. When they confess, or have not yet done so, we must guide them and reassure them that they are not the big leaders. Don't step up the pressure all the time. Say something like 'Don't make us torture you or torture you severely. It's bad for your health, and it makes it harder for us to deal with each other in the future.'

e. If they reveal small matters, encourage them to reveal the big ones. Tell them that if they reveal important matters, the Organisation (Party) will be lenient with them.

f. Tell them that if they slander revolutionaries, such as saying that they are traitors, they fall into the trap of trying to destroy revolutionary forces. Thus their guilt would be just as heavy.

g. If they say that their cronies have been taken into custody and brought here previously, you must praise those cronies and say that they confessed sincerely about themselves and their superiors. We must constantly and consistently accuse prisoners of not yet being sincere, by bringing up their weak points and pinning them down with questions so that it is impossible for them to deny the charges.

h. Avoid using propaganda in such a way that they can grasp an advantage, for example, by knowing we want them to confess about someone in particular or some activity.

i. Make the questions right on the mark and solid. Don't get greedy about dense problems. That will make it difficult for them to respond and difficult for them to know what it is we're asking about.

4. The Question of Torturing

a. The purpose of torturing is to get their responses. It's not something we do for fun. We must hurt them so that they respond quickly. Another purpose is to break them and make them lose their will. It's not something that's done out of individual anger, or for self-satisfaction. So we beat them to make them afraid, but absolutely not to kill them. When torturing it is necessary to examine their state of health first, and the whip. Don't be so bloodthirsty that you cause their death quickly. You won't get the needed information.

b. It is necessary to be fully aware that doing politics is most important. Torture is only secondary, subsidiary and supplementary to some political expediency in certain areas. So politics takes the lead at all times. Even when torturing, it is always necessary to do constant propaganda.

c. At the same time, it is necessary to avoid any question of hesitancy or half-heartedness, of not daring to torture, which makes it impossible to get answers to our questions from our enemies. This will slow down and delay our work. In sum, whether doing propaganda work or torturing or bringing up questions to ask them or accusing them of something, it is necessary to hold steadfastly to a stance of not being half-hearted or hesitant. We must be absolute. Only in this way we work to good effect . . . ■

XII
United Nations Convention Against Torture and Other Cruel, Inhuman or Degrading Treatment or Punishment

The State Parties to this Convention,

Considering that, in accordance with the principles proclaimed in the Charter of the United Nations, recognition of the equal and inalienable rights of all members of the human family is the foundation of freedom, justice and peace in the world,

Recognizing that those rights derive from the inherent dignity of the human person,

Considering the obligation of States under the Charter, in particular article 55, to promote universal respect for, and observance of, human rights and fundamental freedoms,

Having regard to article 5 of the Universal Declaration of Human Rights and article 7 of the International Convention on Civil and Political Rights, both of which provide that no one shall be subjected to torture or to cruel, inhuman or degrading treatment or punishment,

Having regard also to the Declaration on the Protection of All Persons from Being Subjected to Torture and Other Cruel, Inhuman or Degrading Treatment or Punishment, adopted by the General Assembly on 9 December 1975,

Desiring to make more effective the struggle against torture and other cruel, inhuman or degrading treatment or punishment throughout the world,

Have agreed as follows:

PART I

Article I

1. For the purposes of this Convention, the term ' torture' means any act by which severe pain or suffering, whether physical or mental, is intentionally inflicted on a person for such purposes as obtaining from him or a third person information or a confession, punishing him for an act he or a third person has committed or is suspected of having committed, or intimidating or coercing him or a third person, or for any reason based on discrimination of any kind, when such pain or suffering is inflicted by or at the instigation

UN General Assembly Resolution 39/46, UN GAOR Supp. (No. 51), adopted 10 December 1984.

of or with the consent or acquiescence of a public official or other person acting in an official capacity. It does not include pain or suffering arising only from, inherent in or incidental to lawful sanctions.

2. This article is without prejudice to any international instrument or national legislation which does or may contain provisions of wider application.

Article 2

1. Each State Party shall take effective legislative, administrative, judicial or other measures to prevent acts of torture in any territory under its jurisdiction.

2. No exceptional circumstances whatsoever, whether a state of war or a threat of war, internal political instability or any other public emergency, may be invoked as a justification of torture.

Article 3

1. No State Party shall expel, return ('refouler') or extradite a person to another State where there are substantial grounds for believing that he would be in danger of being subjected to torture.

2. For the purpose of determining whether there are such grounds, the competent authorities shall take into account all relevant considerations including, where applicable, the existence in the State concerned of a consistent pattern of gross, flagrant or mass violations of human rights.

Article 4

1. Each State Party shall ensure that all acts of torture are offences under its criminal law. The same shall apply to an attempt to commit torture and to an act by any person which constitutes complicity or participation in torture.

2. Each State Party shall make these offences punishable by appropriate penalties which take into account their grave nature.

Article 5

1. Each State Party shall take such measures as may be necessary to establish its jurisdiction over the offences referred to in article 4 in the following cases:

   (a) When the offences are committed in any territory under its jurisdiction or on board a ship or aircraft registered in that State;

   (b) When the alleged offender is a national of that State;

   (c) When the victim is a national of that State and considers it appropriate.

2. Each State Party shall likewise take such measures as may be necessary to establish its jurisdiction over such offences in cases where the alleged offender is present in any territory under its jurisdiction and it does not extradite him pursuant to article 8 to any of the States mentioned in the paragraph 1 of this article.

3. This Convention does not exclude any criminal jurisdiction exercised in accordance with internal law.

Article 6

1. Upon being satisfied, after an examination of information available to it, that the circumstances so warrant, any State Party in whose territory a person alleged to have committed any offence referred to in article 4 is present shall take him into custody or take other legal measures to ensure his presence. The custody and other legal measures shall be as provided in the law of that State but may be continued only for such time as is necessary to enable any criminal or extradition proceedings to be instituted.

2. Such State shall immediately make a preliminary inquiry into the facts.

3. Any person in custody pursuant to paragraph 1 of this article shall be assisted in communicating immediately with the nearest appropriate representative of the State of which he is a national, or, if he is a stateless person, with the representative of the State where he usually resides.

4. When a State, pursuant to this article, has taken a person into custody, it shall immediately notify the States referred to in article 5, paragraph 1, of the fact that such person is in custody and of the circumstances which warrant his detention. The State which makes the preliminary inquiry contemplated in paragraph 2 of this article shall promptly report its findings to the said States and shall indicate whether it intends to exercise jurisdiction.

Article 7

1. The State Party in the territory under whose jurisdiction a person alleged to have committed any offence referred to in article 4 is found shall in the cases contemplated in article 5, if it does not extradite him, submit the case to its competent authorities for the purpose of prosecution.

2. These authorities shall take their decision in the same manner as in the case of any ordinary offence of a serious nature under the law of the State. In cases referred to in article 5, paragraph 2, the standards of evidence required for prosecution and conviction shall in no way be less stringent than those which apply in the cases referred to in article 5, paragraph 1.

3. Any person regarding whom proceedings are brought in connection with any of the offences referred to in article 4 shall be guaranteed fair treatment at all stages of the proceedings.

Article 8

1. The offences referred to in article 4 shall be deemed to be included as extraditable offences in any extradition treaty existing between States Parties. States Parties undertake to include such offences as extraditable offences in every extradition treaty to be concluded between them.

2. If a State Party which makes extradition conditional on the existence of a treaty receives a request for extradition from another State Party with which it has no extradition treaty, it may consider this Convention as the legal basis for the extradition in respect of such offences. Extradition shall be subject to the other conditions provided by the law of the requested State.

3. States Parties which do not make extradition conditional on the existence of a treaty shall recognize such offences as extraditable offences between themselves subject to the conditions provided by the law of the requested State.

4. Such offences shall be treated, for the purposes of extradition between States Parties, as if they had been committed not only in the place in which they occurred but also in the territories of the States required to establish their jurisdiction in accordance with article 5, paragraph 1.

Article 9

1. State Parties shall afford one another the greatest measure of assistance in connection with criminal proceedings brought in respect of any of the offences referred to in article 4, including the supply of all evidence at their disposal necessary for the proceedings.

2. States Parties shall carry out their obligations under paragraph 1 of this article in conformity with any treaties on mutual judicial assistance that may exist between them.

Article 10

1. Each State Party shall ensure that education and information regarding the prohibition against torture are fully included in the training of law enforcement personnel, civil or military, medical personnel, public officials and other persons who may be involved in the custody, interrogation or treatment of any individual subjected to any form of arrest, detention or imprisonment.

2. Each State Party shall include this prohibition in the rules or instructions issued in regard to the duties and functions of any such persons.

Article 11

Each State Party shall keep under systematic review interrogation rules, instructions, methods and practices as well as arrangements for the custody and treatment of persons subjected to any form of arrest, detention or imprisonment in any territory under its jurisdiction, with a view in preventing any cases of torture.

Article 12

Each State Party shall ensure that its competent authorities proceed to a prompt and impartial investigation, wherever there is reasonable ground to believe that an act of torture has been committed in any territory under its jurisdiction.

Article 13

Each State Party shall ensure that any individual who alleges he has been subjected to torture in any territory under its jurisdiction has the right to complain to, and to have his case promptly and impartially examined by, its competent authorities. Steps shall be taken to ensure that the complainant and witnesses are protected against ill-treatment or intimidation as a consequence of his complaint or any evidence given.

Article 14

1. Each State Party shall ensure in its legal system that the victim of an act of torture obtains redress and has an enforceable right to fair and adequate compensation, including the means for as full rehabilitation as possible. In the event of the death of the victim as a result of an act of torture, his dependants shall be entitled to compensation.

2. Nothing in this article shall affect any right of the victim or other persons to compensation which may exist under national law.

Article 15

Each State Party shall ensure that any statement which is established to have been made as a result of torture shall not be invoked as evidence in any proceedings, except against a person accused of torture as evidence that the statement was made.

Article 16

1. Each State Party shall undertake to prevent in any territory under its jurisdiction other acts of cruel, inhuman or degrading treatment or punishment which do not amount to torture as defined in article 1, when such acts are committed by or at the instigation of or with the consent or acquiescence of a public official or other person acting in an official capacity. In particular, the obligations contained in articles 10, 11, 12 and 13 shall apply with the substitution for references to torture of references to other forms of cruel, inhuman or degrading treatment or punishment.

2. The provisions of this Convention are without prejudice to the provisions of any other international instrument or national law which prohibits cruel, inhuman or degrading treatment or punishment or which relates to extradition or expulsion.

PART II
Article 17

1. There shall be established a Committee against Torture (hereinafter referred to as the Committee) which shall carry out the functions hereinafter provided. The Committee shall consist of ten experts of high moral standing and recognized competence in the field of human rights, who shall serve in their personal capacity. The experts shall be elected by the States Parties, consideration being given to equitable geographical distribution and to the usefulness of the participation of some persons having legal experience.

2. The members of the Committee shall be elected by secret ballot from a list of persons nominated by States Parties. Each State Party may nominate one person from among its own nationals. State Parties shall bear in mind the usefulness of nominating persons who are also members of the Human Rights Committee established under the International Covenant on Civil and Political Rights and who are willing under the International Covenant on Civil and Political Rights and who are willing to serve on the Committee against Torture.

3. Elections of the members of the Committee shall be held at biennial meetings of State Parties convened by the Secretary-General of the United Nations. At those meetings, for which two thirds of the States Parties shall constitute a quorum, the persons elected to the Committee shall be those who obtain the largest number of votes and an absolute majority of the votes of the representatives of States Parties present and voting.

4. The initial election shall be held no later than six months after the date of the entry into force of this Convention. At least four months before the date of each election, the Secretary-General of the United Nations shall address a letter to the States Parties inviting them to submit their nominations within three months. The Secretary-General shall prepare a list in alphabetical order of all persons thus nominated, indicating the States Parties which have nominated them, and shall submit it to the States Parties.

5. The members of the Committee shall be elected for a term of four years. They shall be eligible for re-election if renominated. However, the term of five of the members elected at the first election shall expire at the end of two years; immediately after the first election the names of these five members shall be chosen by lot by the chairman of the meeting referred to in paragraph 3 of this article.

6. If a member of the Committee dies or resigns or for any other cause

can no longer perform his Committee duties, the State Party which nominated him shall appoint another expert from among its nationals to serve for the remainder of his term, subject to the approval of the majority of the States Parties. The approval shall be considered given unless half or more of the States Parties respond negatively within six weeks after having been informed by the Secretary-General of the United Nations of the proposed appointment.

7. States Parties shall be responsible for the expenses of the members of the Committee while they are in performance of Committee duties.

Article 18

The Committee shall elect its officers for a term of two years. They may be re-elected.

2. The Committee shall establish its own rules of procedure, but these rules shall provide, inter alia, that:

(a) Six members constitute a quorum;

(b) Decisions of the Committee shall be made by a majority vote of the members present.

3. The Secretary-General of the United Nations shall provide the necessary staff and facilities for the effective performance of the functions of the Committee under this Convention.

4. The Secretary-General of the United Nations shall convene the initial meeting of the Committee. After its initial meeting, the Committee shall meet at such times as shall be provided in its rules of procedure.

5. The States Parties shall be responsible for expenses incurred in connection with the holding of meetings of the States Parties and of the Committee, including reimbursement to the United Nations for any expenses, such as the cost of staff and facilities, incurred by the United Nations pursuant to paragraph 3 of this article.

Article 19

1. The States Parties shall submit to the Committee, through the Secretary-General of the United Nations, reports on the measures they have taken to give effect to their undertakings under this Convention for the State Party concerned. Thereafter the States Parties shall submit supplementary reports every four years on any new measures taken and such other reports as the Committee may request.

2. The Secretary-General of the United Nations shall transmit the reports to all States Parties.

3. Each report shall be considered by the Committee, which may make such general comments on the report as it may consider appropriate and shall forward these to the State Party concerned. That State Party may respond with any observations it chooses to the Committee.

4. The Committee may, at its discretion, decide to include any comments made by it in accordance with paragraph 3 of this article, together with the observations thereon received from the State Party concerned, in its annual report made in accordance with article 24. If so requested by the State Party concerned, the Committee may also include a copy of the report submitted under paragraph 1 of this article.

Article 20

1. If the Committee receives reliable information which appears to it to contain well-founded indications that torture is being systematically practised in the territory of a State Party, the Committee shall invite the State Party to co-operate in the examination of the information and to this end to submit observations with regard to the information concerned.

2. Taking into account any observations which may have been submitted by the State Party concerned, as well as any other relevant information available to it, the Committee may, if it decides that this is warranted, designate one or more of its members to make a confidential inquiry and in report to the Committee urgently.

3. If an inquiry is made in accordance with paragraph 2 of this article, the Committee shall seek the co-operation of the State Party concerned. In agreement with that State Party, such an inquiry may include a visit to its territory.

4. After examining the findings of its member or members submitted in accordance with paragraph 2 of this article, the Committee shall transmit these findings to the State Party concerned together with any comments or suggestions which seem appropriate in view of the situation.

5. All the proceedings of the Committee referred to in paragraphs 1 to 4 of this article shall be confidential, and at all stages of the proceedings the co-operation of the State Party shall be sought. After such proceedings have been completed with regard to an inquiry made in accordance with paragraph 2, the Committee may, after consultations with the State Party concerned, decide to include a summary account of the results of the proceedings in its annual report made in accordance with article 24.

Article 21

1. A State Party to the Convention may at any time declare under this article that it recognizes the competence of the Committee to receive and consider communications to the effect that a State Party claims that another State Party is not fulfilling its obligations under this Convention. Such communications may be received and considered according to the procedures laid down in this article only if submitted by a State Party which has made a

declaration recognizing in regard to itself the competence of the Committee. No communication shall be dealt with by the Committee under this article if it concerns a State Party which has not made such a declaration. Communications received under this article shall be dealt with in accordance with the following procedure:

(a) If a State Party considers that another State Party is not giving effect to the provisions of this Convention, it may, by written commandments, bring the matter to the attention of that State Party. Within three months after the receipt of this communication the receiving State shall afford the State which sent the communication an explanation or any other statement in writing clarifying the matter, which should include, to the extent possible and pertinent, reference to domestic procedures and remedies taken, pending or available in the matter;

(b) If the matter is not adjusted to the satisfaction of both State Parties concerned within six months after the receipt by the receiving State of the initial communication, either State shall have the right to refer the matter to the Committee, by notice given to the Committee and to the other State;

(c) The Committee shall deal with a matter referred to it under this article only after it has ascertained that all domestic remedies have been invoked and exhausted in the matter, in conformity with the generally recognized principles of international law. This shall not be the rule where the application of the remedies is unreasonably prolonged or is unlikely to bring effective relief to the person who is the victim of the violation of this Convention;

(d) The Committee shall hold closed meetings when examining communications under this article;

(e) Subject to the provisions of subparagraph (c), the Committee shall make available its good offices to the States Parties concerned with a view to a friendly solution of the matter on the basis of respect for the obligations provided for in this Convention. For this purpose, the Committee may, when appropriate, set up an ad hoc conciliation commission;

(f) In any matter referred to it under this article, the Committee may call upon the States Parties concerned, referred to in subparagraph (b) to supply any relevant information;

(g) The States Parties concerned, referred to in subparagraph (b), shall have the right to be represented when the matter is being considered by the Committee and to make submissions orally and/or in writing;

(h) The Committee shall, within twelve months after the date of receipt of notice under subparagraph (b), submit a report:

(i) If a solution within the terms of subparagraph (e) is reached, the Committee shall confine its report to a brief statement of the facts and of the solution reached;

(ii) If a solution within the terms of subparagraph (e) is not reached, the Committee shall confine its report to a brief statement of the facts; the written submissions and record of the oral submissions made by the States Parties concerned shall be attached to the report.

In every matter, the report shall be communicated to the States Parties concerned.

2. The provisions of this article shall come into force when five States Parties to this Convention have made declarations under paragraph 1 of this article. Such declarations shall be deposited by the States Parties with the Secretary-General of the United Nations, who shall transmit copies thereof to the other States Parties. A declaration may be withdrawn at any time by notification to the Secretary-General. Such a withdrawal shall not prejudice the consideration of any matter which is the subject of a communication already transmitted under this article; no further communication by any State Party shall be received under this article after the notification of withdrawal of the declaration has been received by the Secretary-General, unless the State Party concerned has made a new declaration.

Article 22

1. A State Party to this Convention may at any time declare under this article that it recognizes the competence of the Committee to receive and consider communications from or on behalf of individuals subject to its jurisdiction who claim to be victims of a violation by a State Party of the provisions of the Convention. No communication shall be received by the Committee if it concerns a State Party which has not made such a declaration.

2. The Committee shall consider inadmissible any communication under this article which is anonymous or which it considers to be an abuse of the right of submission of such communications or to be incomparable with the provisions of the Convention.

3. Subject to the provisions of paragraph 2, the Committee shall bring any communications submitted to it under this article to the attention of the State Party of this Convention which has made a declaration under paragraph 1 and is alleged to be violating any provisions of the Convention. Within six months, the receiving State shall submit to the Committee written explanations or statements clarifying the matter and the remedy, if any, that may have been taken by that State.

4. The Committee shall consider communications received under this article in the light of all information made available to it by or on behalf of the individual and by the State Party concerned.

5. The Committee shall not consider any communications from an individual under this article unless it has ascertained that:

(a) The same matter has not been, and is not being, examined under another procedure of international investigation or settlement;

(b) The individual has exhausted all available domestic remedies; this shall not be the rule where the application of the remedies is unreasonably prolonged or is unlikely to bring effective relief to the person who is the victim of the violation of this Convention.

6. The Committee shall hold closed meetings when examining communications under this article.

7. The Committee shall forward its views to the State Party concerned and to the individual.

8. The provisions of this article shall come into force when five States Parties to this Convention have made declarations under paragraph 1 of this article. Such declarations shall be deposited by the States Parties with the Secretary-General of the United Nations, who shall transmit copies thereof to the other States Parties. A declaration may be withdrawn at any time by notification to the Secretary-General. Such a withdrawal shall not prejudice the consideration of any matter which is the subject of a communication already transmitted under this article; no further communication by or on behalf of an individual shall be received under this article after the notification of withdrawal of the declaration has been received by the Secretary-General, unless the State Party has made a new declaration.

Article 23

The members of the Committee and of the ad hoc conciliation commissions which may be appointed under article 21, paragraph 1(e), shall be entitled to the facilities, privileges and immunities of experts on mission for the United Nations as laid down in the relevant sections of the Convention on the Privileges and Immunities of the United Nations.

Article 24

The Committee shall submit an annual report on its activities under this Convention to the States Parties and to the General Assembly of the United Nations.

PART III

Article 25

1. This Convention is open for signature by all States.

2. This Convention is subject to ratification. Instruments of ratification shall be deposited with the Secretary-General of the United Nations.

Article 26

This Convention is open to accession by all States. Accession shall be effected by the deposit of an instrument of accession with the Secretary-General of the United Nations.

Article 27

1. This Convention shall enter into force on the thirtieth day after the date of the deposit with the Secretary-General of the United Nations of the twentieth instrument of ratification or accession.

2. For each State ratifying this Convention or acceding to it after the deposit of the twentieth instrument of ratification or accession, the Convention shall enter into force on the thirtieth day after the date of the deposit of its own instrument of ratification or accession.

Article 28

1. Each State may, at the time of signature or ratification of this Convention or accession thereto, declare that it does not recognize the competence of the Committee provided for in article 20.

2. Any State Party having made a reservation in accordance with paragraph 1 of this article may, at any time, withdraw this reservation by notification to the Secretary-General of the United Nations.

Article 29

1. Any State Party to this Convention may propose an amendment and file it with the Secretary-General of the United Nations. The Secretary-General shall thereupon communicate the proposed amendment to the States parties with a request that they notify him whether they favour a conference of States Parties for the purpose of considering and voting upon the proposal. In the event that within four months from the date of such communication at least one third of the States Parties favours such a conference, the Secretary-General shall convene the conference under the auspices of the United Nations. Any amendment adopted by a majority of the States Parties present and voting at the conference shall be submitted by the Secretary-General to all the States Parties for acceptance.

2. An amendment adopted in accordance with paragraph 1 of this article shall enter into force when two thirds of the States Parties to this Convention have notified the Secretary-General of the United Nations that they have accepted it in accordance with their respective constitutional processes.

3. When amendments enter into force, they shall be binding on those States Parties which have accepted them, other States Parties still being bound by the provisions of this Convention and any earlier amendments which they have accepted.

Article 30

1. Any dispute between two or more States Parties concerning the interpretation or application of this Convention which cannot be settled through

negotiation shall, at the request of one of them, be submitted to arbitration. If within six months from the date of the request for arbitration, any one of those Parties may refer the dispute to the International Court of Justice by request in conformity with the Statute of the Court.

2. Each State may, at the time of signature or ratification of this Convention or accession thereto, declare that it does not consider itself bound by paragraph 1 of this article. The other States Parties shall not be bound by paragraph 1 of this article with respect to any State Party having made such a reservation.

3. Any State Party having made a reservation in accordance with paragraph 2 of this article may at any time withdraw this reservation by notification to the Secretary-General of the United Nations.

Article 31

1. A State Party may denounce this Convention by written notification to the Secretary-General of the United Nations. Denunciation becomes effective one year after the date of receipt of the notification by the Secretary-General.

2. Such a denunciation shall not have the effect of releasing the State Party from its obligations under this Convention in regard to any act or omission which occurs prior to the date at which the denunciation becomes effective, nor shall denunciation prejudice in any way the continued consideration of any matter which is already under consideration by the Committee prior to the date at which the denunciation becomes effective.

3. Following the date at which the denunciation of a State Party becomes effective, the Committee shall not commence consideration of any new matter regarding that State.

Article 32

The Secretary-General of the United Nations shall inform all States Members of the United Nations and all States which have signed this Convention or acceded to it of the following:

(a) Signatures, ratifications and accessions under articles 25 and 26;

(b) The date of entry into force of this Convention under article 27 and the date of the entry into force of any amendments under article 29;

(c) Denunciations under article 31.

Article 33

1. This Convention, of which the Arabic, Chinese, English, French, Russian and Spanish texts are equally authentic, shall be deposited with the Secretary-General of the United Nations.

2. The Secretary-General of the United Nations shall transmit certified copies of this Convention to all States.

XIII
United Nations Principles of Medical Ethics

The General Assembly . . .
Desirous of setting further standards in this field which ought to be implemented by health personnel, particularly physicians, and by government officials,

1. Adopts the Principles of Medical Ethics relevant to the role of health personnel, particularly physicians, in the protection of prisoners and detainees against torture and other cruel, inhuman or degrading treatment or punishment set forth in the annex to the present resolution;

2. Calls upon all Governments to give the Principles of Medical Ethics, together with the present resolution, the widest possible distribution, in particular among medical and paramedical associations and institutions of detention or imprisonment in an official language of the state.

3. Invites all relevant inter-governmental organizations, in particular the World Health Organization, and non-governmental organizations concerned to bring the Principles of Medical Ethics to the attention of the widest possible group of individuals, especially those active in the medical and paramedical field.

Principles of medical ethics relevant to the role of health personnel, particularly physicians, in the protection of prisoners and detainees against torture and other cruel, inhuman or degrading treatment or punishment

Principle 1

Health personnel, particularly physicians, charged with the medical care of prisoners and detainees have the duty to provide them with protection of their physical and mental health and treatment of disease of the same quality and standard as is afforded to those who are not imprisoned or detained.

Principle 2

It is a gross contravention of medical ethics, as well as an offence under applicable international instruments, for health personnel, particularly physicians, to engage, actively or passively, in acts which constitute participation in, complicity in, incitement to or attempts to commit torture or other cruel, inhuman or degrading treatment or punishment.

From "Principles of Medical Ethics Relevant to the Role of Health Personnel, Particularly Physicians, in the Protection of Prisoners and Detainees Against Torture and Other Cruel, Inhuman or Degrading Treatment or Punishment," UN General Assembly Resolution 37/194, adopted 18 December 1982.

Principle 3

It is a contravention of medical ethics for health personnel, particularly physicians, to be involved in any professional relationship with prisoners or detainees the purpose of which is not to solely evaluate, protect or improve their physical and mental health.

Principle 4

It is a contravention of medical ethics for health personnel, particularly physicians:

a) To apply their knowledge and skills in order to assist in the interrogation of prisoners and detainees in a manner that may adversely affect the physical or mental health of such prisoners or detainees and which is not in accordance with the relevant international instruments.

b) To certify, or to participate in the certification of, the fitness of prisoners or detainees for any form of treatment or punishment that may adversely affect their physical or mental health and which is not in accordance with the relevant international instruments, or to participate in any way in the infliction of any such treatment or punishment which is not in accordance with the relevant international instruments.

Principle 5

It is a contravention of medical ethics for health personnel, particularly physicians, to participate in any procedure for restraining a prisoner or detainee unless such a procedure is determined in accordance with purely medical criteria as being necessary for the protection of the physical and mental health, or the safety of the prisoner or detainee himself, of his fellow prisoners or detainees, or of his guardians, and presents no hazard to his physical or mental health.

Principle 6

There may be no derogation from the foregoing principles on any grounds whatsoever, including public emergency.

XIV
Statement on Nurses and Torture

Violations of human rights have become more pervasive and scientific discoveries have brought about more sophisticated forms of torture and methods of resuscitation.

Although nurses may not voluntarily participate in any form of physical or psychological torture, they must know what is expected of them and what action they must take to safeguard human rights.

Nurses need to know that, although the apparent motive for much of the treatment during and after torture is the protection of the victim, it is often carried out more as protection of the torturers. The nurse may be called upon to act alone or to assist in the following situations:

- to perform physical examinations on suspects before they are subjected to forms of interrogation, which might include torture
- to attend a torture session in order to intervene when the victim's life is in danger
- to treat the direct physical effects of torture, so that later the interrogation can be continued.

The nurse's primary responsibility is to those people who require nursing care. If the victim of cruel, wanton, degrading or any other inhuman procedure or treatment (in the independent opinion of the nurse) requires nursing care, then no motive should prevail against the nurse giving such care to the highest standard possible.

The national nurses' associations (NNA) need to ensure that their structure provides a realistic mechanism through which nurses can seek confidential advice, counsel, support and assistance in dealing with these difficult situations. Verification of the facts reported will be an important first step in any particular case.

The Responsibility of the Nurse

The nurse shall not countenance, condone or voluntarily participate in:

- any deliberate systematic or wanton infliction of physical or mental suffering or any other form of cruel, inhuman or degrading procedure by one or more persons acting alone or on the orders of any authority, to force another person to yield information, to make a confession or for any other reason
- any treatment which denies to any person the respect which is his/her due as a human being.

From the Meeting of the Council of National Representatives of the International Council of Nurses, Seoul, South Korea, May 1989.

Index